J.B. MACKINNON

J.B. MacKinnon is the author or co-author of four books including *The Once and Future World*, which won the U.S. Green Prize for Sustainable Literature, and *The 100-Mile Diet*, a bestseller widely recognized as a catalyst of the local foods movement. His award-winning writing appears in publications including the *New Yorker, National Geographic* and *Reader's Digest*. MacKinnon is an adjunct professor at the University of British Columbia Graduate School of Journalism and also works in the field of interactive documentaries. He lives with his partner in Vancouver, Canada.

jbmackinnon.com

J.B. MacKINNON

The Day the World Stops Shopping

How ending consumerism gives us a better life and a greener world

VINTAGE

1 3 5 7 9 10 8 6 4 2

Vintage is part of the Penguin Random House group of companies
whose addresses can be found at global.penguinrandomhouse.com

Penguin
Random House
UK

First published in Vintage in 2022
First published in hardback by The Bodley Head in 2021

penguin.co.uk/vintage

A CIP catalogue record for this book is available from the British Library

ISBN 9781784709242

Printed and bound in Great Britain by Clays Ltd, Elcograf S.p.A.

The authorised representative in the EEA is Penguin Random House Ireland,
Morrison Chambers, 32 Nassau Street, Dublin D02 YH68

Penguin Random House is committed to a sustainable future for
our business, our readers and our planet. This book is made from
Forest Stewardship Council® certified paper.

CONTENTS

IV TRANSFORMATION

It is not the
man who has
too little, but
the man who
craves more,
that is poor.

—SENECA

Then he said
to the crowd,
"Take care to
guard against
all greed, for
though one may
be rich, one's life
does not consist
of possessions."

—LUKE 12:15

Earth provides enough to satisfy every man's need, but not every man's greed.

—MAHATMA GANDHI

A consumers'
society cannot
possibly know
how to take care
of a world . . .
the attitude of
consumption
spells ruin to
everything it
touches.
—HANNAH ARENDT

People are drowning in things. They don't even know what they want them for. They are actually useless. You can't make love to a Cadillac, though everyone appears to be trying to.

—JAMES BALDWIN

In a consumer
society there are
inevitably two
kinds of slaves:
the prisoners of
addiction and the
prisoners of envy.
—IVAN ILLICH

I encourage
you all to go
shopping more.
—GEORGE W. BUSH

We must stop shopping
but we can't stop shopping

igh noon in the Kalahari Desert of Namibia, in southwestern Africa. So hot that your lungs turn to leather with every breath. A scrubland that looks like it would cut you—prick you, catch in your clothes—spreads in every direction. Close by, but too far to want to walk to in this heat, is a scattering of thatch-roofed mud huts the same colour as the red-gold sand. Two decades into the twenty-first century, the scene is remarkable for the near absence of *things*: a couple of sunbeaten plastic chairs, faded clothing on a huddle of young hunters, a triangle of scrap metal that holds a battered teapot above low coals. A bow and a quiver of arrows leans in a doorless doorway.

An older hunter sits beneath a woebegone tree, its patch of shade so small that it can hardly hold two people without knocking their knees together. The hunter's name is a difficult one for outsiders. He goes by G‡kao, with the ‡ representing a hard, square sound made by popping the tongue off the ridge behind your front teeth. The result sounds something like "Gitkao," and if it helps to think of him that way, he would surely forgive you. You can also think of him as having a trim grey goatee, a face lined more by laughter than worry, and the lean, muscled look of a long-distance runner.

"Right now, we are mainly eating bush food," Gǂkao tells me. Once in a while, government officials come by with two large bags of cornmeal for each household. People here receive a little cash, too, either by way of government support or from making handicrafts that one or another person will carry nearly forty kilometres—on horseback or on foot—to sell in Tsumkwe, the one-street town that is the hub of the region. But this village, Den|ui (sounds a bit like Dengui), could not survive without hunting and foraging from the desert.

"I have noticed, in other villages, that some men don't hunt and don't even have hunting tools. When the sun rises they are just in their houses until sunset. But in this village, we continue and we will continue," Gǂkao says. "If you come on hard times, if the honeymoon is over, you must be able to do things for yourself."

Den|ui is not untouched by the modern world, of course. Gǂkao sits in a blue plastic chair; he is wearing clothes—including a shining, cowboy-style belt buckle—he bought at a second-hand clothing stall in Tsumkwe. (The fate of many clothing donations to Africa is to be sold by merchants or burned as waste, rather than given to people in need.) But Gǂkao's dinner tonight will be kudu antelope meat stewed in wild vegetables. He doesn't hunt with a gun. He has a bow made of foraged grewia wood that is strung with sinews taken from the spine of an antelope. He makes arrow shafts from the thick, hollow stems of tallgrass, and poisons his arrowheads with beetle larvae he dug out of the ground and crushed. His quiver is a tube of tough bark from the fat root of a false umbrella thorn tree, which he had dug up, cut and then roasted until he could remove its core with only a tap from his hand. Sometimes he makes a smaller quiver and a handful of unpoisoned arrows to sell to the area's few tourists, but these are not skills he preserves for their value in the marketplace. They are the ways and means of his daily life.

Gǂkao will tell you that he is one of the Ju|'hoansi (sounds a bit like "Jukwansi"), which in his language means "True People." Most outsiders, on the other hand, know them as the Bushmen of the Kalahari, or sometimes the San, having seen them and heard their unusual "click language" in *National Geographic* specials or the classic comedy *The Gods Must Be Crazy*.

There's a running debate about the historical baggage of these terms. But as James Suzman, a British anthropologist and writer who has spent much of his career with the Ju|'hoansi, puts it, "As far as they are concerned, the problem is not how others refer to them but rather how others treat them."

In 1964, a Canadian anthropologist named Richard B. Lee, still in his twenties, began more than a year with the Ju|'hoansi, doing research that would later be lauded as among the most important in twentieth-century science. When Lee arrived in the Kalahari Desert, anthropologists, like outsiders in general, saw hunting and gathering as a desperate struggle to survive, a stage of development nearer to wild animals than to contemporary human beings.

Lee decided to test these assumptions empirically. He spent a month recording exactly how each person in the camp used their time, another month totting up the calories in everything the Ju|'hoansi ate, and so on. His findings showed that the hunter-gatherer lifestyle could, in fact, be a good one. By some measures, it might be *better* than life in industrialized nations.

To start with, the Ju|'hoansi didn't work very hard. On average, they put in about thirty hours a week acquiring food and taking care of chores such as cooking and gathering firewood. At the time, a typical person in the "first affluent society"—America—was putting in thirty-one hours a week on the job, then going home to do their share of an average twenty-two hours per household on chores. More strikingly, the hardest-working person Lee observed, a man called ‡Oma (sounds a bit like "Toma"), was logging thirty-two hours a week as a hunter—a far cry from the sixty-plus-hour workweeks that are not uncommon today. Then there was the fact that most seniors and people under twenty usually didn't do any hunting or gathering at all.

Weren't these hungry, malnourished people? Not at all, said Lee. The Ju|'hoansi were eating more than enough for people of their size and activity level. Besides hunted game, they ate a wide range of wild plant foods. When asked why they had never taken up agriculture, one of the Ju|'hoansi told Lee, "Why should we plant, when there are so many manketti nuts in the world?"

There were trade-offs to this life of relative ease. The most obvious—to the eye of one arriving, as Lee had, from the world of Beatlemania and the newly released Ford Mustang—was that the Ju|'hoansi had almost no stuff. Men owned a few articles of animal-hide clothing, blankets (temperatures can drop below freezing in the Kalahari), hunting equipment, and perhaps a simple, handmade musical instrument of some kind; women owned clothes, digging sticks, and a few pieces of jewellery made from wood, seeds and ostrich shells.

Measured by how long they have persisted, the Ju|'hoansi and related cultures in southern Africa are the world's most successful examples of the hunting and gathering way of life. No one yet knows exactly where in Africa our own species, *Homo sapiens*, evolved. What is certain is that soon after that evolution, we were present in southern Africa, which is where the human family split in two. One group voyaged north, eventually becoming African farmers and European sailors and Chinese merchants and Silicon Valley venture capitalists. The other group, among them the ancestors of the Ju|'hoansi, stayed put. They spent the past 150,000 years figuring out the best possible way to live on their landscape.

Lee wasn't the only one to report remarkable well-being where outsiders had never expected it; similar findings trickled in from around the globe. More than nine-tenths of our existence as a species had been spent as hunter-gatherers. Looking around themselves in the 1960s, Lee and other such researchers weren't convinced that their own culture would be as durable: a nuclear arms race was underway, the world population was soaring, and the planetary environment was under siege. Scientists were increasingly concerned about something they called the "greenhouse effect," which threatened to alter the climate. The anthropologists had the same sneaking feeling that many people do today: that somewhere in the drift of cultural evolution we had made a wrong turn, one that would lead, thousands of years later, to a world of robotic cat litter boxes and enamel-whitening toothbrushes and *Storage Wars* and all the rest of the surreal clutter of modern life.

When Lee reported his research at a conference in Chicago in 1966, another anthropologist, Marshall Sahlins, responded to the new findings. "This was, when you come to think of it, the original affluent society,"

Sahlins said. There appeared to be two distinct paths that humans could take to meeting everyone's wants and needs. The first was to produce much; the second was to want little. The Ju|'hoansi and other hunter-gatherer cultures had developed "affluence without abundance," Sahlins said, a lifestyle with few needs, easily met from the landscape around them. (Henry David Thoreau was following in the Ju|'hoansi's footsteps when he allegedly said, "I make myself rich by making my wants few.") Noting that hunter-gatherers frequently accumulated less food and other materials than was readily available, Sahlins wondered aloud about "the inner meaning of running below capacity." Might it be, he said, that such restraint made for a more fulfilling, contented life than endlessly chasing more money and possessions? The scientists agreed this would be a difficult question to answer, for the most brutal of reasons. "The time is rapidly approaching," they recorded in the conference notes, "when there will be no hunters left to study."

The hunter-gatherers themselves had other plans, and they endured despite relentless assaults on their lands and cultures. Den|ui, secluded by the desert at the end of a long, sandy track, is among the Ju|'hoan villages where the "hunting spirit" is still said to be strong. G╪kao gives the immediate impression of having always been a hunter-gatherer, a holdout against the crush of globalized life. In fact, this does not turn out to be true. For a time, he served in the South African army. Later, he held a government job in Tsumkwe, earning money to spend in the shops. He has watched TV, driven in vehicles, eaten food imported from around the world, witnessed the arrival of the mobile phone. Always it seemed to him to be an uncertain, precarious, vulnerable way to live, almost entirely dependent on forces beyond one's control.

Then he stopped. He *chose* to leave it behind.

"All the time I was thinking of going back to the old knowledge. It was always my dream," G╪kao says. "I came back to the village and I will stay forever, hunting."

Is it possible that the rest of us, too, will one day choose to leave consumer culture behind? That we will explore the "inner meaning of running below capacity" instead of the harried busyness of the earn-and-spend cycle, the naked status competition of the age of social media and reality TV, the sheer planetary destructiveness of the system that provides us with our clothing, cars, gadgets and distractions? More and more people believe that a simpler life awaits us, if not through some great awakening then because civilization will collapse beneath its own weight. G#kao's return to a life of few needs, and even fewer wants, illuminates both our hopes and fears about such an outcome: on the one hand, that our ancient human souls may be longing for simplicity, and on the other, that it's a path straight back to the Stone Age.

The twenty-first century has brought a critical dilemma into sharp relief: we must stop shopping, and yet we can't stop shopping. At the turn of this new millennium, according to the United Nations' panel of experts on international resources, consumption quietly surpassed population as our greatest environmental challenge. When it comes to climate change, species extinction, water depletion, toxic pollution, deforestation and other crises, how much each one of us consumes now matters more than how many of us there are. The average person in a rich country consumes thirteen times as much as the average person in a poor one. In terms of environmental impact, that means that having a child in the United States or Canada, the United Kingdom or Western Europe, is equivalent to having thirteen children in a country like Bangladesh, Haiti or Zambia. Raising two children in a rich country is like having twenty-six kids in a poor one.

For decades now, we've witnessed a near-continuous increase in the consumption of every major natural resource, from oil to gemstones, from gravel to gold. We are using up the planet at a rate 1.7 times faster than it can regenerate. If everyone consumed like the average American, it would be five times faster. It's like we're spending all of our salary each year, then taking more than half again as much money out of the savings we'd planned to pass down to our children, and spending that too. At this rate, by 2050, resource use will have tripled in the twenty-first century alone.

Here and there we ban plastic bags or plastic straws; meanwhile, plastic production overall has been increasing by leaps and bounds, growing more than twice as quickly as the global economy. The clothes we buy today add up to an annual mass of apparel totalling fifty million tonnes—a falling asteroid that size would reduce any major city to rubble and trigger earthquakes around the world. In just the past twenty years, the number of garments purchased per person has increased by more than 60 percent, while the lifespan of those clothes has been cut nearly in half. Even if you harbour doubts about how accurately we can measure our voracious consumer appetites, it hardly matters. The numbers could be off the mark by a wide margin and we'd still face a planetary crisis.

In the US, people now collectively spend more than $250 billion each year on digital gadgets, $140 billion on personal care products, $75 billion on jewellery and watches, $60 billion on household appliances, $30 billion on luggage. Yet the stereotype of America as the world's rogue shopping addict is no longer accurate, if it ever was. Several oil-rich countries—such as Qatar, Bahrain and the United Arab Emirates—exceed US consumption per person, and so does Luxembourg. The European Union's shoppers together spend nearly as much as their counterparts in the United States, while Canadians closely rival Americans for the footprint their lifestyles leave on the planet. In China, two-thirds of the population now acknowledge that they own more clothes than they really require. Even the world's poorest citizens buy, as a World Bank report puts it, "what they are willing to pay for—not what they 'need.'" The globe's 4.5 billon low-income people are an enormous consumer market, together spending more than five trillion US dollars each year.

Countertops are bigger, beds are bigger, closets have doubled in size. The technosphere—everything we build and make, our *stuff*—is now estimated to outweigh all living things on Earth. Spread evenly across the surface of the planet, our possessions would amount to a fifty-kilogram heap on every square metre. Picture, say, a pile composed of a small television, a pineapple, a two-slice toaster, a pair of shoes, a concrete block, a car tire, a year's supply of cheese for the average American, and a pet chihuahua.

We haven't even begun to talk about what we throw away. The annual output of garbage in the United States and Canada, loaded into trucks, could circle the equator twelve times. Americans used to toss out far more stuff than Europeans, but nations like Germany and the Netherlands have caught up; an average household in France throws away four times as much waste as it did in 1970. About a fifth of our food ends up in the garbage worldwide, and, remarkably, this is a problem in poorer countries as well as richer ones. Dogs and cats used to help us dispose of leftover food. Today they have their own consumer goods, from beds to toys to clothing to "pet tech" products—a market worth more than $16 billion in the US alone. Our pets produce their own trash.

We have responded to all of the above not by reducing our consumption, but by attempting to "green" it. The focus, globally, has been to replace gasoline-burning cars with electric ones, to recharge our phones with energy derived from the wind and sun instead of coal. Organic food, nontoxic paint, reused computers, energy-efficient televisions and water-saving dishwashers are now widely available.

The environmental harms linked to the goods and services we enjoy would be much worse without these advances. Yet the greening of consumerism has yet to result in an absolute decrease in material consumption in any region of the world. As Joyce Msuya, then the head of the UN Environment Programme, put it in 2019, "At no point in time nor at any level of income has our demand for natural resources wavered." In fact, since the year 2000, the efficiency with which we use those resources has *decreased* overall, while the pace at which we extract them has accelerated.

Yes, there are some hopeful signs. Over the past two decades, as the world witnessed an explosion of natural resource exploitation, the richest countries were responsible for only a small fraction of that increase: with the help of green technology, the planet's wealthiest shoppers really are treading more lightly. Yet they still do by far the greatest damage per person, because they remain the world's heaviest consumers and the rate at which they consume continues to rise. Nothing we have done to green our consumer appetite has been able to keep pace with how quickly that appetite is growing, to the point that the unwavering dedication to greening has become peculiar if not absurd. If we wish to lessen the harms caused by consumption, why not consider . . . consuming less?

The case is made most starkly by our attempts to reduce the carbon dioxide pollution that is heating up the climate. A concerted international effort, billions of dollars in green technology, and an impressive upswing in the supply of renewable energy has yet to reduce the amount of carbon entering Earth's atmosphere for even a single year. Every gain has been lost or neutralized by the growth of global consumption. So far in recorded history, the only times that global greenhouse gas emissions have actually *declined* have come amid major economic downturns—in other words, when the world stops shopping. During the Covid-19 pandemic lockdowns in the first months of 2020, as the doors closed on consumer culture, carbon pollution in most nations fell by one-fifth to one-quarter; countries lagging years behind on their emissions-reduction goals were suddenly years ahead of schedule. It didn't last, of course. (China broke a new record for emissions just one month after the global economy began to return to "normal.") But the speed and scale at which stopping shopping fights climate change was impossible to ignore.

Yet we can't stop shopping. Another core teaching of the twenty-first century so far is that it is our civic duty to buy, buy, buy. Nine days after the 9/11 attacks on New York and Washington, DC, in 2001, George W. Bush addressed the US Congress in a speech heard around the world. He asked people to be giving, calm, tolerant, patient. Then he said, "I ask your continued participation and confidence in the American economy." It's remembered as the moment that Bush told a wounded nation to "go shopping." Forget the fact that he didn't say those words. The implication that buying fresh linens or redecorating your home was a helpful response to a dawning age of terror made such an impression that two words the president had not said—yet—are as famous as anything he did say.

Bush's speech was shocking because we have harboured doubts about consumption throughout most of human history. Moral leaders representing every major religion and political stripe—to the voices in the opening pages of this book could be added Confucius, Benjamin Franklin, Henry David Thoreau, Betty Friedan, Aldous Huxley, Martin Luther King, John Maynard Keynes, Margaret Atwood, Chuck D and many more—have admonished us to be less materialistic, less in the thrall of consumer culture. Even Adam Smith, the eighteenth-century Scottish economist often called the father of capitalism, made the case that materialism was not a virtue but a vice. He excoriated the "lover of toys" who, "in the wantonness of plenty," pursued "trinkets and baubles, fitter to be the play-things of children than the serious pursuits of men." Buying fewer things has always been what we *ought* to be doing, even if few of us actually did.

Those who warn against consumerism have made two main arguments. The first is that a love for money and things indulges the lesser angels of our nature, such as greed, vanity, envy and wastefulness. The second is that every moment you spend thinking about money and things is a moment that could have been spent making a greater contribution to the human community through service, the pursuit of knowledge or the life of the spirit.

Two additional charges against consumer culture began to arouse widespread alarm about fifty years ago. One—captured in the meme "Live simply, so that others might simply live"—is that consuming more than your share amounts to enriching yourself by impoverishing others. The call to reduce this "overconsumption" took on still greater urgency as we awoke to the fact that we were toppling ancient forests to make toilet paper, strangling seagulls with discarded plastic six-pack rings, damming mighty rivers to produce electricity that we used to watch reruns on TV, and, above all else, burning so much fossil fuel that we were throwing the climate into chaos.

After 9/11, however, our long historical unease about consumerism seemed to evaporate. The attack cost the United States at least sixty billion dollars and more than half a million jobs, with most of the damage done not by the terrorists, but by a sudden loss of enthusiasm for shopping in America and around the world. From there, it was only a small step to the conclusion that not-shopping was itself a clear and present danger. As Bush said at the time, "You are with us, or you are with the terrorists."

Bush's speeches changed the way we talked about consumption. It became routine for world leaders to bluntly ask us to get out and shop any time the consumer frenzy slipped below a fevered pitch—as if shopping was less a choice than a necessity. (Bush finally did tell Americans to "go shopping" in 2006, as the economy began to give hints of the coming Great Recession.) When the coronavirus pandemic in 2020 triggered the sharpest decline in consumer spending ever recorded, commentators were soon debating how many deaths might be acceptable to keep the economy "open." By then, the idea that shopping is not just a pastime or a distraction, but the only thing standing between us and the fall of civilization, was perfectly ordinary to our ears.

It also played out before our eyes: shuttered shopping districts, empty airports, boarded-up restaurants, millions of people out of work or facing bankruptcy. Equally undeniable during the Covid-19 lockdowns, though, were the shockingly blue skies over Los Angeles and London, the fresh air in Beijing and Delhi, and the steepest drop in greenhouse gas pollution ever recorded. When sea turtles and crocodiles took over tropical beaches normally invaded by mass tourism, when the vibration of the planet measurably stilled in the absence of our usual rumpus, it raised pointed questions about the costs of business as usual.

It turned out that our older anxieties about consumption have never really gone away. Do we buy and consume as a paltry substitute for something missing in our lives? Does our immersion in stuff distract us from ideas, feelings and relationships that matter more? These thoughts took on new salience as, for a time, people filled the void left behind by the absence of shopping with creative expression, social connection and self-reflection. Millions felt for themselves what a decade's worth of happiness research has been saying: that in the richer nations, and increasingly around the world, the earning and spending we do is no longer adding much—if any—joy to our lives. (As a friend wrote to me from quarantine, "Once you stop for a while, you don't miss it much.") Certainly the issue of the fair distribution of the planet's resources wasn't resolved, as billionaires self-isolated on mega-yachts while others, impoverished overnight through no fault of their own, joined traffic jams for groceries being handed out by charities.

If we slow our consumption, it plainly does have serious consequences for the economy. At the same time, it may not be possible to halt global warming, at least on the urgent timescale that is necessary, without doing exactly that. And climate change is just one on a list of ills, all of them exacerbated by consumer culture, that even cautious experts say could lead to political upheaval or large-scale loss of life.

We must stop shopping but we can't stop shopping: the consumer dilemma has become, quite simply, the question of whether we can sustain human life on Earth.

Suppose that we suddenly listened to all of those voices through history that have asked us to live with less. One day the world stops shopping.

That is the thought experiment I've undertaken in this book. It began when I confronted the consumer dilemma for myself. Like many people today, I'd taken to contemplating how my own consumption contributes to climate change, the destruction of forests, plastic pollution in the oceans, and the many other ecological crises that are making our world uninhabitable. I knew I could choose to reduce my consumption. (When I was younger, I once gave spare change to a panhandler, who took one look at my shoes—duck-billed open at the toes to reveal my stockinged feet—and handed the money back. "You look like you need it," he said.) But how could I stop shopping, when I also believed that if everyone else did the same, it really would lay waste to the global economy? To see if there was a way out of this quandary, I thought, I would need to play out the scenario to its end.

I start at the beginning: What happens in the first hours and days of a world that stops shopping? How do we parse our wants and needs? Whose life changes the most and whose the least? Does the earth begin to heal, and if so, how quickly? From there, I explore the economic collapse that seems inevitable—and also discover how, even in catastrophe, we begin to adapt. Unlike every other such crash in memory, this experiment of mine doesn't end with the world marching dutifully back to the malls. Instead, as the first day without shopping stretches into weeks and months, we change the way we make things, organize our lives around new priorities, find different business models for a global culture that has lost its desire to consume. Finally, I look at where this evolution could lead us over decades or even millennia, from a deeper drift into virtual reality to a planet resurgent with nature to a life more simple, perhaps, than we ever thought to seek.

What does it actually mean to "stop shopping"? Sometimes we say we're "doing the shopping," which usually means we're heading out to buy basic necessities, such as food, detergent, school supplies and—of course— toilet paper. At other times we say, "Let's go shopping," which often means we are on the hunt for goods that we don't really need at all. Most of us today live in societies in which social and economic life is organized mainly around consumption: we are consumers. In everyday conversation, how- ever, a "consumer" is often only that person whose favourite pastime is blowing money on clothes, toys, baubles, holidays, fancy food or all of the above. And "consumer culture" is the daily barrage of ads, sales, trends, fast food, fast fashion, distraction and gadgets-of-the-moment that rains down on us, and our preoccupation with all of it.

For the sake of this thought experiment, I wanted to keep it simple: on the day the world stops shopping, global consumer spending drops by 25 percent. To some, that number will seem conservative, given the enormity of the consumer appetite, from Black Friday shopping riots to mighty rivers that endlessly float plastic water bottles to the sea. Indeed, at a global scale, reducing consumption by one-quarter would only turn back the clock to the spending levels of about a decade ago. On the other hand, when I started writing this book, the idea that global consumption could drop by 25 percent sounded like the wildest of speculations—a fantasy so outlandish that many people I hoped to speak to refused even to entertain it.

Then, of course, it happened. A novel coronavirus appeared in China, and in a matter of weeks our collective patterns of earning and spending, of shopping, travelling and dining out at an epic scale, abruptly faltered. In the United States, household spending dropped almost 20 percent across two months; the hardest-hit industries, such as tourism, sank four times as far. In China, retail sales fell by at least one-fifth. In Europe— where personal consumption in many countries tumbled by nearly a third—$450 billion, usually spent on shopping, instead piled up in banks. Suddenly, the idea that consumption might drop by 25 percent on the day the world stops shopping seemed like a reasonable premise: modest enough to be possible, dramatic enough to be earth-shattering.

To call this book a thought experiment is not to say it is science fiction. Maybe you could think of it as a bit of imaginative reporting: it explores a scenario that isn't real by looking to people, places and times that most certainly are. Throughout history up to the present day, multitudes, sometimes including whole nations, have drastically slowed their consumption. Often the cause was a terrible shock: war, recession, disaster. But there have also been popular movements against materialism, moments of widespread doubt about consumer culture, whole epochs in which weekly sabbaths from commerce were strictly observed. Scholars have pondered the phenomenon of not-shopping, plugged it into computer models, examined it from outer space. They have observed its effects on whales, our moods, the planetary atmosphere. There are entrepreneurs and activists, too, who are designing products, businesses and new ways of life for a world that might one day buy less. From the Kalahari Desert to Finland, from Ecuador to Japan to the United States, I found countercurrents to consumer culture flowing, whispering of other ways we could live. They also flow, I would wager, through most of us.

When I set out to write this book, I had no notion of what I might find. Nothing more, perhaps, than a scattershot of competing visions for how to move past the consumer dilemma, or no way out at all. But as I delved into examples across space and time, I could see that, wherever and whenever humanity has stopped shopping, recurring themes emerge, a pattern that hints at what a world that stops shopping might look like and how it could function. From these shadows past and present, I could sketch a future.

It just might be possible to stop shopping. If so, what remains are more personal questions. Do we want to? Would life really be worse—or better?

I

FIRST DAYS

FIRST DAYS

What we give up and
what we hang on to

Among the first to realize that the world has stopped shopping is an army of effortlessly cool young people feeling anxious about their job security. They are the global tribe of clothing retail clerks, and they have failed—catastrophically—to meet their daily sales goals.

There are, for example, nearly three thousand Levi Strauss & Co. shops across a geography quiz of countries from Azerbaijan to Moldova to Zambia, selling the company's famous blue jeans. In nearly every one of these places, the number of people who bought something, the number of items purchased per shopper, the number of shoppers, period—all have dropped precipitously. It isn't that no one on Earth needed a new pair of jeans that day, but the vast majority did not. Most of us already have a pair, or three, or fifty.

At day's end, nervous shop managers report the situation to alarmed district managers, who forward the news to unhappy regional directors, who place calls to corporate vice presidents. No more than eighteen hours after it began, a data alert from the day the world stops shopping is on the desks of Levi's three global-region presidents, in Brussels, Singapore, and a surprisingly human-scale brick building tucked between Telegraph Hill and the waterfront in San Francisco, California.

Paul Dillinger, vice president of global product innovation at Levi's, is one of the few who could say that he saw it coming. It is part of Dillinger's job, from an office cluttered with fabric samples in the San Francisco head-quarters, to contemplate apocalyptic scenarios. "Doom as a design brief," as he put it. When Cape Town, South Africa, announced in 2017 that it might run out of water, Dillinger saw an opportunity to observe what a future of resource scarcity might look like. He had an idea for a fashion statement: a denim jacket with specially designed pockets, one for a water bottle and another for a handgun.

Dillinger is not, as you will have deduced, your typical corporate veep. When I joined him in a Levi's meeting room to spin out how the day the world stops shopping would unfold in a multinational apparel company, he was dressed in a black hoodie, black sneakers, and a black watch cap that pinned down the out-turned ears that he has in common with his great uncle John Dillinger, the notorious Depression-era bank robber. He was also wearing Levi's, of course, which, in order to conserve the world's water, he had not washed in several years. (He freshens them with spritzes of vodka.) Quick-thinking and just the right amount of awkward, Dillinger is the adult version of the home-schooled prodigy who mastered the piano in between studying *Marx for Beginners* and *Capitalism for Beginners*.

The World Resources Institute has labelled consumption "the new ele-phant in the boardroom"—a problem too large to be mentioned by the corporations that sell us the stuff we buy. They fear a "Ratner moment." Twenty years ago, a British jeweller named Gerald Ratner achieved infamy when he said that the secret to his shops' ability to sell a cut-glass sherry decanter, six glasses and a serving tray for just a few pounds sterling was that they were "total crap." Forced by an outraged public to leave the company, he lost an eight-hundred-thousand-dollar salary and became legendary as "Mr. Crapner" (though he has since become a successful jeweller again). It was a sharp reminder to other businesses that, in a consumer culture, you must never admit that what you're selling may not be worth buying.

Dillinger, then, is a rarity. He has been known to publicly declare that the apparel industry is "propped up on unnecessary consumption." The greatest threat to Levi's, he said, was not that people would stop buying apparel, but rather the opposite: that the endlessly growing appetite for trousers and shirts and dresses and jackets would one day run up against the planet's finite capacity to supply the water, petroleum and cotton needed to make them. Years before the coronavirus outbreak, Dillinger had played out in his mind what might happen if an especially severe recession or global pandemic caused demand for clothing to crash. He concluded that sales would inevitably bounce back to normal, then continue to climb ever higher.

That doesn't happen on the day the world stops shopping, of course. Instead, the appetite for consumption itself disappears—and it doesn't come back. "Stop shopping for a week, and it would be a market event," Dillinger said. "No shopping for a month, and this industry falls apart."

The most telltale point about stopping shopping is that we hardly ever do it. On those rare occasions when we do, we immediately face the ancient and troublesome question of needs versus wants—what to keep buying and what to give up.

In recent years, historians and anthropologists have tried to draw a clear line in history to mark when humans first became consumers. It has proved impossible. The psychological foundation of consumer culture is materialism, or a set of values and beliefs that centre on the importance of wealth, possessions and social status—it is the strength of a person's materialism that predicts, more than any other quality, how much of a consumer they will be. Most of us think of a materialist as someone whose obsession with money, self-image and things is extreme: a greedy, shallow show-off. In fact, all of us are materialists to some extent. The reason materialism has been useful in the course of human evolution is that it pushes us to meet our material needs and maintain our standing in the community. It is an essential part of being human.

Traces of every behaviour that we associate with materialism can be found far back in time. At least 1.5 million years ago, long before our own species, *Homo sapiens*, evolved, our forebears were adding touches of style to tools like hand axes, hinting at consumer choice and self-expression through our belongings. Hunting and gathering peoples who had almost no possessions might still jealously compare their possessions to those of others. The Maya, who began their rise in Central America some four thousand years ago, formed powerful attachments to their goods and infused them with meaning, even to the extent of recognizing them as having conscious will of their own. (In one foundational Maya story, mistreated belongings—cooking pots, tortilla griddles, dogs and turkeys, even houses—rise up against the first human beings.) Nearly five hundred years ago, in the richest trade regions of China, *shiyang*—the "look of the moment"—was already changing regularly, even in villages.

Istanbul, Turkey, had more than ten thousand shops and stalls by the early seventeenth century. Ordinary British households were filling with pottery, mirrors, clocks, utensils and separate sets of tableware for special meals even before the mass production of the Industrial Revolution made these things more affordable. In the 1800s, anticipating Amazon.com by two centuries, a shopper with money to spend in Zanzibar or Tahiti could flip through a catalogue and place an order for worldwide shipping. By the First World War, Europeans looking to buy an object as basic as a chair had thousands of designs to choose from. Advertising surrounds and even tracks us today, yet the amount of money spent on marketing as a percentage of the US economy peaked a hundred years ago during the Roaring Twenties.

We didn't *become* consumers, history seems to say—we *are* consumers. Our economic lives have been disrupted by forces ranging from plagues to world wars to colonialism, but most of us, in every corner of the globe, have gradually accumulated more stuff.

The thought that human beings have always consumed offers some relief from the sense that there is something aberrant about how we consume today. It also ignores gaping differences in scale. That hunter-gatherers and today's shoppers share threads of consumer psychology doesn't mean we are all in this together. Beginning in the United States at the end of the Second World War, household spending in the wealthier countries began to rise rapidly. From 1965 onward, it absolutely shot for the stars. The surge in shopping coincided with what some call the "great acceleration," a full-tilt jump-up in the world's population, overall wealth, urbanization, resource exploitation and pollution. Only then did a popular understanding emerge that a "consumer society" was spreading around the globe, one in which we are first and foremost consumers, earning money and spending it.

The first real test of this new enthusiasm came in 1973, when Mideast oil producers, unhappy with American policy in their region, imposed an embargo on the United States, causing one of the sharpest shocks a major economy has sustained in modern times. In a televised address, Richard Nixon linked the oil crunch in part to American consumerism. "We are running out of energy today because our economy has grown enormously and because in prosperity what were once considered luxuries are now considered necessities," the president said. When Jimmy Carter took office in 1977, the embargo was over but oil supplies remained tight. In an image that came to define the era, Carter donned a beige cardigan, sat in front of a wood fire, and asked Americans to make "modest sacrifices" and "learn to live thriftily." Later, he made a more damning statement. "Too many of us now tend to worship self-indulgence and consumption. Human identity is no longer defined by what one does, but by what one owns."

Americans didn't only have presidents from the left and right of the political spectrum asking them to stop shopping. The 1970s had kicked off with twenty million people participating in the first Earth Day, led by a rising environmental movement that—aghast at the waste produced by consumer culture, which polluted rivers so badly they caught on fire, turned rain into acid, and littered the nation's highways—called for a simpler way of life. During the energy crisis, the public debated what to sacrifice in order to make America less dependent on foreign oil. Should Christmas lights be banned? Should government officials be forbidden from driving limousines? Should the Indianapolis 500 car race be discontinued? (It wasn't, but the Daytona 500 was temporarily reduced to 450 miles.)

"It's the first time that you have this invoking of the need to cut back, which is a radical shift to the American mentality," Princeton historian Meg Jacobs, who studies the 1970s oil crises, told me.

Americans responded by *increasing* household spending throughout the decade. Reflecting on this unshakeable dedication to consumption, former energy secretary James Schlesinger said, "Remember, we are talking about the habits of the American people. Moralists may find these habits reprehensible, but the public finds them satisfying."

In 2009, American consumers—who had kept shopping through the Second World War and the Vietnam War, through the social upheaval of the 1960s, through oil shocks and the rise of environmentalism, and through eleven other recessions—finally put down their wallets. The Great Recession was the first time since the Great Depression, seventy-one years earlier, that the total amount Americans spent on consumption actually declined. The people of many other nations also bought less. It created a modern portrait of how we divide between needs and wants, unclouded by a catastrophe like a war or pandemic.

Economists discovered long ago that there are things that we plainly do not require for our basic survival that we nonetheless treat as essential. Typical examples are small pleasures (or addictions) like coffee and alcohol; others, like electricity and gasoline, feel fundamental to the times that we live in. Called "necessity goods," they are sometimes described as the last things people will give up buying.

As a classic advertisement for the huge four-wheel-drive Hummer said, "Need is a very subjective word." In a consumer culture, what we consume is essential to how we express our values and identity to others; our belongings constantly signal both that we are a part of the wider social order and that we stand apart from it as unique individuals. These signals are a language that, whether consciously or not, those of us who live in consumer societies speak with remarkable fluency—so much so that we notice it most when the message is overly obvious: the meek man with the oversized truck; the nouveau riche home cluttered with gilded statues.

The idea that we are consumer zombies, buying what advertisements command us to buy, has been debunked. Consider the mysterious—but not at all uncommon—phenomenon of the shopper who goes to the mall and comes home empty-handed. Suppose we want a pair of blue jeans. In jeans, we know we will fit in (on any given day, by anthropologist Daniel Miller's estimate, half the people on Earth are wearing them), and they're comfortable, durable and generally affordable. But there is so much more that we want our jeans to tell the world about us: whether we prefer hip-hop or country music, lean toward rebellion or conformity, work with our hands or our head, and so on. "The shopper has a quite extraordinarily precise idea of themselves in relation to the vast array of consumer goods," Miller wrote in his book *Consumption and Its Consequences*. If we can't find a pair that does enough for us, we might—despite ads on our phones, influencers on social media, and hundreds of available styles—buy no pair of jeans at all.

Saying that anything can be a need is not the same as saying that everything is one. Yes, collectible porcelain dolls, shoes specifically designed for exploring canyons, or daily trips to McDonald's could, for any given person, be something they would continue to pony up for until life became truly desperate. During the Great Recession, however, patterns in the US—a nation with fine-grained household spending statistics—showed that when the going gets tough, Americans do divide needs from wants in broadly similar ways.

What did they give up first? The community of Elkhart, Indiana, offers one clear answer. The Recreational Vehicle Capital of the World, also known as Trailer Town, produces as many as four-fifths of made-in-America RVs—motorhomes, caravans, campers, land yachts, ships of the open road. This fact has long made Elkhart an early warning system for any tremor in consumer confidence. In the 1973 energy crunch, for example, people stopped buying RVs "like somebody shut off a switch," one manufacturing executive said. Four months later, as the crisis eased, "nobody could build them fast enough." The Great Recession began in Elkhart more than a year early—at one point, recreational vehicle sales dropped 80 percent *in a single week*. When it comes to stopping shopping, motorhomes are the first to go.

(As an aside that proves the point that what is dispensable in one case may be indispensable in another, sales of RVs and camperized "vanlife" vans, often costing a hundred thousand dollars or more, soared during the coronavirus pandemic among those who wanted to travel while avoiding shared spaces like restaurants, hotels and planes.)

Alongside recreational vehicles as the most expendable purchases in the Great Recession were all-terrain vehicles. Next in line were sport utility vehicles and pickup trucks, which declined in sales by nearly a third, followed closely by "pleasure aircraft," motorcycles and recreational boats. Then came cars. Americans spent 25 percent less on them. These seem intuitive—big-ticket purchases that most people can hang on to for a few more years before truly needing something new. Next on the chopping block were carpets.

After that we start into more everyday items. Americans cut back by 15 to 20 percent on jewellery, flowers and house plants, musical instruments and furniture, and by 10 to 15 percent on textbooks, major household appliances like refrigerators and washing machines, courier services, airfares, tools and hardware, watches, sports equipment (including guns, which, again, were in high demand during the pandemic), cookware and tableware. "Yep, yep, yep," said Alan Zell, a commercial real estate agent with decades of experience in Phoenix, Arizona, as he remembered the boarded-up stores. "Those are the extra expense items that you might not need to buy."

Some goods and services—land-line telephones, camera film, video rental stores—were already trending downward, and the recession gave them the final shove into the dustbin of history. Yet it would be inaccurate to say that people cut costs across the board: the Great Recession had widely shared necessity goods as well. Television sales soared as people traded up to the newer, bigger flat-screen models. The amount we spent on cell phones, personal computers, digital gadgets and internet access all climbed through every year of the downturn. Spending on restaurant meals declined, but only by 6 percent; in many countries, dining out is no longer an extravagance but an essential part of contemporary life. Nail parlours, with their promise of affordable luxury, held their own, though Zell marked the seriousness of the Great Recession in part by the fact that they suffered at all. "Usually, they are an unaffected type of business. It just seems that they roll along."

A decade after it ended, in Phoenix the recession was still visible from the air: dotted around the adobe-coloured city, like tissue paper on shaving cuts, were the blank squares of empty big-box stores. Phoenix lost thirteen linen stores alone, split between the big-box plazas and the malls. Yet Phoenicians quickly forgot what used to fill the abandoned spaces. Circuit City, Linens 'n Things, Kmart—stripped of their brands, the buildings all look the same, their paint paling under the Sonoran Desert sun. They were symbols of what Americans decided they could live without.

A recession, though, even a great one, offers only a rough sketch of the end of shopping. In a typical economic downturn, many people don't buy fewer things, only cheaper things; richer people continue to spend freely on their wants, while the poorest cut back even on basic needs. Overall in the Great Recession, household spending by Americans dropped by only 3.5 percent—hardly the end of consumerism.

The day the world stops shopping would be different. While the things we cut back on would likely track the Great Recession, the magnitude of the drop in spending would more closely mirror the global coronavirus shutdown. Even it had necessity goods, many of them the kinds of products we might also turn to in a sharp turn away from consumer culture: bicycles, bread-making lames, gardening gloves. Reduce global consumerism by one-quarter, though, and there's no avoiding the fact that humanity is buying less of nearly everything.

About forty-eight hours after the world stops shopping, Dillinger said, the entire clothing and fashion industry would be abuzz with speculation about the sudden collapse in consumer confidence. That's when the shock wave would ripple out in new directions, affecting tens of millions of people.

The apparel trade as a whole is valued at $1.3 trillion. If Fashion Nation was an actual country, it would have the world's fifteenth-largest economy and employ a global workforce roughly equal to the population of the United States. The cotton industry alone provides wages to 250 million people in eighty countries, or about 3 percent of the world's population. Levi's uses less than 1 percent of the cotton produced each year, but that still means that cutting Levi's sales in half—clothing tends to be harder hit than consumption as a whole when shopping drops—results in lost income for roughly 1,250,000 people worldwide, including in the United States, which is the world's third-largest cotton producer.

In a typical year, Levi's buys fabric from cotton mills in sixteen countries, including the major manufacturing centres you know from your clothing labels—China, India, Bangladesh—but also reaching as far as Bahrain, Lesotho and Nicaragua. Add in the factories that dye, sew and otherwise make Levi's products, and the supplier list totals more than five hundred, many with thousands of employees. The message that Levi's planned to dramatically cut back production would trickle down to real companies that are owned by and employ real people, firms like Splendid Chance International, based in Phnom Penh, Cambodia; Sleepy's, in Guadalajara, Mexico; and Keep It Here Inc., in Commerce, California.

"How quickly can that message get to the zipper maker and the cotton mill?" said Dillinger. "How quickly can the mill get it to the people they're procuring cotton from? And those cotton people are getting the cotton from a field somewhere. The field is going to be the last to know, and it was probably already planted, right?"

Ironically, the fast-fashion clothiers that constantly spin out cheap new styles would respond more nimbly than traditional firms. Some fast-fashion labels can design a garment, manufacture it and put it on sale in a matter of weeks; they can stop the cycle just as quickly. For slower-churn companies like Levi's, it would be months before existing orders are completed and loaded onto cargo ships in mega-ports like Singapore and Shanghai. "We're not going to stop the boats and just have them sit in the water. So they do come in. They do drive a serious inventory problem." In Levi's warehouses, unsold jeans and other garments would begin to pile high.

Similar ripples convulse almost every industry. Smartphones are a modern necessity good, but in a lower-consuming world, more of us would hang on to our phones for another year or two—at least—before we upgrade. Who's affected? Research into the iPhone supply chain once found contributions ranging from designers in California to software developers in the Netherlands to camera-tech companies in Japan to manufacturers in China. Nearly eight hundred businesses in two dozen countries were involved, and that's not including the mining and processing of the raw materials that go into the phones, including nineteen chemical elements ranging from familiar ores like gold, lead and copper to rare earth minerals such as yttrium and praseodymium.

In the 1970s energy crises, truckers—the major delivery system for goods at the time—were dubbed the "first victims" of the slowdown in American consumption; today, it would be Amazon. The company's headquarters in Seattle, Washington, is a downtown in and of itself, populated on the city's typically rainy days by crowds of people, from coders to couriers, carrying the company's cheerfully totalitarian-looking orange-and-white umbrellas. The company has spent tens of billions of dollars in Seattle alone, and its army of employees spreads its money to coffee shops, craft breweries, vegan eateries, gyms and dozens of other businesses.

Amazon boomed as shopping moved online during the pandemic, but the company is ultimately powered by household consumption. From the moment the world stops shopping the orange-and-white umbrellas would begin to close. In New York, where home delivery quadrupled in the 2010s, a 25 percent drop in online orders would mean 375,000 fewer packages a day. Almost overnight, the worst gridlock in the United States would ease, raising traffic speeds in the most congested parts of Manhattan above a jogger's pace for the first time in years.

By far the worst chaos and loss, though, would fall on people in poorer nations who now make most of the world's products and provide many of its services, too. Sarah Labowitz, a Houston-based human rights advocate, worked for years to improve conditions for such workers. When she visited Bangladesh after the Rana Plaza disaster of 2013, in which a factory collapse killed more than a thousand people making clothes for brands based in Britain, Spain, Italy, the US, Canada and beyond, Labowitz asked garment workers if they had a message for consumers in the West. "They would say, 'Yes. Keep placing orders,'" Labowitz said. The workers wanted better labour laws, but their greatest fear was the collapse of the industry that kept them in paycheques.

Dillinger's mind turns immediately to countries where violent Islamic fundamentalists have attracted significant followings—and where the apparel industry is a major contributor to national economies. A consumer slowdown is a jolt that moves from wealthier countries, where most of the consuming happens, to poorer ones, but there is also a risk of blowback in the opposite direction. "We should all be worried about what happens when the money from Western consumption stops flowing into Turkey, Egypt, Tunisia, Pakistan," Dillinger said. "Our outside consumption has actually been something that's purchased political stability in areas where we are disliked."

A straight line between stopping shopping and a spike in international terror. George W. Bush's words begin to seem prophetic: *You are with us, or you are with the terrorists.*

One place that doesn't feel the sudden blow of a world that stops shopping is your closet. A day without shopping? "No one would be running around pantless," Dillinger said. A week? "Still, everyone's got pants on." A month? That's enough time for some people's bodies—pregnant women, for example, or growing children—to change enough to need something new. "But by and large, pants on everyone." Fashions don't fundamentally change on timelines anywhere near that fast. Dillinger likes to show people a photo of the cast of the 1990s television hit *Seinfeld* alongside a photo of the cast of the 2010s show *Modern Family*. Though the programs are separated by twenty years, you could swap the actors' attire from one photo to the other and scarcely notice the difference. In fact, Dillinger said, by modifying clothes that already exist we could clothe everyone without any additional shopping whatsoever, even as the world's population climbs to ten billion and beyond. "We have all of the raw materials we need. Your closet is already full of them," he said.

He is supported by the numbers. In 2016, the global consulting firm McKinsey & Company reported that six out of ten articles of clothing end up in a garbage dump or trash incinerator within a year of being made. Only a small portion of those garments are scrapped because they fail to sell—most really are clothes that we buy and then throw away. They are the clothes that we get as gifts but don't actually like, promotional T-shirts and hats handed out at events, things that we buy as one-offs because we need something green to wear for St. Patrick's Day. More and more, however, they are simply clothes that we purchase because they are cheap, without much thought to whether we will keep them.

Many of today's clothes are not, in any case, made to last: socks and tights that fall apart in a matter of hours, shirts that lose buttons, trousers that tear, sweaters that pill, clothing that shrinks or stains or is ruined at the cleaners, T-shirts that get those tiny, mysterious holes that are a staple of internet threads. (*Do I have moths? Bugs?* No, you have planned obsolescence. The holes are caused by today's thin fabrics rubbing at the belt line, against countertops, and what have you.) The ultimate in clothing turnover is the white T-shirt, which is cheaply made, stains easily, and sells poorly in second-hand stores because no one wants to wear your cheap and stained white T-shirt.

Imagine, then, that you have been buying ten articles of clothing a year. Take away the six you typically get rid of within a year and you end up with four. Now imagine that you're buying half as many garments, or five each year. You're still left with four to keep, and one to throw away.

It's the consumer dilemma in a nutshell. Buy half as many clothes and it's an asteroid strike on the world economy. Your wardrobe, on the other hand, hasn't even begun to shrink.

We don't shop equally,
so we won't stop equally

Six thousand kilometres south of the Levi's headquarters, Fernanda Paez rolled through the sunburned midday streets of Quito, capital city of the South American nation of Ecuador. "I'm not so poor and not so rich," she said, laughing. "I'm fashionably average." On the day the world stops shopping, that makes her a figure of international importance.

Paez is a *taxista*, or taxi driver, which is just as unusual a job for a woman in Ecuador as it is anywhere in the world. When we met, she was driving a basic sedan—a taxi-yellow Chevrolet Aveo Family. She bought the car second-hand and put a hundred thousand kilometres on it in just two and a half years, and when she told me this, she sat up taller in the driver's seat. Paez is not tall. She is small and featherweight and appears younger than her thirty-something years. Despite this she conveys toughness. She has a habit of locking eyes over the rims of her sunglasses when she wants to give weight to her words.

"Yes, I have a television," she said. "What I don't have is a television in every room."

You have heard it said that if everyone on Earth lived like the average American, we would need five Earths' worth of resources to sustain our lifestyles. The obvious problem is that we don't have five Earths. We only have one.

A nonprofit organization called Global Footprint Network has been fine-tuning these calculations for nearly two decades. They begin by breaking the planet down into the hectares—units a little larger than a typical soccer field—that are biologically productive for human uses, then assigning each one an average amount of that productivity. The parcels are called "global hectares," and if they were split equally among all humankind, we would each get 1.6 of them. Think of that as roughly the share that would be available to every individual if the world's land and water resources were shared equally—which, of course, they are not.

Besides needs and wants, there is another way to draw lines around what it means to stop shopping: whether or not we are consuming beyond what the earth can sustain. According to Global Footprint Network, humankind is now consuming 2.7 global hectares per person on average. This is the size of our "ecological footprint," and it is 170 percent larger than the planet can provide for over the long term. (Ecological footprints, like most global data, are a crude metric. The network's scientists call it "a minimum reference value for the magnitude of human demand on nature.") To figure out how many planets we would need if we all lived like the average American, researchers start with the number of global hectares' worth of resources an average American needs to meet the demands of their consumption. The average American's ecological footprint is 8 global hectares. Since that is five times the 1.6 global hectares' worth of resources available to each person worldwide, we know that it would take five worlds to sustain Planet America.

The same calculation can be made for other countries, and doing so makes plain how unequally consumption occurs around the globe. Suppose we all lived like the average citizen of Afghanistan, one of the world's poorest countries; we could shrink Earth by half and still have enough resources to maintain everyone at that standard of living. We'd need a little more than two planets if we all lived like the average Chinese, roughly two and a half if we were all Spanish, British or New Zealander; three if we lived on Planet Italy, Planet Germany or Planet Netherlands; three and a half to live like they do in Russia, Finland or Norway; and four or more to enjoy the way of life in Sweden, South Korea, Australia or Canada. And if we lived on Planet Ecuador, we would need just one Earth—the one that actually exists.

Ecuador's consumer lifestyle is considered "globally replicable," meaning that all of us could consume like the average Ecuadorian—Fernanda Paez, for example—without us ever running out of natural resources. It's sometimes called "one-planet living."

What does this lifestyle look like? That is, what is a sustainable standard of consumption on Earth, not in some imaginary future of wind-powered airplanes and clothing made of kale, but right now?

It takes half an hour to drive from Quito, which is tossed like a salad in a bowl of Andean mountains, to the suburban barrio where Paez lives. Called Carapungo, it sprawls across a bench of land between the peaks that surround Quito and a slashing gully that falls away to the Middle of the World—Ecuador is named for the fact that it is split by the equator, the line that divides the planet into north and south, which passes just north of the capital. The neighbourhood is scruffy and graffitied, with a main street lined with small shops in front of which the business owners are forever sweeping their patch of broken sidewalk spotlessly clean.

"People here struggle, but they don't suffer," said Paez.

The outline of her life seems familiar enough. She had a partner named Henri, two children (a boy and a girl—she has since added another boy), and a standard schnauzer named Locky. They were living on the top storey of a melon-coloured condominium owned by her in-laws, who occupied the lower floors. Everyone had enough to eat, and their clothing—the family favoured soccer-themed sportswear—wouldn't look out of place in any but the ritzier districts of Europe or North America.

Yet to many in richer countries, Paez's lifestyle would seem inadequate. Hot water did not run from the taps in her apartment; the family used an on-the-spot electrical heating system for the shower. Her children shared a bedroom and received a daily allowance of $1.50 (Ecuador uses American dollars as its currency). The family had a refrigerator and a washing machine, but no dryer; they hung clothes to dry on the terrace. At Christmas, the bonus that Henri received from the factory where he worked making seats for GM cars was paid not in money, but in nearly a year's worth of rice, sugar and cooking oil. The whole family had one desktop computer, and only the adults had mobile phones. "Technology has become indispensable," Paez said. "It is necessary to have those things." They were running a tight budget, but it was not without its luxuries. Paez owned thirty pairs of shoes.

The family rarely went to restaurants, and in their spare time they played soccer (all of them) or gathered with family and friends. Though many people in Carapungo did not own cars, Fernanda's family was able, sometimes, to drive in her taxi to one of Ecuador's national parks, or make the plunging descent from their home, nearly three kilometres above sea level in the Andes, to the beaches along the Pacific coast. But no one in the family had ever flown in an airplane.

Much of Ecuador is like this: a lifestyle that resembles that of richer nations, but seems to have shrunk in the wash. The country does not have a "third world" feeling. Poverty is visible, especially in urban slums, but the breadth of middle-class life is impossible to miss: people train for marathons, families go out for Chinese food, there's a lot of fresh-poured pavement. ("We have the best highways in South America," one man said to me, "but not the best drivers.") Toilets flush, lights turn on.

Yet the bathroom of even a four-star hotel offers a Lilliputian bar of soap and an eye-dropper bottle of shampoo. Air conditioners are rare. Meals are filling and tasty, but there isn't much meat in them, and it isn't unusual for street stalls to serve food on real crockery, with metal utensils, rather than in throwaway containers. As a general rule, shops, restaurants, cafés and bars aren't busy. A surprisingly large number close on weekends, and it's rare, outside of the richest neighbourhoods, to meet anyone who says they enjoy shopping as a pastime. The residents of Quito are known as *quiteños*; tell them that you're getting around town on foot, and they smile and say, "Ah, like a quiteño."

The United Nations classifies countries on a curve from "low human development" to "very high human development." As of 2018, none of the sixty-two very highly developed nations—the list includes all the countries you'd expect and many you might not, such as Chile, Kazakhstan and Malaysia—were living at a one-planet level. Yet there is some good news. A few "high human development" nations *are* living one-planet lifestyles. Ecuador is one of them.

Make no mistake: the gap between "very high" and merely "high" human development is significant. For citizens in many nations with very high human development, a shift to the average Ecuadorian standard of living would come at a cost of about five years' expected lifespan and education. Compared nation by nation, the differences narrow. People in the US live only two years longer than Ecuadorians. People in Canada, a very highly developed nation, exceed Ecuador in years of schooling by only one year. And while income inequality in Ecuador is greater than in most "very high" countries, including all of the European Union, it is similar to the United States. In fact, Ecuador has less unequal income distribution than a number of US states and territories. It is considerably more equal than Puerto Rico, for example—or Washington, DC.

By the latest count, nine countries had both a high level of development and were consuming at or very close to a one-planet level: Cuba, Sri Lanka, Armenia, the Dominican Republic, the Philippines, Jamaica, Indonesia, Egypt and Ecuador. They share one other trait in common: all of them have per capita incomes that are radically lower than in the rich world. According to World Bank figures, the average person in Ecuador has purchasing power equal to someone earning $11,500 in the United States. Meanwhile, the per capita income in the US is over $65,000.

People with less purchasing power have less to spend on goods and services. Put bluntly, poorer people are not the problem when it comes to consumption. There are at least fifty-three entire countries where the average person consumes at or below a one-planet level. (Planet India would need to be only three-quarters as large as Earth. If we all lived like the average resident of Eritrea, an impoverished nation on the Horn of Africa, we could survive on a world just a little larger than the moon.) Taken together, these countries account for nearly half of the global population.

An uncomfortable truth emerges: as measured by their ecological footprints, the day the world stops shopping would demand tremendously deep cuts in consumption in the richer corners of the globe. Meanwhile, billions of people have yet, really, to *start* shopping. Some are already consuming no more than their fair share. Many others are *underconsuming*—still waiting for the day when they are able to meet their basic needs.

Even in the richest countries there are people who consume at or below the one-planet level. These are not, for the most part, urbanites with vegan diets and the muscular legs of avid cyclists. They are people who don't earn a lot of money.

The Economic Policy Institute in Washington, DC, studies the cost of living across the United States to determine what families need to earn in order to attain a "modest yet adequate standard of living." They call this the "family budget."

"It's not poverty," Elise Gould, a senior economist with the institute, told me. "There are a lot of people in this country—millions—who are living paycheque-to-paycheque. It reflects that kind of idea."

A family-budget household in America spends 25 percent less than average—for the purposes of my thought experiment, they have effectively stopped shopping. These are people who can afford not only to survive, but to participate in the social and economic life of their times—to achieve, as consumer affairs pioneer Caroline Ware called it back in the 1940s, "economic citizenship." They may not own the latest iPhone, but the adults in the house will own cell phones of some kind. If they're in the city, they probably live in an apartment; if in the country, perhaps a small house. "They would typically have a television, they would have a dining room table, they would have places to sit in their homes. You're not walking through a house that's bare," said Gould.

Their lives would look familiar to Fernanda Paez, just as her life in Ecuador would seem ordinary to them. The family-budget household has at least one extra bedroom for the kids, a single computer and one car. The fridge and cupboards are stocked with food (probably not organic food, because "they're looking for deals"), but the family rarely dines in restaurants. Their clothes are not the latest fashions, but not out of fashion, either. "They're able to buy winter coats in the winter and put shoes on their feet, but you're not talking about keeping up with the trends," Gould said. They make up a large fraction of the 53 percent of Americans who rarely or never travel by airplane. Places in the US where the cost of living is close to the family-budget standard include DeFuniak Springs, Florida; Friendsville, Tennessee; and Kansas in general—the kinds of places that the typical tourist never visits. For cities, we're talking Detroit and Houston, not New York or Los Angeles. About half of Americans consume at or below the family-budget level.

The lifestyle will also ring a bell for anyone who remembers the twentieth century. Restaurant meals as a rare treat, hand-me-down clothing, holidays close to home, the sluggish pace of commercial life, the sense that it is the exception rather than the rule to spend any money at all on a typical day—most people alive today can still remember when these were widespread norms. According to Global Footprint Network, 1970 was probably the last year that the human race as a whole was still engaged in one-planet living. The richer nations went into overshoot earlier, of course: the network's analysts estimate that the average US lifestyle exceeded global replicability sometime between 1940 and 1960. The same is true of the UK, Canada, Germany and most other rich countries, though a few crossed the line later, such as Spain, Italy and Japan in the mid 1960s, and South Korea as late as 1979. Think of it this way: the US population is 60 percent higher today than it was in 1970, but consumer spending as a whole, adjusted for inflation, is up 400 percent. Compared to 1965, it's up nearly 500 percent. Turn back the clock only as far as Generation X, and you shed whole planets' worth of overshoot.

The standard at which a person feels like an economic citizen is constantly rising. We eat at restaurants more and more often. We own more shoes for more occasions. The pandemic accelerated a trend toward fully furnished "outdoor rooms," in some cases complete with big-screen TVs. Cars are newer and larger; the percentage of cars sold worldwide each year that are SUVs has doubled since the year 2000. Whole new realms of consumption are widespread that hardly existed two decades ago— Amazon-style delivery of all things, foodyism and its ever-expanding compendium of kitchen gadgets, an ironically large number of products to help us declutter our homes. Not only clothing, but housewares, furniture and even the basic structure of homes (size of rooms, number of walls) now move quickly through fashion cycles. Between work, play and family, many people today fly as much as only the elite—diplomats, film stars, politicians, the Pope—did at the turn of the millennium. These days, even a family-budget household might be awash in dollar-store junk bought on maxed-out credit cards and loans. We consume radically more than we did, but it feels as though nothing has changed.

Ecuador has been attracting people who consider an earlier standard of living not only tolerable, but better. I met Bruce Finch, formerly of Austin, Texas, living in Cotacachi, a quietly busy small town at the foot of a volcano about two hours from Quito. Silver haired and square-jawed, in a Panama hat, T-shirt and shorts, he had the look of the classic gringo, but he hadn't come to Ecuador so much as he had left America behind. Part of what drove him out, he said, was "political correctness and all the bullshit that goes with that." But it was also the American lifestyle. He didn't recognize it in his home country anymore. In Ecuador, he did.

"It takes me back to when I was a kid growing up. I lived in a small community in south Texas, where everybody knew everybody, you knew the grocers' names. It was just a nice feeling. It's the same here," he said. "It's not that way in Austin—you don't know anybody, you have to get in the damn car to drive just to the grocery store. Here, I walk everywhere. I've lost thirty pounds! And not from trying to, just from living this type of life."

Finch had moved into an apartment on one of Cotacachi's downtown streets. He had no plans to go home again.

"These are basically happy people," he said. "They don't have as many things as Americans do, but that's all Americans pursue is things—they're materialistic. These people are not as much that way. They do like things, of course. But it doesn't play on their souls to have them."

"It is said so often and in such ignorance that Mexicans are contented, happy people. 'They don't want anything.' This, of course, is not a description of the happiness of Mexicans, but of the unhappiness of the person who says it."

So wrote John Steinbeck after he sailed, eighty years ago, up the long, open artery of Mexico's Gulf of California, encountering men who, he said, seemed able to acquire a canoe, fishing harpoon, pair of trousers, shirt and hat and consider themselves "fairly well set up in life." Steinbeck didn't trust his observation. Were these people truly happy?

It has long been a cliché that people from the manic, materialistic West travel to poorer countries and admire the simple, happy life they see there. (Very few of those travellers return home and promptly give up materialism.) Today, thanks to global surveys, we can say something more objective on the matter. At the time I visited Ecuador, it ranked fiftieth among nations for self-reported happiness. That was lower on the list than most wealthy countries, but higher than some, such as Kuwait, South Korea, Japan and Russia.

Where Ecuador and many other developing countries shine is in generating happiness at a more sustainable level of consumption. The Happy Planet Index, compiled by the UK-based New Economics Foundation, combines measures of self-reported well-being, life expectancy, inequality and ecological footprint. By those standards, Ecuador was a top-ten nation. Most very highly developed countries don't even make the top twenty, with the United States plummeting to 108th out of 140 measured countries, and Canada sinking to 85th place. In effect, the richest countries have an efficiency problem: they are squandering consumption without transforming much of it into joy. As American consumption rose 25 percent in the past fifteen years, did it produce 25 percent more happiness? Did it, in fact, produce more happiness at all?

For nearly five years during the 2010s, Ecuador had a Minister of Happiness—that's what the international media called him, anyway. Or the Minister of Good Living, or State Secretary of Well-being. He was Freddy Ehlers, a TV personality rarely seen without his trademark *sombrero de paja toquilla* (a Panama hat, which every Ecuadorian will tell you, correctly, was actually invented in Ecuador), and his actual title was *Secretario del Buen Vivir*. Ehlers considered it untranslatable. There is, he told me, no term in

English for *buen vivir* that does not imply living "better," a fact that said a lot to him about Western culture.

"If you use the word 'better,' you have to compare to something," Ehlers told me, sitting in a boardroom in his secretariat's offices, located in an eerily abandoned airport. "And with what do you compare? I want to live better than my grandfather. I want to live better than my dad. I want to live better than my brother, better than my neighbour—especially the neighbour. I want to live better than the way I lived twenty years ago, ten years ago, five years ago. We don't propose to live better, because living better is destroying the planet. We propose to live well."

Ehlers was a controversial figure, signing documents not with his name but with a sketch of a smiling tree, and convincing visitors (including colonels in the national army) to join him in Zen meditation during the lunch hour. "Poverty is not who has a little and who has a lot. Poverty is wanting more and more and more and never being satisfied with what you have," he said. It was a hard sell in a country where many could not afford the essentials but saw the lifestyles of the rich every day on television. When a new government was elected, Ehlers was fired on its first day in office. Ecuadorians had rejected the idea that they have buen vivir.

Fernanda Paez was an exception. "I think we do have buen vivir," she said.

When Paez was a girl, her family lived in a mechanic's garage in Quito as caretakers. It was not the safest playground. At the age of nine, she climbed onto the back of a derelict bus and—as children do—fell off. She was bedridden for six months with a broken pelvis. Her parents used that time to build a house in Carapungo, which at the time was countryside. The new house Paez moved into had no running water, no electricity, but it was, she said, a profoundly peaceful place to live.

"People used to say, Who will come to live in Carapungo? Who will come to live in such a castaway place? And look!" She gestures to the entrance of the barrio, where dozens of people now wait for buses and taxis along the curb of the Pan-American Highway at all hours, or mill about the little-bit-of-everything shops called *micromaxis*. "We lack for nothing in Carapungo."

Even so, she and Henri had bought a vacant property in a nearby *cuchara*—in Ecuador, the Spanish word for "spoon" is also the word for "cul-de-sac"—where they planned to build a new home. "I think we will build a small house," Paez said. "Because the children will grow up and leave, and then their rooms will be too big." Still, it would be one of the few stand-alone houses in Carapungo. Paez and her family were becoming above-average Ecuadorians. On the day the world stops shopping, even they might have to consume a little less.

Across the globe, the day the world stops shopping would play out in nearly 8 billion individual stories. In the poorer parts of the world, most households would hardly alter their daily habits, while a minority of wealthier citizens sharply reduce their consumption. In the rich world, the pattern is reversed: a few scarcely notice the difference, while the majority plunge into a torrent of change. It would be a shock so great that it would seem to bend time itself.

It's not that time turns weird,
it's a different kind of time

The parking lot of the Garden State Plaza, where you can buy everything from a McDonald's Extra Value Meal to a luxury Tesla SUV, fits eleven thousand vehicles. This day, it is nearly empty, a sweep of graphite-coloured asphalt curving around the mall. Kids play street hockey in front of a shuttered Macy's store. Blue jays caw from the plaza landscaping. Only an occasional vehicle beetles by on the six-lane highway. The stillness, the quiet, has an apocalyptic air, like a scene from the coronavirus lockdowns. The mall is closed? Something serious must be happening.

"This was once just as commonplace as anything American," Judith Shulevitz, author of *The Sabbath World*, told me. The Garden State Plaza is in Bergen, the last county in the US that still bans shopping on Sundays.

We have seen that it is almost unheard of for people to stop shopping by choice, but Bergen County does, once a week. It is not, incidentally, some isolated religious enclave where fashions haven't changed since the seventeenth century. Far from it: Bergen lies just across the Hudson River from New York City; you can get there in half an hour from Times Square. Why did Sunday closing laws endure in Bergen County? "Paramus," said Paul Contillo. "That's the answer I can give you: Paramus. The sheer volume of what goes on here."

The town of Paramus is the economic hub of Bergen County, and Contillo is a Bergen legend, now in his nineties, who at one time or another has held nearly every political position available in the district. White-haired, blue-eyed and patrician, he'd be perfectly cast as a Roman senator in a movie. When he first moved to Bergen from Brooklyn, in 1955, Paramus was a rural borough—"deer, fox in the backyard"—and people did their shopping on Main Street in county centres such as nearby Hackensack. Today, Paramus is a community of bosky streets, white colonial houses—and an absolute meg-apalooza of malls, outlet shops and big-box stores.

Beginning in the 1950s, discount outlets luring New York shoppers began to toadstool along Paramus's highways; Bergen also became home to one of the first preplanned suburbs to feature shopping malls. Local mom-and-pop shops, afraid they'd have to work seven days a week to compete, formed a lobby with church groups and residents concerned about traffic congestion, and before the first real mall had even opened, Paramus had passed its own "blue laws" limiting Sunday sales. (Historians say that this American term for Sunday closing laws stems from the colour of paper that early Puritan settlers used to print their own sabbath rules, or else from a slang term for Puritanism in that era.)

By the end of 1957, Paramus was home to the nation's largest shopping complex. The impact on small, local retailers in the county really was sub-stantial. Within three years, 10 percent of Hackensack's Main Street busi-nesses closed. New Jersey lawmakers decided to let each county in the state hold its own referendum on a blue law that would forbid the sale of cloth-ing, furniture, appliances and building materials on Sundays. More than half the state's counties opted in, including Bergen, which went on to pro-hibit Sunday shopping almost completely. The United States as a whole gradually became the most sabbatarian nation on Earth. By the 1960s, there were Sunday closing rules of some kind in every state but Alaska. It's easy to overlook how radical this really is. Sunday closing sounds quaint to modern ears, but if it were implemented tomorrow, it would amount to an immediate 15 percent drop in shopping time.

Only in Bergen has a full suite of blue laws survived—not *in spite of* the rise of consumer culture, but *because of it*. Six days a week, Bergen, and especially Paramus, is a hypermodern bazaar of sales, trinkets, trends, fashions, distractions and technologies, all packed into the kind of malls where your boot prints are quickly mopped to a sparkle behind you. One day a week, it stops. Relaxing in his home on a Sunday morning, Contillo said that the shutdown is popular across partisan, religious and cultural lines. "It's a family day," he said. People get together to eat, or talk, or drink, or do sports, or make a trip together to the Jersey Shore. "Or just do nothing."

Is it an act of anti-consumerism?

"We use a different word for it," Contillo replied. "We call it 'quality of life.'"

What do people actually do when they stop shopping? Until the coronavirus outbreak brought consumerism to a grinding halt, we had largely forgotten. For more than a generation, we had lived in a 24/7 economy, with a growing list of shops and restaurants that stayed open 365 days a year. Even if you lived in some exotic place—Bhutan, say, or Antarctica— where consumer culture had yet to invade every moment of daily life, you could always watch a movie on your phone or spend $2,300 shopping online for a programmable, app-connected shower head for your bathroom. The ability to buy things whenever, wherever, became so much the water we swam in that we soon forgot it had ever been any other way.

But this way of life was both new and unusual. Among the globe's richest countries, Sunday closing was widespread just thirty years ago, recent enough that many people can remember learning to drive in empty mall parking lots on Sundays, or roaming as teenagers through shuttered downtowns. On the day the world stops shopping, an older, even ancient, architecture of time is revived, one founded on hours no longer spent working or spending. It is the first change that begins to make way for personal transformation.

Even the earliest human cultures enjoyed days of rest from economic life, but the idea of marking out a single day each week as a break from practical work in order to make room for spiritual work began with the founding of the Jewish sabbath—what the Israeli poet Chaim Nachman

Bialik called "the most brilliant creation of the Hebrew spirit." In that tradition, the sabbath was a day to cease from creating, a day defined by a sensation of *shinui*, or change. It was an early act of resistance against the idea that every moment of our lives be filled with busyness, commerce and trade—in other words, against time as we have come to know it.

The Jewish sabbath falls mainly on Saturday, but Sunday was the sabbath that took over much of the globe. It began 1,700 years ago, when the Roman emperor Constantine, a Christian, banned official business and manufacturing on Sundays. The Sunday sabbath has been many things since: a day of music, feasting and boozing; a day of moral purity, when such crimes as vigorous horseback riding could be punished with arrest or even flogging; a day to watch sports on TV. Always, though, it was a day to stop working—and shopping.

In the late 1940s, a social research organization called Mass Observation set out to determine just what people were getting up to on the sabbath in Britain. There was a last-chance urgency to the research. In London, pubs, public transportation, museums and cinemas had already begun opening on Sundays, and so had recreational facilities such as swimming pools. Still, most things remained closed, restaurants and cafés included, and organized sports were forbidden. Outside of London, the shutdown was almost total. In Scotland, even children's swings were put out of use, a sight we wouldn't see again for seventy years, when playgrounds were closed behind CAUTION tape during the pandemic lockdowns.

Christianity had not been the dominant force behind Britain's sabbath for decades. By the time Mass Observation hit the streets, just three out of every twenty people were attending church on Sunday—fewer than went to the pub, and less than half the number who worked in their gardens. In another quirk of resemblance to the pandemic, most people didn't leave their homes at all. The main Sunday activity, if it can be called that, was not the pursuit of happiness but rather the pursuit of aimlessness.

People chin-wagged. They napped and slept in. They played cards, drank tea, did odd jobs, wrote letters. They recovered from Saturday night's hangover. Some visited with friends, the elderly or the disabled. In good weather, which there wasn't as much of in pre-climate-change Britain, they journeyed in droves to parks, beaches and the countryside. Young people, especially, made day-long excursions by bicycle that seem improbable by today's standards of fitness—riding 140 kilometres round-trip from London to Southend-on-Sea, for example. They made their own fun: the district of Hammersmith had a bicycle speedway, built where German bombs had levelled several houses during the Second World War, around which competing youth clubs raced for glory in helmets, gumboots and what is described as a "pseudo-leather body covering."

Mass Observation summed up Britain's overall attitude toward Sundays in the words of one fifteen-year-old: "Nothing particular ever happens, and yet I would not call it dull." Two out of three people liked the day as it was, and many more had at least mixed feelings about it. Just a few years earlier, a pair of homesick British soldiers, jailed in Singapore's Changi prisoner-of-war camp, had written a song about Sunday in London. It lists the various entertainments that weren't available, all the goings-on that were not going on. "It may seem rather funny," the song says, "but we like it that way."

Sunday wasn't just life with the volume turned down; it was a different kind of day. It had shinui. There was the "Sunday orgy of newspaper reading," as Mass Observation put it. Nine out of ten people read at least one newspaper on Sunday, and more than a quarter read three or more. They read differently, as well. During the busy workweek, people mainly followed the daily news. On Sundays, they read more deeply (longer articles that gave context to the events of the day) but also more shallowly (entertainment news, gossip and scandal). They listened to a lot of radio, too.

People ate differently, preparing larger, more elaborate meals—one group notable for their ambivalence about Sundays was housewives, for whom it was extra work. They dressed differently, putting on their "Sunday best" whether or not they went to church. They even drank differently, sipping beer in the pubs at a measurably slower pace. A conclusion becomes unavoidable: *the people themselves were different on Sundays.* This is captured in the full-moon-like transformation of a police officer and his public wards over glasses of beer in an English steel town:

A fifty-year-old Police Inspector comes into the bar every midday and drinks two or three halves of bitter—treating nobody and nobody treating him. On a Sunday midday he has as many as nine halves of bitter—being treated, and, in his turn, buying rounds. This happens every Sunday.

There is a sense in the Mass Observation report of people who were practised at using this different kind of time—who were good at it. When the Covid-19 shutdowns began, we learned that, for the most part, people today are not. Faced with yawning expanses of time no longer filled with commuting, work, shopping, travel, restaurant meals and countless other distractions, many of us felt something approaching fear. Almost immediately, media overflowed with ideas for self-improvement: we could come out of isolation with a flatter stomach, perfectly organized closets, a diploma in homemade Hollandaise sauce, and fluency in a foreign language. If the original notion of a sabbath was to do no deliberate activity (baking, or even kneading, a loaf of sourdough would have been prohibited), the gold standard during the first weeks of the pandemic was to do nothing but. There was a widespread failure to take hold of what so many of us had said we were hungering for.

The term "time famine" is sometimes used to describe the twenty-first-century feeling of unrelenting busyness. At the heart of that feeling is a contradiction: strictly speaking, the number of hours the average household puts into paid labour and housework has changed little over many decades. The problem is that we now fill every free hour we've got. If people in sabbatarian England pottered about, it's because there was nothing much else to do. Today, of course, you can sit in a café, meet friends at a restaurant, visit a water park, shop your way down a laneway of boutiques, take a parachuting lesson, or support your local theatre's production of *Death of a Salesman*—on top of older pastimes like needlework, gardening, dog-walking and keeping up your social contacts. The fate of free time is well represented by the smartphone, which, like the washing machine, had the potential to be a time-saving device. Offered unprecedented abilities to organize our lives on the fly, we responded not by getting the same number of things done in less time, but by fitting in more things. As anthropologist David Kaplan said at the turn of this new millennium, "Being a consumer in such a society *is* work."

Many people, either through their own ambitions, the demands of coercive employers, or the financial desperation of poorly paid work, really do lack leisure time. What has been in universally short supply is listless, unhurried, genuinely *free* time, days and hours that seem to expand rather than contract. That changed when, due to the coronavirus, millions of people began to spend weeks at a time in their homes. Suddenly, everyone was talking about how plastic time had become, sometimes passing like a leaf in the wind, at other times gaping like a wound. The problem wasn't only that our familiar patterns and schedules were disrupted. We were dealing with a different kind of time entirely: noncommercial time.

In America, Sunday closing was repeatedly tested in US Supreme Court. The most important of these legal challenges was decided in 1961. Employees of a Maryland department store had been fined for selling, on a Sunday, a three-ring binder, a can of floor wax, a stapler and staples, and a toy submarine. The accused argued that Sunday closing laws caused them economic harm by imposing the tenets of the Christian religion. The court disagreed. In its decision, Chief Justice Earl Warren wrote that what was protected by Sunday closing was not a religious sabbath, but a "special atmosphere" that had comfortably survived the transition to a secular, multicultural society.

"The State seeks to set one day apart from all others as a day of rest, repose, recreation and tranquility—a day which all members of the family and community have the opportunity to spend and enjoy together, a day on which there exists relative quiet and disassociation from the everyday intensity of commercial activities, a day on which people may visit friends and relatives who are not available during working days," the court declared. In the US, that day had come to be Sunday. The court upheld Sunday closing as a form of freedom enjoyed by all.

The people surveyed by Mass Observation in Britain in 1949 understood their sabbath in much the same way. At the time, a popular movement was calling for the "staggering" of days off from work—the system we have today, in which different people take different days off. There were also calls to "brighten" Sundays with wider opportunities for enjoyment of galleries, cinemas, sports, cafés, restaurants and even shopping. The dilemma was immediately apparent: "If demands for brighter Sundays are met, will this develop into a day in which half the population works to entertain the other half? What is the answer?" wrote Mass Observation.

At stake was noncommercial time: "the old duality of life," in the words of the author D. H. Lawrence. For more than a century, people in the world's richest economies had agreed to an "ingenious compact," as Frank Trentmann describes it in *Empire of Things*, his world history of consumer culture. Six days a week were dominated by an accelerating commercial culture; one day was defined by a near-total rejection of it. Today it sounds ridiculous that one could not rent a bicycle or get a latte or spend three hours in a paint shop deciding which shade of white—Linen White? French Macaroon?—to paint the walk-in closet. It sounds comical when you hear that, in the 1980s, Paramus tried to prohibit the Sunday operation of computer mainframes. But the core concern was not piety; it was the thorny fact that every new commercial activity on Sunday pushed noncommercial time—in which almost no one worked or consumed—closer to extinction.

The most persistent modern epidemic, loneliness, was also anticipated by Mass Observation's interviewees. Their Sundays were typically spent with other people. In Britain in 1949, there were fifty-two Sundays a year, plus holidays, in which you could be sure that everyone you knew, and everyone you didn't, was off work and doing nothing much more than reading a pile of newspapers. A sixty-six-year-old road sweeper, who actually disliked Sundays and found them boring, still strongly opposed staggered days off. "It would be worse than a Sunday," he said. "It would mean being out of contact with everyone."

When we staggered time off and "brightened" Sundays, we effectively made commercial time never-ending. People didn't stop napping or walking or playing cards in their downtime, at least not entirely; the crucial difference is that today we all do these things according to individual schedules.

Meanwhile, every other form of resistance to perpetual productivity and consumption, from store closings on Thanksgiving and Christmas and at night, to New York's three-martini lunch and London's workday-afternoon pints, has gradually been vanquished. In Israel, the sabbath is now the busiest shopping day of the week. Politicians in Spain have chipped away at both Sunday-closing laws and the nation's traditional daily break from work and shopping, the siesta. Historical sabbatarian strongholds, such as England, Germany and France, have weakened Sunday shopping limits in major cities almost out of existence. When Germany's highest court upheld blue laws a few years ago, media from across the political spectrum applauded. "Sunday is Sunday because it is unlike other days," read an editorial in one newspaper. "It is a day to synchronize society." Yet the court decision only restricted shops from opening on Sundays more than three weeks in a row.

Of course, the biggest blow to Sunday closing had been struck long before. On August 11, 1994, a man in Philadelphia ordered a Sting album, *Ten Summoner's Tales*, from a cyberspace shopping mall based in Nashua, New Hampshire—the first known digitally secure online retail sale. The *New York Times* reported the historic event under the headline, "Attention Shoppers: Internet Is Open."

Bergen County's blue laws, too, are frequently under assault. One recent opponent, Mitch Horn, heard his call to action in a Babies "R" Us store. Three Sundays in a row, Horn had found himself making the forty-five-minute round trip from his home in Bergen to neighbouring Hudson County to pick up the wants and needs of contemporary parenting. On any other day of the week, he could drop by his local Babies "R" Us, less than five minutes from his front door. In any other county in the US, he could legally do so on a Sunday.

"It's all about our liberties," Horn told me. "We should have the right to sell goods and to buy goods on any day or at any time that we choose."

Horn saw encouraging signs in widespread disobedience of the blue laws. Drinking coffee on a Sunday at Starbucks (cafés are permitted to open), Horn suddenly turned to an employee as she removed an item from a shelf.

"That's a French press?" he asked. "Someone's actually going to buy that today?"

"Yes," the employee replied.

"That's a cooking item," Horn told me with satisfaction. "That's a prohibited transaction."

It's easy to feel hostile toward Horn for seeking to erase this last trace of defiance. Bergen County's sabbath is, as biologists say of the last living representative of a species on the cusp of extinction, an "endling." Yet Horn only wants what most people in the rest of the world already have, and his reasons are the same ones that toppled the sabbath everywhere else: the advance of commercial time has made noncommercial time intolerable. As families with two working adults became the norm and business hours extended into night work and other nonstandard job hours, the inability to shop on Sundays became inconvenient. As civic life became synonymous with consumption, shopping-as-recreation emerged. A day at the mall became as much a family outing as a day at church or the ballpark.

Two points are remarkable for their absence in Mass Observation interviewees' comments about the sabbath. The first is that no one, or at least not enough people to warrant mention, appears to have complained about the inconvenience of Sunday closing. Everyone, it seems—despite lives that, even then, were frequently described as a "mad rush"—found that six days out of seven was enough to get the shopping done. The second point is that no one seemed to care what effect Sunday closing might be having on corporate sales figures or the British economy. Reams of studies since have failed to demonstrate any clear economic effect of Sunday closing. Bergen County, for example, is among New Jersey's wealthiest counties and home to one of the United States' top ten postal codes for retail sales. Perhaps British citizens understood this through experience. Another possibility: that stepping outside commercial time once a week gave them the necessary perspective to see that maximizing economic potential might not be the one and indivisible meaning of life.

Until the pandemic, it was fair to assume that the sabbath was as good as gone and would never be back. We were left to wonder: Did people in the past, with one long day each week to spend staring at the four walls inside their own heads, have lives that were richer than ours in some way? Do we reflect less carefully on ourselves and our own behaviour? Are we less thoughtful, more trivial people? It seemed possible that these questions could no longer be answered, because "that Sunday feeling" seemed gone forever. Even if noncommercial time made some kind of resurgence, we were constantly connected, endlessly pursuing goals and ambitions, too distracted for solitude or long fireside chats about the meaning of life. "It just does not seem like we are fated for a return. I can't imagine it happening," Judith Shulevitz told me when we first spoke, long before the pandemic. "It's a very forlorn plea that I was issuing in *The Sabbath World.*"

If the sabbath has never been easy to keep, however, we also found it difficult to lose. Long before the pandemic, people had started to push back against what Shulevitz called the "valorization of busyness." It's just that they did so only within their own lives and households, rather than in society at large. Ironically, much of that resistance took the form of consumption: spas, meditation retreats, vacations at all-inclusive resorts, and decluttering products, but also drugs, alcohol and other means of escape.

The historian David Shi, whose book *The Simple Life* traces resistance to the materialist lifestyle from the founding of America to modern times, counts busyness itself among the core problems with consumer culture. "Money or possessions or activities themselves do not corrupt simplicity, but the love of money, the craving for possessions, and the prison of activities do," he said. As the period of quarantine turned from days to weeks, more of us seemed to leave that prison behind. The focus on achievements and constantly scheduled tasks receded, and, like sabbath-day citizens of the past, many of us gained skill at not just living with less, but doing less. It was only then that time ceased to stretch fearfully, a hollow to be filled, and instead began to broaden and slow down. When it did, a small miracle took place: life itself began to grow longer.

A month into the lockdown, I surveyed as widely as possible within my own network, ranging from close friends to near-strangers, and heard back about a growing tiredness with productivity, a widespread sinking-in to time. "I am noticing more," one person said, describing the change in the simplest of terms. "We have had a chance to really notice and enjoy spring in a way that might not happen again," said another. Many comments seemed almost to echo the lost world described by Mass Observation seventy years ago. "It is interesting to see how now one has a chance to delve into topics with people," wrote one woman. "It reminds me a little of being on the cross-country train, and the quality of interactions." A few, entirely unprompted, described the closure as a kind of sabbath.

Since the pandemic, it has become impossible to look at near-empty freeways and malls lost in their vacant parking lots, like those in Bergen County, without thinking of disaster. They also, though, serve as a reminder that those first lockdowns contained a kind of liberation. Spend a weekend in Bergen County and the first thing you notice on Sunday is the traffic. There's a lot less of it, of course, just as we witnessed during the corona-virus outbreak. But again, it isn't merely an absence; Paramus police will tell you that Sunday traffic is *different*. People drive more slowly, less aggres-sively, and there's less rat-running—the term is a comparison to the way laboratory rats try to get out of a maze—through the backstreets.

The philosopher Rousseau described idle moments as an escape from grown-up time, and, sure enough, skateboarders practise kickflips and par-ents teach their children how to ride bicycles on the vacant swaths of pavement. On the other end of life's spectrum, the coronavirus reminded us of how little time we had been setting aside for our elders, in their iso-lation and vulnerability. In Paramus, the parking lots of eldercare homes have always been full on Sundays.

As the lockdowns eased, many people solemnly pledged to hang on to this freer sense of time. Shulevitz, who during the pandemic fled New York for the small-town home in the Catskills where she plans to retire, correctly predicted that few people would be able to keep those promises. "I just don't think it can happen alone," she said. "This works only because everyone else is doing it at the same time. You definitely need it to happen en masse. You're not going to get less traffic, you're not going to be able to find people at home, you're not going to be able to socialize with your neighbours who otherwise are taking their kids to soccer games or shop-ping, unless this is done as a group." A sabbath is like a ceasefire: unless everybody participates, it doesn't really exist. Everyone needs to stop working. Everyone has to stop shopping. When we do, a form of time emerges that begins to remake the world.

One of the most instantaneous of those changes takes place in the planetary atmosphere, where in the first split second of stopping shopping we accomplish what we've been unable to do for decades: reduce the global carbon pollution that is causing climate change.

4.

Suddenly we're winning the
fight against climate change

f we could see our carbon dioxide pollution—suppose CO_2 was as visible as smog, but instead of being brown, it was the rich indigo colour of good fountain-pen ink—then the threat of climate change would at least be beautiful. A car would drive by, its exhaust pipe trailing faint blue vapours of humankind's main contribution to global warming. From a factory smokestack, a blue smudge like the fingerprint of an accusing god. Above it all, depthless clouds the colour of the Mediterranean Sea would roil, a storm that never breaks.

The air surrounding most of us would be an enchanted cerulean mist. When we talk about carbon dioxide in "the atmosphere," it sounds as though it's high above us. In fact, carbon dioxide is densest near ground level, where most of it is emitted; the gas then slowly mixes with higher layers. Climb into the sky in a commercial airliner (a streak of indigo stretching behind it), and at cruising altitude, about ten kilometres above sea level, the air would be clearer—up there, the atmosphere remembers a time when humanity pumped out a lot less carbon. You might begin to see another blue above you: sky blue.

Look down from space, and the indigo atmosphere would mesmerize: blue plumes rising from our cities and industrial centres, then bleeding into the paler blue of the accumulated CO_2 that has spread nearly evenly around the globe. You'd see blueness streaming across prairies and oceans, pouring through hill-country passes, eddying behind mountain ranges like water around a midriver boulder.

Both the natural and human contributions of carbon dioxide are greatest in the Northern Hemisphere. In summer, the blue atmosphere around us would lighten and brighten as forests and grasslands burst into green life, absorbing CO_2 and emitting the oxygen we breathe. As winter approached, however, blue would seem to steam up nearly everywhere, not only from cities but also the land: the vegetation stops taking in carbon and instead releases it as plants and leaves fall and rot. The annual peak in atmospheric carbon comes at winter's end, when the top half of the world would be lost beneath a thick, whirling indigo cloak. In spring, it would start to fade again. A NASA spokesman—my description is based in part on the agency's data visualizations—described this cycle to me as a heartbeat, "the lub-dub of the planet."

But it's humankind's emissions that drive carbon dioxide accumulation in the atmosphere, wreaking havoc with the climate. In a world with visible carbon pollution, our centres of consumption and industrial production— Western Europe, Southeast Asia, the eastern seaboard of North America, as well as smaller urban and industrial centres like California and Japan— would look from space as though they are endlessly venting blue smoke. The Southern Hemisphere would hardly smoulder. Only in the dry season would great swirls of blue rise from Africa, South America and Australia— not from human activity but from wildfires. (Though the fires have been worsened by climate change.) Each year, with more and more CO_2 added to the atmosphere, the sky would grow a darker indigo worldwide.

And from the moment—the very instant—that the world stops shopping, the air would begin to lighten. In a matter of days, the ground-level blue fog would be noticeably paler. The blue bonfires that burn across the Northern Hemisphere would send up less smoke.

Beneath the deep indigo sky of accumulated carbon pollution, a layer of clearer air would form, the way a clean tide flows beneath the mouth of a muddy river.

———

We can't see carbon dioxide, of course—it's a colourless gas. As we learned during the pandemic, though, declining carbon emissions are unmistakably visible.

Particle pollution, which is the brownish-yellow smog often seen in cities, belches out of the same factories, coal or gas-fired power plants, and fossil fuel burning vehicles that also produce greenhouse gases. When the coronavirus shut down the global consumer economy, the haze began to clear. The bluer-than-blue sky that appeared with shocking suddenness over the world's cities was perhaps the most widespread reckoning human-kind has ever had with the fact that our everyday actions have planetary consequences—and it meant that the carbon emissions we can't see were fading, too.

At first, the change was obvious mainly in the world's most polluted places, almost all of them in India, China and Pakistan: they are the places that produce many of the world's consumer products. Within days of entering lockdown, blue skies were reported even in Ghaziabad, India, which had the world's worst air quality in 2019. In a typical April, fifty-five of the one hundred most polluted cities have air quality ranging from "very unhealthy" to "hazardous" due to particle pollution; near the end of April 2020, only three did. (Those cities—Hanoi, Vietnam, as well as Guangzhou and Chengdu, in China—had been hit early by the first wave of corona-virus and were already rebooting industrial activity.) In satellite images measuring pollutant plumes, it really did look like the flames of a burning planet were subsiding.

The rich world already had relatively clean air, in part because few goods are manufactured in wealthy nations anymore; these countries have largely offshored polluting industries to other parts of the globe. Yet before long, a blue that the eye somehow knew was more true, as if we had been wading in the shallows and now looked into deeper waters, had appeared even above cities like Vancouver, which had some of the planet's freshest air to begin with. There were days when London and New York had *the cleanest urban air in the world.* Toronto smelled like the oak and pine savannah it had been before the city existed; Los Angeles awoke to mornings with the fresh scent of sagebrush after rain. That nearly all of us have been breathing air that is sootier than we might have imagined was suddenly understood. As a stand-in for invisible climate pollution, the absence of visible haze was telling to the point of being chilling.

Many people said the air had cleared because everyone was staying home. A more precise cause is that the consumer economy had stalled. Factories were closed. Planes weren't flying. Shipping lanes were empty. Our daily commutes to earn money, or to spend it, were called off. It was the consumer dilemma made piercingly clear: our economies are driven by consumption, yet consumption drives our carbon emissions. The relationship is so strong that climate scientists have long used growth in one as an indicator of growth in the other. Accelerate the fashion cycle, and you accelerate climate change; cut back on the Christmas spending spree, and fewer CO_2 molecules enter the atmosphere that year. Yet addressing climate change by reducing the scale of our consumption has never been seriously considered by political leaders.

Ever since the Club of Rome published *The Limits to Growth* in 1972, warning the world of the dangers of infinite growth on a planet with finite resources, there has been debate over whether or not we can have both a perpetually growing consumer economy and a clean, healthy natural world. Could humans live with all the comforts to which we have become accustomed or we aspire—air conditioning, three-car households, constantly updated wardrobes, endless new stuff, globetrotting holidays—without doing environmental harm? The report didn't rule out the possibility. "It is success in overcoming limits that forms the cultural tradition of many dominant people in today's world," it reads.

That dominant worldview never changed, and the idea that all our economic activity—from clothing factories to football games, from cattle ranching to mass tourism—can be "decoupled" from environmental harms, the way a boxcar is decoupled from a train, is now the guiding light of governments and corporations around the globe. It is the cornerstone of the faith that technology can resolve climate change without the need to substantially change our lifestyles. It is the holy grail known as "green growth": a perpetually growing economy that does not damage the environment.

In the mid 2010s, the promise of decoupling seemed suddenly real. When the annual data on global carbon dioxide emissions trickled in for

2014, they showed that CO_2 emissions had remained flat. We had not pumped *less* carbon into the atmosphere than we had the year before, but at least we hadn't pumped *more*. Then the same thing happened in 2015, and again in 2016. "There is reason for optimism," Laura Cozzi told me at the time. Cozzi was the head of the team that crunched the data at the International Energy Agency, or IEA, which represents thirty of the globe's major economies.

There was reason for pessimism, too. Emissions were still wildly, recklessly high. When annual emissions first stalled in 2014, they did so at a record-setting high. To picture what this means, think of the atmosphere as a bathtub. Now put a bunch of ping-pong balls in your imaginary bathtub. The ping-pong balls represent carbon dioxide that has accumulated in the atmosphere. The trend had been to add more and more ping-pong balls every year, until we set a record of (let's say) ten ping-pong balls in 2013. In 2014, we once again added ten ping-pong balls, but at least we didn't add eleven, or twelve. In 2015, we added ten more, and the same again in 2016. The total amount of ping-pong balls in the bathtub—that is, carbon dioxide in the atmosphere—continued to increase, but the rate at which we were adding more had finally plateaued.

Much better was the news that, while we were flattening the curve on carbon pollution, 170 million people had been added to the world population and the global economy grew by 10 percent. Instead of increasing in lockstep with one another, growth and CO_2 emissions finally appeared to be travelling along different paths, with emissions standing still while growth continued to rise.

The slowdown in emissions happened for several reasons. The first was that the world's richest nations, along with China, were making significant cuts to their CO_2 pollution. Europe had been leading the way for years, but the United States, the world's second-greatest carbon polluter, had joined the fight. In large part because of offshoring by Western countries, China, the world's greatest manufacturer, is also the world's worst carbon polluter, despite the fact that the average Chinese consumer is responsible for fewer emissions than the typical resident of almost any wealthier nation. Yet China, like the West, was burning less coal and more natural gas, and had made an even bigger push toward renewable energy and nuclear power. Greener growth really was occurring.

Yet there was another key reason that CO_2 pollution had plateaued, one that rarely made the headlines. Economic growth overall had slowed, *especially* in China, the US and Europe. It wasn't only green technologies that had stalled emissions; we had reduced consumption, too. "We're at a fragile stasis in emissions," said Rob Jackson, an environmental scientist at Stanford University, at the time. Jackson was then the head of the Global Carbon Project, a major carbon-tracking agency involving a network of climate scientists. "If the global economy were booming, emissions would not be flat."

One of Jackson's Stanford colleagues bet him ten thousand dollars that carbon pollution had not peaked and emissions would soon rise again. Jackson didn't take the bet. He did say, however, that we might never again see carbon emissions rise by 2 percent or more in a single year.

The following year, 2017, emissions increased by 2 percent according to Global Carbon Project calculations. In 2018, with the global economy surging, they increased by nearly 3 percent. Coal use was inching up again. Oil and gas burning continued unabated. Despite all the talk of decoupling, it was still more accurate to say that economic growth and carbon emissions remained tightly coupled, only slightly less so than in the past.

The day the world stops shopping amounts to a deliberate reduction in carbon emissions at a global scale. This is something we have never before accomplished.

Since the Second World War, global carbon dioxide pollution has fallen only four times: in the mid 1980s, the early 1990s, 2009, and 2020. In none of these cases was the decline the result of decoupling, green growth, or any other purposeful action to protect the planet; each involved severe and widespread economic downturns. Emissions fall when the world stops shopping. The sharpest drop came during the Covid-19 outbreak, which reduced global emissions by 7 percent for the year. But the pandemic may not prove to be the most enduring decline.

"The biggest suppression we really ever saw of carbon emissions was during the '90s with the collapse of the Soviet Union. A large part of the global economy shrank," said Richard York, a sociologist at the University of Oregon who studies how the structure of societies influences their consumption and pollution.

The Soviet Union collapsed in 1991. Across much of the decade that followed, the former communist empire underwent what York called "demodernization." Carbon dioxide emissions in the former Soviet bloc ultimately declined by nearly a third, more even than the 25 percent reduction measured in China across the four weeks of its strictest pandemic clampdown. The Soviet decline was so drastic that, in combination with a severe recession in much of the West, total emissions for the entire planet decreased for two years and grew only slowly throughout the decade. Though it is widely forgotten, some nations in Western Europe, such as Germany and the Netherlands, were already working to reduce their emissions at that time, but none came close to as deep a cut as the former Soviet republics. "It tends to suggest that it's hard, at the very least, to get major reductions in emissions without some change in the scale of the economy," York said.

The problem, of course, is that economic declines of the kind seen in the former Soviet Union or during the pandemic involve terrible hardship for millions. Laszlo Varro grew up in Budapest, Hungary, when it was still behind the Iron Curtain. Far from Moscow, Budapest had the look and feel of a European capital. Even under communism, Varro was, in the 1980s, able to watch *Star Wars* and drink Coca-Cola nearly as freely as young people in the West. In terms of material well-being, many Hungarians were actually better off in the Soviet era than they are today in a free-market economy.

Still, when the Soviet Union collapsed, one in every five people in Hungary lost their jobs. Under communism, energy had been free; some households, unable to pay their new natural gas bills, were reduced to burning firewood. Hungary fared better than many parts of the Soviet bloc, yet consumption still declined by at least 25 percent, far worse than almost anywhere in the US during the Great Recession.

"It was an exceptionally serious social and political shock," Varro said. "This is not the type of climate policy that has any political viability.

Nobody—*nobody*—would want to do this intentionally. It might happen to you, but you don't want to live in one of these states."

Today, Varro is the chief economist of the IEA. An important part of the energy agency's work is mapping out how the world as a whole might begin to draw down its annual carbon emissions. All such scenarios, Varro said, have green growth as their goal. The IEA never includes the possibility that people might voluntarily reduce their consumption in order to prevent climate change. In other words, they consider decoupling an endlessly growing economy from climate pollution to be realistic, while "degrowing" the economy—making a planned reduction in its size and scale, even to the smallest degree—is treated as unthinkable.

"I'm not aware of a country where a government won a democratic election with a program of, 'We want to intentionally reduce your consumption,'" Varro said. "We took an assumption that we don't think that human nature could change."

In 2008, the IEA sounded the klaxon that, if the world community failed to take aggressive steps toward decoupling, energy demand would increase 15 percent by 2018, and the resulting increase in emissions would have "shocking" consequences for our future climate. To look back on that report in 2018 made for uncomfortable reading. The IEA's predictions had come true. They released new scenarios for tackling the climate crisis that year. The most achievable vision they promoted this time would see demand for energy increase by a quarter in the next two decades, while maintaining a growing global economy and population. To make that dream real, energy efficiency would have to increase so radically that there would be no increase in demand for energy in any of the world's wealthy nations. All the growth would occur in developing countries, where millions of people still need a better standard of living.

To control emissions under this scenario, the adoption of natural gas, wind energy and solar power would need to expand at rates astronomically higher than ever before. Again, only developing economies, mainly in Asia, could add new coal-fired power plants. The amount of oil we use to run the world's cars would have to peak within five years, though oil use overall would still be expected to increase (mainly for producing petrochemicals, shipping by trucks and freighters, and air travel). The amount of plastic we recycle would need to double, which still wouldn't be enough to keep up with humanity's rising hunger for plastic products.

The IEA's most realistic scenario, in other words, would require a staggering, globally coordinated effort—and in the end, we'd be farther from solving climate change than we are today. Carbon dioxide emissions would continue to rise, though more slowly than they have been. The IEA itself acknowledged that the vision was "far out of step with what scientific knowledge says will be required to tackle climate change."

In 2020, the IEA provided a new scenario that may be in step with what's required to tackle climate change. This alternative vision sees carbon emissions drop to zero, or nearly so, by 2050. Achieving it would require a transition to ultra energy efficiency, renewable sources of power, trains instead of planes, and so on, all at a speed and scale that can only be described as the reinvention of global society. By 2030, total emissions would need to fall 45 percent—and remember, they have yet to decline *at all* through our efforts at decoupling. Demand for energy, which has been steadily rising, would instead need to fall to where it was in 2006, when the world economy was half the size it is otherwise predicted to be in 2030. The rate at which we burn coal would return to 1970s levels, when the world population was half what it is now. As examples of the kinds of changes to everyday life that would be needed, by the end of the current decade all flights of under one hour would be grounded, and journeys of less than three kilometres (a cross-town trip in many cities) would be done on foot, bicycle or low-carbon transit. Annual sales of electric vehicles would need to soar by nearly 2,000 percent, and—perhaps hardest of all to imagine—we would have to accept lower speed limits for those trips still made by car. If we did all of the above, and much, much more, we might meet our targets to prevent truly dangerous global warming.

There was, of course, one bit of "good" news in 2020. The worldwide economic slowdown caused by the pandemic reduced demand for energy and set emissions on a lower course of growth than had been anticipated before the health emergency. Still, the IEA once again dismissed the idea that slowing the consumer economy could contribute to the fight against climate change. Among our leaders, the notion that we can rapidly achieve even more extreme technological and cultural changes than we have consistently failed to make over the past three decades continues to be more plausible than the idea that the world's citizens could be persuaded to buy a little less stuff.

As Varro said, "In the past five thousand years there are very, very few historical evidences of people doing that willingly."

It's hard to predict how much climate pollution would drop on the day the world stops shopping. In the first year of the pandemic, an economic downturn that affected nearly every consumer, carbon dioxide emissions shrank more than the world economy did. In the hardest year of the Great Recession, on the other hand, total emissions fell slightly less than the economy. While ups and downs in consumption tend to closely track the economy as a whole, there certainly are some exceptions.

Let's say the two fall by roughly the same amount: a 25 percent decline in consumption causes emissions to drop 25 percent. Set aside, for the moment, the economic chaos that we know would result and focus instead on the climate crisis. On day one of stopping shopping, we would witness not a flattening of the upward curve of emissions, but an absolute reduction of it. Rather than plateau at a record high, which is the best outcome we've achieved in pursuing green growth so far, global carbon emissions would rapidly drop to 2003 levels.

We would still be adding ping-pong balls to the bathtub. In order to stabilize Earth's temperature, most climate scientists agree, we need to reduce humanity's carbon dioxide emissions to zero. Shockingly, then, even reducing consumption worldwide by 25 percent would only get us a quarter of the way there. Still, it would be a monumental accomplishment, buying us a few more years to take further action before we hit 1.5 degrees Celsius of global warming—the limit beyond which climate scientists coolly predict "large risks for natural and human systems." On our current trajectory, we will reach that temperature increase in the early 2030s. "We'd have a lot more time to change," Jackson said.

It is depressing that even a major drop in consumption doesn't come close to solving climate change. That's just how tough a challenge climate change is. Yet, as we have learned over recent decades, it is also extremely challenging to pull it off by depending on green technology and clean energy. Every percentage-point reduction in emissions that we achieve by slowing consumption or degrowing the economy narrows the gap that has to be closed with decoupling. This was another surreal milestone of the pandemic. With four billion of the world's people under full or partial lockdown in April 2020, the global economy downsized enough that we came closer than ever before to being able to power our modern civilization with renewable energy.

Five years ago, when emissions were flat, Jackson was unsure whether economic growth itself, and the consumption that drives it, should be part of the discussion when it comes to stopping climate change. "Gosh, what a large box to open," he said. "I don't think the notion of degrowth is politically possible—though that doesn't make it wrong." When I spoke to him again just ahead of the pandemic, with emissions once again at record highs, his frustration was palpable. And his perspective had shifted. "I think it has to be part of the answer," he said.

We need to get used to the night again

As recently as February 20, 1962, most of Earth was pitch black at night. On that date, as the astronaut John Glenn, the first American in orbit, crossed from the day-lit Earth to the dark side of the planet, the world below awaited answers to its questions. Could a lightning storm be seen from space? How visible were the lights of cities and towns from 200 kilometres above them? Even a few physicists predicted that nothing at all would be visible. For a while Glenn hurtled over the blackness of the Indian Ocean. At last he said, "Just to my right I can see a big pattern of light, apparently right on the coast. I can see the outline of a town."

It was Perth, Australia, ready to greet the astronaut. Knowing Glenn would pass overhead, the city council had voted to leave its street lights on (not so very long ago, many cities shut theirs off at night), and the people of Perth pitched in, turning on porch lights and headlights, or just pointing flashlights into the sky. The local BP refinery even turned up its gas flare—"a very bright light," said Glenn. While the rest of the sprawling Australian land mass was cloaked in darkness, Perth gleamed. "The lights show up very well and thank everybody for turning them on, will you?" Glenn said to his ground crew.

How times have changed. By 2020, nearly a quarter of the land area of Earth outside the polar ice caps was lit by skyglow from artificial lights. In NASA's "black marble" images of our planet at night, pinpricks of light are spreading even in the Arctic, the Sahara Desert, and the heart of the Amazon rainforest, while true darkness has disappeared from whole swaths of the globe, including eastern North America, Western Europe, the Nile River Valley, much of India and eastern Asia—and Perth, which now dubs itself the "city of light."

The moment the world stops shopping, that brilliance begins to dim.

Adam Storeygard has seen it happen.

An economist at Tufts University in Medford, Massachusetts, Storeygard uses the world's lights to measure changes in economies, especially where other sources of data are limited. As it turns out, lighting is tightly linked to the consumer economy and, in much the same way as carbon emissions, has tended to grow rather than shrink as energy efficiency and green technology have progressed. We've been living on an ever-brightening Earth.

With few exceptions, both the amount of lighted area and the overall brightness of a nation—its radiance—correspond to the size of its economy. The number of people in a country matters much less. Bangladesh has a higher population density than the Netherlands, for example, but many more unlit areas, and while Canada and Afghanistan have similar numbers of people, Canada is much brighter. The world's light, like so many products of human endeavour, is far from evenly distributed.

Lighting is something we shop for—we consume light. On average, more economic activity means more lighting, for the simple reason that the production and consumption of most goods and services takes place either indoors or at night, with the lights turned on. "Humans tend to use as much artificial light as they can buy for approximately 0.7 percent of GDP," wrote a team of light-pollution experts in the journal *Science Advances* in 2017. In the most brightly lit country on Earth—the United States—that would equal $140 billion each year, or about $450 per person to keep homes, factories, restaurants, malls, museums, stadiums, parks and so on bathed in illumination. The average resident of the southern African nation of Zimbabwe, on the other hand, benefits from about $10 in annual lighting.

When consumer economies decline, the lights dim. It can happen swiftly. Using data collected by satellites, Storeygard and his colleagues measured the brightness of booming Indonesia just before it plunged into a financial crisis in 1997; one year later, the country was dimmer by 6 percent. In Zimbabwe, the economy collapsed by an immiserating 50 percent in the first decade of the twenty-first century; the country darkened dramatically.

What does the loss of light look like on the ground? "People are driving less, and cars and trucks and such are fewer," Storeygard said. "And then businesses, right? Some businesses specifically open in the evening. If you have places with restaurants or where people gather outdoors with lighting and signage—if they go out of business, they're less likely to have lights on."

The effect is strongest in the developing world, but as consumption declines, even wealthy places begin to dim. In 2012, after a long economic lull, the city of Detroit began to turn off some street lights to save money, and that was on top of the nearly half of Detroit's remaining lights that were broken. On the outskirts of downtowns, where outlet malls, auto dealerships and chain restaurants glow, blocks of darkness begin to appear—picture Phoenix with its dozens of abandoned big-box stores. "It wouldn't surprise me to see lights shrinking in toward cities to some extent in the US," Storeygard said.

Some of the brightest individual lights seen from space are oil and gas wells (similar to the "very bright" refinery flare John Glenn saw near Perth). One place starred with flaring wells is North Dakota's Bakken Shale, among the largest oil and gas deposits in the United States. Wells here are so dense, and cover an area so large, that the landscape looks—by night, from orbit— almost pixelated. Oil and gas companies are loath to close down (in industry parlance, "shut in") wells, even in such serious economic slowdowns as recessions; instead, they dial back the amount of oil they pump to the surface, which dims the wells' gas flares. Yet Storeygard predicted that a world without shopping might lead to such a decline in fuel use (in industry parlance, "demand destruction") that shut-ins in the Bakken Shale would soon be apparent. The pandemic proved him correct. By the second month of wide-spread lockdowns, pixels in the Bakken Shale and other oilfields had not only dimmed—they were visibly winking out one by one.

Whole towns might disappear. In 1998, light from the tiny truck stop of Ilakaka, Madagascar, could not be detected from orbit at night. That year, large deposits of sapphires and rubies were discovered nearby, and five years later, Ilakaka was a bright blob of light surrounded by hand-dug mines with names like Swiss Bank. In a world that has stopped buying gemstones, the opposite of what John Glenn saw in Perth occurs. Instead of lighting itself out of the darkness, Ilakaka could fade to black.

Imagine Chicago with 90 percent less light. Imagine most American cities, in fact, with lighting reduced by a factor of three, or five. Picture Madrid or Milan, their gleaming streets and plazas darkened by half. Picture Shanghai, where the multicoloured glow of the floodlit skyline casts a rainbow upon the Huangpu River, or Hachiko Square in Tokyo, bathed in the glare from giant video screens—imagine these places cooled and shadowed. Imagine London dim enough that the M25 motorway that rings the city can no longer be seen from space. What would life look like in such cities if a steep decline in consumption was darkening the globe?

It would look like life in Berlin, Germany, on any ordinary night.

"At least in terms of what we can measure from a satellite, Germany is a lot darker than most of the other places that are wealthy," said Christopher Kyba, a physicist and light pollution researcher at the GFZ German Research Centre for Geosciences. "I don't think we really understand why that is yet. Some of it has to do with street lights, but some of it has to do with culture."

I have been one acquainted with the night, wrote Robert Frost. "That's definitely me," Kyba said. He enjoys candlelit restaurants, and even when summer lingers far into the fall, as it does too often these days in Berlin, he shows no sign of a tan. His clothing is in shades of black and grey; he wears a T-shirt that reads Because Every Day Needs a Night. By the age of five he was aware of light pollution, because his family lived in a small town south of Edmonton; he could see the stark difference between the night sky to the south and the city skyglow to the north.

Berlin, Kyba said, has a policy of "only as much light as is sensible and necessary." The street lights turn on only at the point of true twilight, rather than the first hint of evening dimming as in other cities. Plazas that would shine white in London or Las Vegas, in Rome or Seoul, instead have the soft, grainy light of a vintage smartphone photo. Shop signs and street advertisements are generally smaller and less bright than in other cities. Even standing in an especially glaring part of Berlin (near the floodlit Kaiser Wilhelm Memorial Church, which was bombed in the Second World War and movingly preserved in a state of partial ruin), Kyba estimates that he could count half again as many stars as in most cities' downtowns.

Until recently, Berlin was home to more than forty thousand gas lamps, more than any other city. Though it is replacing them with brighter, more energy-efficient lights, many Berliners have resisted the change, preferring the gas lamps' golden glow—so soft it is almost louche. To Kyba, it's a clear indication that city dwellers don't necessarily see bright lighting as the ideal.

Berlin's parks have no lighting at all. "You have this feeling that you're going into this really dark place, and it's intimidating at the start," said Kyba. "It looks like once you're in there you won't see anything." Instead, your eyes swiftly adjust to the darkness, and what you see is: people. Teenagers gathered around a bench, their faces blue-lit by their phones. Men and women, walking alone or with their dogs. Pairs murmuring in the darkness. "Berliners are somehow more used to this idea of dark," Kyba said.

The night is rarely truly black. In 1900, American ethnographer Walter Hough recounted to a scientific congress in Paris the "many manifestations of light in nature coming to the aid of the denizens of Earth during the hours of darkness." We all know the moon, of course, and the stars— though most of us see a sky robbed of many of them by light pollution. But Hough reminded his audience of others: the northern and southern auroras; zodiacal light, which is a hazy, glowing pyramid on the horizon caused by sunlight reflecting off cosmic dust; the Magellanic Clouds, a pair of galaxies visible as smudges of light in the Southern Hemisphere; electrically charged luminescent clouds; phosphorescent plants, fungi, minerals, waters and "gaseous emanations"; fireflies on land, and in the sea, the 150 species then known to produce their own illumination. "Under the clear night sky of the Arizona deserts the atmosphere seems charged with star mist; eminences miles away may be outlined, the dial of a watch may be read, and a trail followed with little difficulty," Hough said. He noted that, in certain circumstances, the planet Venus alone casts enough light that a traveller in open country needs no other. (Kyba once tweeted that if he had a bucket list of things he must do in his life, seeing his Venus shadow would be on it.)

The blacker night of a world without shopping would be beneficial in many ways. A surge in light pollution research over the past decade has revealed that many living things depend on natural darkness for their well-being, probably including humans. Some scarab beetles, the creatures famous for rolling balls of dung back to their nests to feed their families, navigate according to the position of the Milky Way in the night sky. The beetles are literally lost without it—and today, the Milky Way is invisible in many places, washed out by skyglow that might originate hundreds of kilometres away. More than a third of the world's people can no longer see the Milky Way where they live. Given that it is the imprint of our own galaxy in the night sky, might we, too, be in some way lost in space?

Another example of light pollution's effects: it is late June, and as night falls over the vastness of Lake Erie, weather radar picks up an ominous cloud that is rapidly growing in size in the darkness. Then the cloud begins to move toward Cleveland, Ohio. "Oh. My. God," tweets a local newscaster.

The storm is made up of millions—probably billions—of mayflies. The good news is that the flies, which are harmless to humans and a favourite food of fish and many other creatures, are hatching again in huge numbers after decades in which lakes and rivers in the eastern US were too polluted with toxins for the species to survive. The bad news is that the flies are now drawn straight toward light pollution sources—"light bombs," as one entomologist put it—like Cleveland, where they mistake floodlit asphalt and parked cars for moonlit water, causing them to uselessly lay their eggs on dry land and then die. In fact, scientists now suspect that lighting is causing population losses in a wide variety of species all over the globe. The World Health Organization, meanwhile, has identified sleep disturbance in humans as a probable cause of cancer, while other research links light pollution to depression, obesity and other health problems.

On the autumn streets of Berlin, the leaves turn their fall colours of red, orange and yellow, but where branches hang close to street lights, some tree branches stay green far longer. On the artificially lit side of a tree, it is summer; on the dark side, it is fall. No one knows yet whether such effects come at a cost to the trees. What is clearer is that Berlin's darkness does benefit some species. "Berlin is a really important location for night-ingales," Kyba said. This humble brown bird, famous for its nocturnal singing, has declined by half in some parts of Europe in just the last decade; it remains common in Berlin. One reason is that Berlin still offers a night to sing in.

For years now, a technological fix has been available to reduce both light pollution and the staggering amount of energy we consume by lighting our lives. Unfortunately, it hasn't been enough—because our lights are caught up in our consumer mindset.

If you dump plastic into the ocean, or poison soil with mining tailings, or pump carbon dioxide into the atmosphere, the effects play out for years if not centuries, making these problems difficult to truly solve. Not so when it comes to light pollution. "You can literally turn them off," said Kevin Gaston, a British ecologist who studies the effects of artificial light. "You can regain some of what you've lost quite easily."

The same goes for saving energy. While green technology is advancing slowly on many fronts, energy-efficient light-emitting diodes (LEDs) are widely available and affordable. They commonly burn at least 75 percent less energy than older models of lights, and well-designed fixtures also prevent light pollution by directing their brightness only to those areas that need to be lit. A worldwide system of environmentally friendly lighting is so achievable that light scientists have argued that we should pursue it as a way to inspire confidence that we can resolve tougher global challenges.

Instead, the opposite is happening. As LEDs gain popularity, there are growing indications that we're spending the money we save on energy costs to buy: more lighting. A boom in "media architecture"—enormous video screens that play out across the facades of buildings—is now underway around the world. The two towers of the International Youth Cultural Centre in Nanjing, China, are a standout example: 700,000 LED lights cover the sixty-storey buildings' exteriors, which are also floodlit from the ground. The "Mighty Lights" on the Hernando de Soto Bridge in Memphis, Tennessee, involve 10,000 colour-controllable lights that cover the entire bridge structure. Meanwhile, on the famous Bahnhofstrasse, an upscale shopping street in Zurich, Switzerland, video screens increased by more than forty times in the past five years alone. A similar explosion in decorative lighting is taking place in private yards and homes. "If we improve the energy efficiency of all the outdoor lighting by switching to LED lights, but increase the total amount of advertising and floodlighting, then we might not actually save much energy on a global scale or national scale," said Kyba.

When Kyba and his colleagues looked at changes in the amount and brightness of light around the world between 2012 and 2016, they found that most places were gradually growing brighter. Only a few nations were dimming, almost all of them war-torn or in the throes of economic decline. They were places where consumption had slowed.

Can we become reacquainted with the night?

Over the past decade, many British towns and boroughs began to save money by dimming lights late at night, or even turning them off. Recent research showed no change in the number of traffic accidents and no increase to the crime rate. (Some evidence suggested that crime *declined* in communities that had dimmed their lights.) Most people simply didn't realize or care that their street lights had been turned off. "It's just one of them things, street lights, doesn't really make much difference," said a bartender who regularly heads home from work after lights out in one rural English county.

That the return of darkness might go largely overlooked should not surprise us, Kyba said. Most visitors to Berlin don't realize that the city is unusually dimly lit unless it's brought to their attention; when Vienna turned down its lights by 50 percent for one hour each night, almost no one but astronomers took note of the fact (and the astronomers were delighted). Similarly, LED bulb lifespans are often measured according to how long it takes for the bulb's light to fade by more than 30 percent, which is the point at which most people will realize that the bulb is no longer performing properly. That's a decline in brightness of a third before we're even expected to notice.

What does catch our attention is the night itself. In the UK surveys carried out where lights had been turned down, the most common reaction was pleasure at seeing the nighttime sky; when air and light pollution sharply declined during the pandemic, people in cities worldwide thrilled at the crispest view of the stars some had seen in their lifetimes. The spread of light around the world in the past century has been described as the "conquest of the night," and as in any conquest, there were losses as well as gains. When street lights first began to spread through Japan, one writer worried that the Japanese would lose their appreciation of shadows. When Paris became the original *ville lumière* in the 1860s, lighting itself with twenty thousand gas lamps, the loss of night was a matter of debate: some felt it created a pressure to conform; others that it would be the end of the "safety of darkness."

In 1998, thirty-six years after his original orbits around Earth, astronaut John Glenn returned to space. He witnessed a nighttime world transformed: nearly every one of the world's cities and towns is now a "city of lights." Still, Perth and its citizens once again put on every light for him. What Glenn said this time around was not recorded by the ground crew. According to his fellow astronauts, though, when the spacecraft he was travelling in once again hung over the city, Glenn said, "Wow. Perth is a lot bigger than the last time I saw it." Then he said, "Okay, guys, you can turn them off now."

A world that stops shopping is a darker place, and maybe that's an idea whose time has come. Still, there is something symbolic about stepping back into darkness that worries us. The widespread taming of fire, some half a million years ago, was one of the most consequential moments in human evolution, banishing the night, and lighting the darkness with electricity is still seen as a milestone of development. In the UK, even those who enjoyed walking by the newly visible starlight were also troubled by whether it represented a backward step for civilization and progress. There was even something eerie, during the pandemic, about the vanishing oil wells as seen in images taken from orbit. They looked like stars being blotted out of the sky, the same way that real stars have been disappearing from our brightly lit nightscapes.

The first days after the world stops shopping have this same duality. There is a spreading quiet and calm, a sense of time stretching and older lifeways returning. There's still food on the table and clothes in the closet. It's peaceful, nostalgic, maybe even a little too slow. Beyond it all is a gnawing sense that much, much harder times are coming.

II
COLLAPSE

The end of growth is not the end of economics

t was a balmy afternoon in Toronto when I told Peter Victor that household consumer spending in Canada had dropped by 50 percent overnight. Victor, an economist retired from York University, raised his eyebrows. The voices through history who have called on us again and again to pursue a simpler, less materialistic life, never seemed to talk about what would happen if we all took up the call. Economists filled in the blanks. Stop shopping, they said, and the economy stops growing and begins to shrink. The inevitable result is imploding markets, rampant joblessness, shuttered storefronts, broken supply chains, and perhaps even a slide into mob rule and famine.

Victor agrees with that assessment, up to a point. A specialist in modelling how change plays out in economies, he regularly simulates recessions, depressions and market crashes on his laptop. When it comes to consumption, Victor's work neatly reveals how much of the shopping that you and I do is strongly influenced by much larger economic forces, such as prices, taxes, distribution of wealth, interest rates and so on. Dial these up or down in specific ways—as governments have significant power to do—and you can pick the economy's winners and losers, or even toggle its fate between boomtime and disaster. Victor knows that stopping shopping can send economic growth into a tailspin. He also knows that there is more to the picture than just: things fall apart. Steps can be taken to prevent a crash from becoming a collapse.

"Let's see what happens," he said, and began tapping at his keyboard.

Victor uses the system dynamics approach pioneered by Massachusetts Institute of Technology professor Jay Forrester in the 1950s. It is designed to explore how variables relate to one another in systems that are too complex to hold in our mind's eye. We are immersed in such systems today, which leave us constantly wrestling with the unforeseen and unintended outcomes of our actions. Some such cases seize the world's attention: the sale of wild animals in a market in Wuhan leads, three months later, to the shutdown of the global economy. More often, they pass unnoticed, troubling only to those who are close to the facts. When advances in technology made solar and wind power less expensive, for example, these renewable energy sources were supposed to become more competitive with fossil fuels—but something else happened as well. Fossil fuel companies began to use renewable energy to power the production of oil and gas. In other words, wind and solar power were used to make fossil fuels more competitive with wind and solar power.

The system that Victor studies is the Canadian economy. For more than a decade, he has been building models of it on his computer, adding detail after detail as though making a ship in a bottle. Using his most recent version, developed in collaboration with British economist Tim Jackson, he can, with the push of a button, draw links across space and time. What effect will an uptick in the tax rate today have on greenhouse gas emissions thirty years from now? Victor and his laptop can make an informed prediction.

His goal all along, however, has been to answer a different question: Is it possible to have an economy that grows very little—or does not grow at all, or even shrinks—and still have a livable system, and maybe even still a capitalist one? Victor is a longtime Canadian, but originally from the UK, and the dark muse for his inquiry is former British prime minister Margaret Thatcher. The so-called Iron Lady was one of capitalism's great defenders, but her perspective on it was grim. She described the economic system as we know it today as a totalizing ideology—a kind of prison, though one that is comfortably appointed for many of its captives. Her

vision of unregulated markets, individualism, private enterprise and aus-
terity had as its central pillar a perpetually growing economy. It became
known as the doctrine of TINA, short for one of Thatcher's oft-repeated
phrases: "There is no alternative."

"That was such a mind-numbing view of the world," Victor said.

It remains the predominant view of the world. "It is easier to imagine
the end of the world than the end of capitalism," goes a recent catchphrase.
The question of growth is at the heart of the consumer dilemma, because
the one argument that seems to make it impossible to slow consumption
is that doing so will end growth. To endlessly expand the consumer economy is the objective of politicians from town councils to presidential
offices, and everything from the creation of national parks, to proposed
immigration laws, to the decision whether to accept a greater or lesser
number of deaths from Covid-19 has been tested against whether it will
stifle growth or boost it.

This is puzzling, Victor said, because low or no economic growth was
the norm through nearly all of human history.

From ancient times until the eighteenth century, the global economy grew
very slowly—probably at an average rate of about 0.1 percent each year.
Almost all of that annual growth was due to a gradually rising population.
If you add people to a society, more goods and services are produced and
consumed, and the economy expands. The amount of goods and services
per person, however, hardly budged from year to year. If you lived in any
era up to the end of the 1700s, you would probably have gone through life
with about as much in the way of belongings as your parents, grandparents
or great-grandparents. In fact, a lot of what you owned, including clothing,
would have been handed down to you from them.

Only with the Industrial Revolution in the early 1800s did economic
output per person begin to rise sharply. Then, in the hundred years between
1913 and 2013, annual global growth increased at thirty times the rate that
it had throughout most of history. Each year more and more stuff was
made and sold. The consumer economy had been born.

The idea that growth should be the main indicator of economic success is even newer than that. Near the end of the Great Depression, a Russian Jewish immigrant and brilliant economist named Simon Kuznets developed America's first national accounts. For the first time, it was possible to say how much the US economy had shrunk during the crash: by half. The finding helped to inspire Franklin Roosevelt's New Deal—in large part an attempt to regrow the economy through government spending, including by putting money in consumers' pockets.

Kuznets's measure of the nation's total economic output came to be known as the gross domestic product, familiar today as the GDP. By the 1950s, influential economists had embraced GDP growth as a magic solution to the age-old tension over what share of economic benefits should go to investors and entrepreneurs versus the share that should go to working people and society as a whole. At last, there seemed to be a way to increase everyone's wealth without taking from the rich to give to the poor, and that was to make more money and stuff per person each year. Supporters were soon describing "growthmanship" as "a rising tide that lifts all boats."

Yet GDP faced criticism from the start, including from Kuznets himself. The welfare of a nation can "scarcely be inferred" simply from a measurement of national income, he stated in his first report to Congress on the subject. He specifically pointed out that his new statistic had nothing much to say about the distribution of wealth. It was clear from the Depression, for example, that although growth's rising and falling tides did indeed lift and lower most boats, some were lifted far higher than others, or lowered much further, depending on how society and the economy were structured.

Kuznets also recognized that not all economic growth is created equal. "Goals for 'more' growth should specify more growth of what and for what," he would later write in *The New Republic*, also noting that, in dictatorships, growth was sometimes achieved through oppression or by goading people to work harder out of fear and hatred of foreign enemies. Kuznets wanted national ledgers to have both plus and minus columns, though the kinds of economic activity that went into each was open to debate. Kuznets himself thought that military spending should be subtracted from GDP, rather than added to it as it is today, because defence spending is something a nation is compelled to do by its potential attackers; the money could otherwise be used to improve citizens' standard of living. Kuznets was no great fan of consumer culture. Echoing Adam Smith, who felt that some forms of economic activity were undesirable and destructive, Kuznets declared that GDP should reflect economic goals "from the standpoint of a more enlightened social philosophy than that of an acquisitive society." Among the activities that he felt should be red-inked as "disservice rather than service" were advertising and financial speculation. He wondered aloud whether the unpaid work of housewives was among the activities that should be included in national accounts.

Kuznets was later echoed by Robert F. Kennedy in a speech he made just three months before his assassination in 1968 as he pursued the United States presidency. Noting that material poverty in the US was matched by an even greater "poverty of satisfaction, purpose, and dignity," Kennedy decried GDP as a poor measure of the state of the nation. "Too much and for too long, we seemed to have surrendered personal excellence and community values in the mere accumulation of material things," he said. The GDP was buoyed, he noted, by cigarette advertising, ambulances, home security, jails, the destruction of redwood forests, urban sprawl, napalm, nuclear warheads and the armoured vehicles used by police against riots in American cities. "It does not include the beauty of our poetry or the strength of our marriages, the intelligence of our public debate or the integrity of our public officials. It measures neither our wit nor our courage, neither our wisdom nor our learning, neither our compassion nor our devotion to our country. It measures everything, in short, except that which makes life worthwhile," Kennedy said.

Today's critics of GDP—there are more every day, ranging from the current president of the World Bank to a growing "degrowth" movement—have expanded on the concerns raised by Kuznets and Kennedy. The fruits of economic growth continue to be enjoyed wildly unevenly. While some poorer nations, such as China and India, are gaining ground against the historical winners of the growth game in Europe, North America,

Australasia and Japan, it is important not to overstate the case. Spread evenly, the wealth produced by the global economy each year could pay everyone on earth about $12,000. In Canada and the United States, home to just 5 percent of the world's people, the average income is 400 percent higher than that.

Even as inequality between nations gradually decreases, it is increasing within them. As the French economist Thomas Piketty has noted, this is most glaringly visible (on paper, that is; in real life it can be quite hard to see) not among the world's richest 1 percent of people, but in the richest 0.1 percent. In the US, this top one-thousandth of income earners has seen its after-tax income increase by 420 percent in the past forty years, while the GDP per person increased just 79 percent. (The entire lower half of American workers saw gains of 20 percent.) In recent years, this hyper-upper class has been creeping toward earnings a hundred times higher than the national average. Income in the US is, as Piketty puts it, "about as unequally distributed as has ever been observed anywhere." But even in much more equal countries, such as in Western Europe, the top 10 percent still earns far more than the bottom 50 percent.

Since Robert F. Kennedy's day, the claim that GDP needs to learn to subtract has been bolstered by a long list of oddnesses and weirdosities. When governments dump taxpayers' money into failing banks, as witnessed in the Great Recession, that adds to GDP. Inefficiency, which wastes money to accomplish results that could be achieved for less, is good for the GDP. As financial journalist David Pilling has pointed out, the GDP would rise if every mother shifted from breastfeeding her babies to buying formula to feed them—against the recommendations of nearly every pediatrician on the planet. Replacing the world's volunteers with paid labour would be terrific for economic growth. During the coronavirus pandemic, the business of providing masks, ventilators, personal protective equipment, vaccines, liquor and virtual meet-up software were among the GDP bright spots, though all of them were markers of desperation or isolation. The moral bottom-feeders who hoarded vital supplies during the pandemic and then profiteered through price gouging were actually doing good works from the perspective of GDP growth.

In 2019, New Zealand became the first country to officially drop GDP as its main measure of economic success, while Scotland and Iceland have declared that they plan to track citizens' well-being as their principal metric. Many other nations and regions now also tally the genuine progress indicator, or GPI. (The US state of Maryland has calculated it annually since 2010.) The GPI attempts to take into account social and environmental costs in the economy. Where the GDP counts the productivity of a nation's factories only as positive growth, for example, the GPI will also subtract the cost of their air pollution.

Two decades of research show that GDP and GPI have followed different paths. For one, genuine progress rises more slowly than GDP. For another, GDP and GPI typically increase together as a nation's economy develops, but only up to a certain point. In the world's wealthiest countries, GDP has climbed steeply since the Second World War, while GPI has muddled along, growing slowly if at all, since the mid 1970s. For the last several decades, the world's strongest consumer economies have done a poor job of turning economic growth into a more satisfying life for their citizens.

At this point, there is no claim to growth's benefits that has not come under fire. For example, the argument that economic growth has lifted millions out of poverty is incontestable: a smaller percentage of the earth's population lives in dire poverty than did so before the era of rapid growth. While the fraction of impoverished people is lower than ever, though, the raw number of poor has increased. After two centuries of growing economies, there are as many deeply poor people on the planet today as there were people, period, when the nineteenth century began.

Sitting under his favourite oak tree on a pleasant day in his sleepy neighbourhood, Peter Victor did not relish having to shock his computer-model Canada with the end of shopping. To simulate my scenario, Victor first dialed down what economists call our "marginal propensity to consume," a measure of how much of each additional dollar the average person earns will be spent on consumption. If their propensity to consume was left to follow the trajectory it has taken throughout most of the twenty-first century so far,

Canadians would be consuming 170 percent more fifty years from now than they are today. (If such an increase sounds unimaginable in a country already as rich as Canada, simply picture the typical Canadian household, which now earns $60,000 each year, instead living the lifestyle of a household that earns about $160,000.) Victor turned that down by 50 percent—the overnight abandonment of an economy driven by consumption.

He then made a few more adjustments to ensure that shopping did not make a comeback. Normally, when consumption slows down, powerful economic forces try to speed it up again. Governments offer tax cuts and start spending public money on job-creation programs such as fixing roads and bridges. Banks offer loans and credit at rock-bottom interest rates. Shops and restaurants lower their prices. But if the desire to spend money is simply half as strong as it used to be, then none of that will work. Victor looked apprehensive.

His cursor hovered over a button marked RUN.

A moment later various graphs appeared, their lines bending upward or downward, or leaping back and forth between the two. Victor studied them. Unemployment and debt are so high they're off the charts, he announced. Investors lose enormous amounts of money. The average household ends up paying 60 percent of its income in taxes as the government struggles to keep civilization from going medieval. Despite the fact that the population continues to climb, fifty years after the day the world stops shopping, Canadians will be consuming significantly less than they do today. Remarkably, in this state of chaos, greenhouse gas emissions are still rising, though at a much slower rate than they otherwise would have. Taken as a whole, the model predicts a series of severe recessions with brief (and quite mysterious) windows of better times in between.

Victor leans back in his patio chair. A cardinal, brighter than red velvet, flits into and out of Victor's favourite tree. In a world without shopping, he might soon be burning that tree for firewood. "I think you might be killing capitalism," he said.

Victor's Stop Shopping model resembles two things. One is the economic crisis precipitated by the coronavirus lockdowns. Another is an older scenario Victor developed, nicknamed the No Growth Disaster. In the No Growth Disaster scenario, Victor imagined a sudden freeze in both economic and population growth in Canada. The result was a steep decline in GDP, skyrocketing unemployment, serious government debt and surging poverty, with the only upside being a 14 percent drop in greenhouse gas emissions. The Stop Shopping scenario, he said, would be even worse. "What this brings out is why policymakers attach so much importance to rising consumption," he said. "Everyone's income derives from someone else's expenditure. If we all cut expenditures, then incomes go down. There are major hazards in deliberately and dramatically slowing the rate of growth."

There is more to the story than that. Economists, like environmentalists, have what Piketty calls an "overly developed taste for apocalyptic predictions." Since the era of high economic growth has also been the era that created the world that we know today, the two are often assumed to be inextricably linked: the end of one would be the end of the other. Yet when Victor first began running models of the Canadian economy, he soon came to a heretical conclusion. It is entirely possible to manage without growth.

Why don't we take a look, he said, at a consumer slowdown of 4 percent—what we might call the Slow Shopping scenario? "Coming from a culture where the ambition is always to consume, it's not trivial," he said. He runs the new numbers. The result, while not a complete disaster, is an enduring Canadian recession, with the familiar miseries of lost jobs, lost investments and lost government revenue.

Victor leaned in to make further adjustments. When people consume less, there's less demand for goods and services, so economic activity declines. There's less work to go around. To avoid mass unemployment, Victor took steps to share the remaining work among as many people as possible. He shortened working hours until most people would be working just four, rather than five days a week. He then slowed the growth rate of the Canadian population, which is currently increasing only because of immigration; this step, too, limits the number of people who are seeking the available jobs. (As people are always aging out of the workforce, some new immigrants can still be accommodated.) Next, Victor increased green investment, which can produce jobs and income while lowering the amount of resources that go into the goods and services that we still have a propensity to consume. He adjusted tax rates, too, in order to more equally distribute the wealth that the economy is still producing.

In the end, Victor managed to keep joblessness within historic bounds, provide an adequate standard of living for most people, and reduce pressure on the climate and environment even more than by a reduction in consumption alone—he reaped the benefits of both decoupling and degrowth. Unemployment still surges at times, even in his smoothed model, but by directing more government spending toward Canada's poor (leaving less for other big-ticket expenditures such as education and the military), poverty doesn't worsen. In theory at least, it is possible to put the brakes on consumption and growth, possibly quite dramatically, without facing anything like collapse: "slower by design, not disaster," as Victor describes it in his book *Managing without Growth*.

None of this happens automatically: it's the result of decisions by people in power—in this case Victor is the great puppet master, but in real life it would be political leaders and government officials. Much more brutal options are available. If there are fewer hours of work and less income to go around, for example, governments could allow both to concentrate in the hands of a privileged few. They could allow poverty and joblessness to worsen in order to protect investors. The amount of shopping that stops could itself be spread unfairly: people who are not overconsuming might nonetheless be forced to cut back in order to spare those who are grossly overconsuming from having to make deep reductions. All of the above, in fact, is more in keeping with global consumer society as we know it today.

The Slow Shopping model is similar to one of Victor's recent scenarios, known as Sustainable Prosperity. In it, GDP growth gradually declines nearly to zero across fifty years. Using the same tools as he did to manage a 4 percent drop in consumer spending, he was able to prevent any serious worsening of the employment rate, while reducing working hours and income inequality. Government debt did rise, but only to a level that has been far surpassed in the real world without resulting in economic collapse. The overall wealth of households continued to increase, though less than it would have with more robust growth in the economy.

Is the system still a capitalist one? With its strong policies of wealth redistribution, many people—especially in the United States—would call Victor's system socialism. Yet in this scenario there are still investors. They earn less money than they do today, but not a lot less, and the division of spoils between business and labour remains within historically normal bounds. Meanwhile, carbon emissions in the Sustainable Prosperity scenario hit net zero in less than a quarter century—much sooner than by focusing on renewable energy and green technology to slow climate change in a growing economy.

Victor is quick to emphasize that models are imperfect. To give just one critically important example, they cannot predict whether people would accept the tremendous changes he plugs into them. Yet every tool that Victor applies to his model is already used by highly developed nations, most recently to prevent widespread misery or explosive social discontent during the pandemic. We really could, it seems, begin to slow the consumer economy, deliberately and at any time.

Of course, none of this step-by-step gentling takes place in my thought experiment. Instead, the world stops shopping abruptly, and the ensuing fall is sudden, rapid, long and hard. To know what happens then, you have to go somewhere that has lived through it.

Somewhere like Finland.

7.

The consumption disaster begins,
the disaster of everyday life is over

An eight-year-old girl, her blond hair darkening in time to late autumn's shorter days, watches her father butcher half a pig on their kitchen table. She wears homemade clothes. At the door, never worn inside the house, is the girl's one and only pair of shoes, which she will use until they fall apart. She is by turns fascinated and disgusted with the blood and guts in front of her, the exposed pig brain like some wondrous pink coral.

It sounds like a scene from a faraway time: the Second World War or the Great Depression, an age before the age of affluence, brands and fast fashion. Other details, though, are incongruous. The girl's homemade garments include a tiger-print fun-fur jacket. In a kitchen nook sit a video-cassette recorder and television. In her bedroom she keeps a light-up magic wand, a souvenir of her family's trip, just two years earlier, from Finland's black winter to subtropical Florida. They visited Disney World.

Varpu Pöyry, the millennial who keeps these memories, seems too young to remember economic times as hard as this in one of the world's richer nations. Pöyry is seated, along with her baby, Rosa, in Café Aalto on the tasteful esplanade that reaches into the heart of Helsinki, the Finnish capital, from its harbour. The café is named after the architect and designer

Alvar Aalto, and brims with his particular vision of consumer culture, a blend of hard, modernist lines warmed by leather, wood and brassy light from hanging lanterns. It's a cold-country kind of beauty, and the Finns around us are dressed in fall clothing out of habit rather than necessity; the weather outside—an October heat wave—defies belief.

Pöyry is an engineer and creator of *Her Finland*, a Finnish-lifestyle blog. But in 1990 she was a girl growing up in the small, forest-girdled community of Kuhmoinen. Like many children, she was not very serious about macroeconomics. She played in fields and forests, attended a tiny school, and loved the classic Finnish cartoon The Moomins. "I truly had the best childhood that I could have had," she said. It wasn't until her mother began timing the family's grocery-shopping trips to the expiry dates on packets of meat, in order to buy them at half price, that she recognized their creeping poverty.

Suddenly, half of Kuhmoinen seemed to be unemployed. Her mother and father were lucky enough to keep their jobs but now had to support her paternal grandparents, who had gone bankrupt. "I still don't know why, because we don't talk about money—it's a very Finnish thing," said Pöyry. "But they had lived beyond their means." Only months earlier, her family had regarded fishing and cutting firewood as simple pleasures of country life; now, they relied on them for food and heat. They planted a huge vegetable garden, a potato patch just as large, and filled the "coffin fridge"—a standalone freezer—with wildfowl and moose meat. There would be no more trips to Disney World. Instead, the year's most vivid memory would be of pig brains.

The Finnish Depression began in 1990 and lasted four years, though it was seven years before any real upswing in the economy. It was the greatest "consumption disaster"—a drop in consumer spending by 10 percent or more per capita—to strike a wealthy, democratic nation in recent memory.

"It came very, very, very hard," said Lasse Jääskeläinen, who was a financial journalist in Helsinki at the time. In the 1980s, Finland's stock and housing markets soared on a heady cocktail of financial deregulation, easy credit, frothy investment and the perennial boom-time faith that none of it would come to an end. Just as in the rest of the rich world, it was the era of the yuppie (juppi, in Finnish), correct in detail down to the Lacoste-brand polo shirts and Corvette convertibles. Late in the decade, *Businessweek* warned that "the system is tilting from investment to speculation." Today we find it normal to view the housing and stock markets more like vast casinos than arenas of trade in real and useful things, but in the 1980s, that view had not been widely held since the Roaring Twenties. It had *never* been widely held in Finland. Late to join the Industrial Revolution, many Finns could still remember tasting their first imported orange in the 1950s, and meat was a luxury into the 1960s. Less than twenty years later, lifestyles had changed so much that it was perfectly ordinary to drink wine with dinner or fly somewhere warm in the winter.

"You get blinded with the speed," recalled Jääskeläinen. "Everyone was at the bar trying to look like somebody." Jääskeläinen himself was just eccentric enough not to follow the herd—he is the definition of the sardonic Finn, and his passions include (but do not combine) martial arts and Himalayan cats. "I had this little voice inside me that said, 'Just stay out of it.'"

Economies went bust worldwide in the late 1980s and early '90s, but Finland's crisis was intensified by the decline of its largest trading partner, the Soviet Union. In the first month of the crash, Jääskeläinen's home lost a third of its value. As Finland stopped shopping, businesses all over Helsinki began boarding up their windows. "Just imagine that in New York there would be, in two years, something like forty thousand to fifty thousand small businesses going under."

The term "consumption disaster" captures how elemental consuming has become: just slowing down our shopping creates an economic reality comparable to wars, famines and terrible earthquakes. Most often, such catastrophes are combined. According to Robert Barro, a Harvard economist who has scoured the global database of macroeconomic crises, brutal consumption disasters swept Europe and much of Asia during the Second World War, including some of the fiercest in recorded history, with declines of 54 percent in the Netherlands, 58 percent in Russia, 64 percent in Greece and Japan, and a dire 68 percent in Taiwan. Until the pandemic, however, some nations hadn't experienced a consumption disaster in generations.

In fact, by the time the Finnish Depression began, many people across the industrialized world believed that the era of peacetime economic catastrophes was over. Yet Finland suffered a crash even greater in its history than the Great Depression, and it did so in a dawning era of globalization, cell phones, video game consoles and the World Wide Web.

Finns parsed their needs and wants in much the same way as Americans did in the Great Recession, but with details all their own. The sudden appearance of breadlines—people waiting for handouts of food—was shocking in Finland, one of the world's strongest social welfare states. Bars where topless women served "half and half" beer (served at half the size and half the alcohol content as before) emerged as an inexpensive decadence. Yet spending on mobile phones and the internet increased by a factor of ten during the Finnish Depression, becoming the new necessity goods—"like bread," in the words of one Finnish economist. As the economy collapsed around them, people bought cats and dogs, seeking comfort and the feeling of being vitally important to at least one other living thing. Three decades later, during the Covid-19 outbreak, this was echoed in surging demand for "pandemic pets."

By the time their 1980s boom went bust, most Finns were so strapped by high mortgage or rent payments that they had little to spend on frivolous shopping. Nonetheless, the same bank lobbyists and politicians who had enabled the bubble economy accused ordinary citizens of having caused the crash through greed and excess. Swept by a wave of shame, many in the historically thrifty nation cut their spending even more than they needed to.

"It was psychological," said Juha Siltala, a lantern-jawed, glacier-eyed historian who seems to have just stepped out of the swirling snow of one of Finland's epic pagan poems. "When people enjoy life at a level more than the previous generation experienced, they suspect that they have exceeded the norms and the economic collapse is a sign of God's wrath. They had to pacify angry spirits and destiny by flagellating themselves, by abandoning everything." Some households were forced to sell nearly all they owned; some gave up on having children because they could not afford to raise them. It was during the Finnish Depression that the nation became infamous for an especially high rate of suicide—one of the most widely known facts about a little-known country.

Consumption in the Finnish Depression fell only 14 percent across four long years—it is stunning how severe the consequences of a moderate decline in household spending can be. The Great Recession in the US snatched away jobs, homes, businesses and savings, but on paper it didn't make the cut as a national disaster; neither, in 2020, did the pandemic. In the last 150 years, the US has experienced true consumption disasters only twice. The first was in 1920 to 1921, when federal spending cutbacks after the First World War triggered a consumption drop of about 15 percent. A decade later came the Great Depression, with a 21 percent decline across several years. If many Americans wondered why daily life in the Great Recession or coronavirus crisis didn't look as bad as in the Great Depression, one reason is that neither was as serious a catastrophe, even with tens of thousands of individual Americans facing crushing hardship.

Another reason that recent economic crises don't seem as severe is that most of the population in wealthy nations have a long way to fall before they hit rock bottom. In the 1930s, when a quarter of the average person's household budget was spent on food, people who lost their jobs faced actual starvation—there are stories of people eating rotten bananas and animal feed. In the Great Recession, many American consumers simply bought fewer songs on iTunes, ate in less expensive restaurants, switched to cheaper phone and cable TV plans. Cut American consumption today by 14 percent, the same amount as in the Finnish Depression, and—adjusted for inflation—it would only take us back to the level at which Americans were consuming five years ago. It would also be one of the greatest economic disasters in history.

A paradox of catastrophes is that we often look back upon them fondly. The reasons why we do began to be pieced together in the 1920s, when a small group of social scientists created the field of "disaster studies."

Among its key early findings was that, contrary to what we see in Hollywood films, people stricken by cataclysms like war, earthquakes or hurricanes are more likely to take care of one another than take advantage of each other, and to act with reason and purpose rather than with primal fear.

One disaster studies pioneer, the sociologist Charles E. Fritz, arrived in Britain five years into the terror and privation of the Second World War. "One might expect to find a nation of panicky, war-weary people, embittered by the death and injuries to their family members and friends, resentful over their prolonged lifestyle deprivations," he later wrote. "Instead, what one found was a nation of gloriously happy people, enjoying life to the fullest, exhibiting a sense of gaiety and love of life that was truly remarkable." Epitomized by the enduring motto "Keep Calm and Carry On," the British case is well known. Far less remembered is the fact that similar resilience was recorded in many countries, including Germany, where an assessment of the psychological effects of aerial bombing found that the most heavily bombed cities had the highest morale. There are limits: no one claims that the world's desperate refugees are in any way living the good life. But other than in cases of absolute scarcity, people facing disaster have consistently and rapidly adapted to living with less, often while becoming friendlier, more tolerant, more unified, more generous.

As the American writer Rebecca Solnit points out in her book *A Paradise Built in Hell*, inspired in part by her own experience of a powerful earthquake in San Francisco, the reason these ways of being feel so profound to us in the midst of catastrophe is *because they are normally absent*. In ordinary times, many of us struggle with social isolation, constant time stress, sharply felt inequalities of income and opportunity, or a sense that our lives have little purpose or meaning. "Everyday life is already a disaster of sorts, one from which actual disaster liberates us," Solnit writes.

Unfortunately, economic disasters seem to be different. As happened in Finland, victims of market crashes or recessions are often blamed for their own fates, while big-picture causes—typically the actions of powerful players in business, society and politics—are overlooked. Instead of filling our lives with meaning, economic crises often deepen isolation, strip life of purpose, and bring everyday anxieties like job security and paying the bills even more forcefully to bear.

There is a notable exception to this doom and gloom: economic disasters often relieve the status pressures associated with consumption. Even though income inequality may deepen in a recession, for example, shows of wealth are often seen as tasteless; people tend to dress down and purchase less ostentatious homes and cars, while thrift becomes more acceptable. Finns as a whole have little nostalgia for the Finnish Depression, but many who were young in that era remember it as liberating. As was the case across Europe and North America during the global recession of the 1990s, the brightly coloured clothing and heavily advertised brands of the '80s were abandoned in favour of basic black, leather jackets, and jeans, the more worn out the better. With job opportunities closed off, ambitions were frustrated but the pressure to succeed also dissipated. "A lower-consumption lifestyle—you avoid lots of problems," one woman told me. "You don't have to worry about what to wear, whether your car is up to date, whether your house is up to date." This sense of relief is one of the most important psychological shifts in a world without shopping.

In 1899, Thorstein Veblen, a Norwegian-American social and economic theorist, wrote *The Theory of the Leisure Class*, a coolly observant book about the behaviour of the upper classes. In it, Veblen coined the term "conspicuous consumption" to describe consumption that serves its purpose mainly when it is plainly visible to others. His classic example revolves around the question of why anyone would bother to own a hand-wrought silver spoon, which in Veblen's day cost about twenty dollars, when it didn't bring soup to your mouth any more effectively than a machine-made aluminum spoon that cost twenty cents.

Veblen anticipated the obvious argument in favour of the silver spoon: that its function is not simply to scoop soup, but also to provide the pleasure of using a beautiful, well-made thing. He responded, witheringly, with three points. First, that the difference in "intrinsic beauty of grain or color" between silver and polished aluminum is not enough to justify a price a hundred times higher for the silver spoon. (Many people are unable to tell the two metals apart by sight, and both aluminum and silver reflect light so well that they are used in high-end mirrors, such as those in telescopes). Second, that if the supposedly handmade—artisanal, as we might say today—silver spoon were suddenly revealed to have been manufactured by a machine, then it would immediately lose 80 percent or more of its value, though the product itself was unchanged. Third, that if the aluminum spoon were manufactured to exactly equal the silver spoon in every way but the difference of weight between the metals, it still would not come close to equalling its price. The silver spoon's value, Veblen concluded, derived mainly from the fact that you had to be wealthy to own one—and everyone knew it.

"The case of the spoons is typical," Veblen wrote. "The superior gratification derived from the use and contemplation of costly and supposedly beautiful products is, commonly, in great measure a gratification of our sense of costliness masquerading under the name of beauty."

Ever since Veblen put a name to it, conspicuous consumption has been widely recognized. It is familiar from the yuppie culture of the '80s, the bling and Instagram cultures of the twenty-first century so far, and the ascendency of a billionaire US president whose private jet's seatbelt buckles were plated in twenty-four-karat gold. Publicly applying an expensive lipstick, driving a Lamborghini, carrying a five-thousand-dollar Chanel "hobo bag," flying business class on a short-haul flight—all of these are typical modern examples of classic conspicuous consumption.

Conspicuous consumption is what advertising most often advertises; it's what we're usually talking about when we talk about shopping. "Peer group influence is always higher for visibly consumed products than for those we consume in private," notes Juliet Schor, an American sociologist who in the 1990s led a resurgence of research into conspicuous consumption. Yet more and more consumption is becoming conspicuous. Goods that Schor did not consider to be "visibly consumed" in the 1990s, such as furnaces, hot water heaters or bedroom curtains, can easily be found being conspicuously consumed in photographs on Facebook or Instagram today. In the recent past we rarely knew exactly how friends or family, let alone total strangers, were consuming on their holidays or at restaurants; today we often do, in real time. As it happens, Veblen anticipated that this would occur. "The conspicuous consumption of goods should gradually gain in importance," he wrote, "until it had absorbed all the available product, leaving nothing over beyond a bare livelihood." Almost everything now is a "Veblen good."

Veblen thought a lot about why we engage in such behaviour. The cultural shorthand for his theory usually goes like this: poorer people envy richer people, and therefore strive either to become rich or to mimic the things that rich people do. What Veblen called conspicuous consumption has since been described as competitive consumption, status consumption, even invidious consumption—consumption that is likely to inspire resentment, envy or indignation in others. Veblen was more compassionate than that. The essential reason we participate in conspicuous consumption, he said, is not because we are greedy, envious or even competitive. We do it in pursuit of "the complacency which we call self-respect."

Sadly, most of us don't seem to develop a sense of self-respect simply from putting food on the table, clothes on our backs and a roof overhead. Instead, we are doomed to dissatisfaction if we don't also feel that we are living as well as the people with whom we compare ourselves. Those people are not necessarily, or even usually, the rich. Instead, they are what we might today call our circle or our network.

We now know that the question of who we look to as our comparators is vexingly complicated, ranging from friends, workmates and neighbours—keeping up with the Joneses—to celebrities—keeping up with the Kardashians—to complete strangers on social media. Because we constantly use consumption to position ourselves in relation to those around us, today's scholars often refer to "positional consumption." We position ourselves so carefully, in fact, that some conspicuous consumption has become strangely inconspicuous: a pair of Hiut jeans, a Robbe & Berking spoon, or a T-shirt featuring the animated *susuwatari* dustballs from the Totoro universe will send an immediately recognizable signal to some, while remaining completely invisible to the vast majority of others.

Some commentators argue that the way we consume today is so elaborately personal that it is no longer useful to talk about conspicuous consumption by any name. Yet a lot of today's consumption still involves fairly naked status competition. Houses, for example, are such important status symbols that researchers have found that, given the choice between owning a three-hundred-square-metre home in a neighbourhood where most homes are two hundred square metres, or a four-hundred-square-metre home in a neighbourhood where most homes are six hundred square metres, most people will choose the three-hundred-square-metre home—because it is larger than their neighbours'. The results of research into which brands were considered "high status" in the 2010s could, for the most part, have been beamed in from the 1980s, and those brands are more often mentioned on social media in parts of the United States that have wider gaps between rich and poor. Here's the top ten: Gucci, Mercedes, Louis Vuitton, Rolex, BMW, Chanel, Apple, Prada, Armani, and Versace. We remain well aware of visible indicators of wealth. We still do use consumption to mark our place in the pecking order. Another important finding: almost all of us will claim that we, personally, do not engage in positional consumption, while the data shows that almost all of us do.

Positional consumption is one of consumerism's clearest causes of unhappiness. A study from forty years ago revealed the strength of the effect in an unexpected way. The researchers attempted to determine whether the spread of television across the US in the 1950s had led to an increase in crime, given that crime is so often depicted on TV. They found that it had not, with one exception. Wherever television was introduced, an increase in larceny—the theft of personal property, a crime that is rarely featured in television programming—soon followed. After ruling out other possible causes of the stealing spree, the researchers attributed it to "factors associated with viewing high levels of consumption—perhaps relative deprivation and frustration." At the time, 85 percent of all TV characters were depicted living middle- and upper-class lifestyles. A spike in exposure to conspicuous consumption had been enough, it seemed, to drive some people to commit crimes.

In private interviews, even the very rich told Veblen that conspicuous consumption was both a pleasure and a burden—they sometimes felt they were bending their backs beneath the "elaborate and cumbrous" weight of their "dwellings, furniture, bric-a-brac, wardrobe, and meals." But the phrase "relative deprivation and frustration" applies here as well. Whether struggling to get by or perfectly well-to-do, if we have the sense that we are keeping up, we will feel some peace of mind; if we're out ahead, even better. ("Extremely gratifying," as Veblen puts it.) Any feeling that we're falling behind—that our place in society is becoming less equal—strongly dampens our happiness.

Modern research confirms that inequality helps drive consumerism, mainly by intensifying status competition so that obvious markers of wealth and success, whether they be more expensive phones, luxury cars or globe-trotting adventures that we post on social media, become more important, which in turn makes the pursuit of money more important. Simply put, inequality pushes materialistic values. Our reactions to what inequality researcher Richard Wilkinson calls the "ordeal of performance" demanded by status competition are varied: some people become classic, conspicuously consuming materialists; others, their self-esteem ceaselessly under assault, slide into depression or anxiety; still others respond by escaping into drugs, alcohol or consumption itself. (Shopping really can provide temporary "retail therapy" for status anxieties.) Looking at our own lives, most of us probably recognize some mixture of all of the above.

The journalist Anu Partanen moved from a wealthy but relatively equal country, Finland, to a nation with some of the worst income inequality in the rich world, the United States, and ultimately wrote a book—*The Nordic Theory of Everything*—about her observations. Sitting in a Helsinki café, she recalled how, before she left Finland, she had never felt much pressure to show outward signs of success; she felt financially secure, and other people's lifestyles seemed roughly similar in scale to her own. In fact, Finland's wealthy sometimes complained that they could not publicly enjoy their wealth and were only respected if they lived moderately.

When Partanen moved to New York City, American materialism struck her as both obvious and irresistible. She constantly encountered people who plainly had more expensive clothes, bigger and better apartments, flashier cars. In the media, celebrities engaged in the most conspicuous of conspicuous consumption. "They want to show off their big houses, there are TV shows built around that, so it's something to admire and something to want. And it's very excessive. It's not enough to have one Ferrari, you have to have ten Ferraris," Partanen said.

At the same time, she saw on the streets and subways of New York a depth of poverty unlike anything she'd ever witnessed in Europe, and realized that unemployment or even a poorly paid job in the US could lead to abject homelessness, hunger and desperation. Compounding Partanen's anxiety was the fact that, while poverty was often visible, wealth frequently was not: she eventually realized that many of the people whom she thought of as her peers were not living on their earnings, but on inheritances or family support. Worst of all, it really did seem difficult to earn enough to own a home, send her kids to college, or have reliable health-care insurance. Paradoxically, as her insecurities added up, she found herself wanting to spend more money, rather than less.

"It was striking to me that I, who had grown up in a Nordic country and had not felt that before, got caught up in it quite quickly after moving to America. I felt like I should be consuming more," Partanen said. "You want to buy more things that will make you feel like you're making it, and like you are safe."

Her experiences closely mirror inequality research. A large body of studies now supports the theory that people become more materialistic when they feel insecure about meeting their material and psychological needs, and that inequality aggravates those feelings of insecurity. Wide gaps between rich and poor also create more obvious opportunities to compare one's own lifestyle with others', which in turn leads us to focus on what possessions or experiences we might need to have in order to attain Veblen's "complacency which we call self-respect." In the end, Partanen moved back to Finland. Immediately, she said, she felt like she could put aside the success-signalling wardrobe that she wore in New York. No longer feeling pressured to focus on status, she felt freer to think about what she truly wanted to accomplish. As a British politician once said, "If you want the American dream, go to Finland."

Modern Finland, though, is a much less equal country than it was before its 1990s crash. Until then, the nation's guiding vision had been of a society in which, as one geographer told me, "everyone lives the same reality and therefore can understand each other." Income inequality rose during the juppi-era 1980s, but not by a lot, and in the Finnish Depression, homelessness and starvation were largely kept at bay through government support and higher taxes on those still earning income—the kind of actions Peter Victor uses to smooth disasters in his economic models. There were no riots or even mass protests in the streets.

As the Finnish Depression ground on, however, the country's richest and most powerful pushed for the kind of market-driven policies then being advanced by their peers in Europe and North America. Since then, the gap between rich and poor in the country has continued to widen. Finland today would be a tougher place to endure a consumption disaster than it was thirty years ago. The breadlines never disappeared.

But what, you may ask, about Finland's famous suicides? Surely those speak a terrible truth about the costs of the Finnish Depression. Almost completely unknown—even within Finland—is that the number of people committing suicide didn't actually increase during the economic crisis; it peaked at the height of the 1980s economic boom. Once the Finnish Depression began, the suicide rate decreased, a trend that has continued to the present day. (It is still higher than in most of Western Europe, but about the same as in the United States, and below Japan or Korea.) In fact, the question of Finns' mental health during the consumption disaster is an open one; no studies indicate anything like a deep decline, and some suggest it improved by most measures.

No one can say exactly why this might be. A common explanation, though, is that amid the roaring consumer culture of the 1980s, Finns found themselves competing with and comparing themselves to one another more fiercely than ever before. There had never been such a strong sense that the nation was dividing into winners and losers. Old Finnish wisdom warns against young people dying by their own hand not in the long darkness of winter, but with the arrival of spring. "They see a world of possibilities," one woman told me, "and they kill themselves." They come face to face with the disaster of everyday life.

Varpu Pöyry, she of the homemade clothes and pig-butchering memories, clearly recalls the moment when she knew the Finnish Depression was over. During the hard years, Pöyry would watch TV to see what was in fashion, then draw designs that her mother and grandmother would sew for her.

When she was eleven, everyone on TV was wearing neon, and she requested a pair of neon-green pants and a neon-pink shirt. "I was so proud, I was so stylish," she said. But by then, things were looking up in Finland.

The following year her family went to Greece, and there, on a beach, she met girls from Helsinki wearing the trending brands of the day, like Diesel and Miss Sixty. "I was wearing my homemade clothes, and I really felt like, oh my god, I'm so horrible," Pöyry said.

Many Finnish millennials like herself, Pöyry said, are anxious about how they consume today. She's not sure what weighs on them more, their childhood memories of the Finnish Depression, or the fact that the world's environmental problems are now so undeniable. Like concerned people everywhere, they are making individual choices that they hope will reduce their footprint on the planet. They ride bicycles and use public transit. They eat *nyhtökaura*—vegan pulled pork. They take trips by airplane, and then feel guilty about it.

But another hand-me-down from Pöyry's childhood is that she does not fear another crash. "I didn't feel like I was deprived of anything," she told me. "I think it's huge that I *didn't* get everything I wanted. It teaches me that I can still have a great life." She has the skills to survive, she said. She can grow food and raise farm animals and catch fish. She can make jam and sew clothing and knit socks.

A surprising memory surfaces in her mind: you might think that, as a child during the hard times, she would have longed to live in a big house or busy city. Instead, she had daydreamed about living even more self-sufficiently than her family already was. She pictured a simple cottage with solar power and livestock, with moss instead of toilet paper. Although she was a happy girl, she had picked up on the anxious mood of the Finnish Depression. Dark times, she thought to herself, must be on the horizon. She didn't realize they were already here.

Can advertising turn into
the opposite of itself?

nyone passing through the Clapham Common subway station in
London will typically walk past 65 advertisements on their way
from the train to the street or the street to the train. For a daily
commuter, that's 130 ads a day, 650 a working week, just in the minute or two
that they spend each day moving through the station. On the escalator alone,
they pass 54 ads: for clothes, perfume, films, shoes, phones, shows.

Suddenly, those ads have disappeared. Instead, the walls and even the
turnstiles are plastered with images of cats: a classic black-and-white tom,
a kitten in a purple collar, a magisterial long-haired tabby with green eyes.
The cats have nothing to sell. There is nothing they want from you. They
are there simply because, as the internet has emphatically shown, cats tend
to make people feel *good*, while advertising tends to makes people feel insecure or lacking in some way—in other words, *bad*. So why not more cats
and fewer ads?

This scene with the cats in the London Underground really happened.
In 2016, during a rare September heat wave in England, a group of rebel
advertising creatives, as the people who come up with ads call themselves,
hired out the entire Clapham Common station and replaced the posters
selling stuff with a celebration of all things feline. It was a glimpse—the

group of creatives was called Glimpse—of what becomes possible when advertising fades from the mental and physical environment.

This we know: a world that stops shopping is a world with fewer ads. If there is an industry that, on that fateful day, would stand out for the severity of its collapse and the unlikelihood of its recovery, it is the advertising and marketing industry.

When consumers stop consuming, advertising is one of the first things businesses spend less on. During the pandemic, even advertising on the internet—where people were spending more time than ever before—plunged by nearly 40 percent in just two months. While the general public mourned many of the business losses that piled up during the crisis, media reports on fading ad campaigns were typically greeted with cheers. Ironically, most of those same media reports were supported by advertising.

The pattern is old and consistent. In 2009, the bottom of the Great Recession, global advertising spending fell by 10 percent—far more than consumer spending. In the United States, the number of jobs in marketing crashed to 1995 levels, turning back the clock by nearly fifteen years. The recession wasn't even the greatest ad blackout in recent history. That took place during the grinding downturn of the early '90s, when marketing plummeted five times as quickly as the economy as a whole across the richer nations of the world. Worst of all, of course, was Finland, where a decline in advertising spending of more than a third stretched across several years.

Consumption and advertising are clearly tightly coupled. Fly from a nation like Ecuador to any American airport, and the bombardment by ads, so much less heavy in poorer countries, is a shock. Marketing even declines when income inequality decreases, because people buy less stuff when they feel they're keeping up with the lifestyles of those around them.

The role of advertising, and its effect on us, is endlessly debated. There is no consensus among those who study the subject even on whether we can say that advertising *works*, because ads clearly are effective only some of the time, or on some people at a time, and in many cases have no measurable impact at all. That we know in our guts that advertising is a powerful social force, however, is shown by the fact that more than six hundred billion dollars is now spent on it in a typical year worldwide. Marketing is like climate change. We can't say that a September heat wave in London is because of global warming, but we do know that global warming increases the likelihood of September heat waves in London. Not every purchase we make is because of advertising, but the omnipresence of advertising makes it more likely we'll buy stuff.

The ways that marketing can sell to us are as diverse as the ways we value our things. An advertisement can be designed to convince us that a product will be useful, or solve a problem, or bring meaning or beauty to our lives, or make us more attractive, or mark an important life event, or indulge our daydreams and fantasies, or dispel our guilt and insecurities, or express who we are, or give us status, or strengthen our ties to people we care about, or connect us to the past, or act as a gift—and so on. Ultimately, meeting any of these wants and needs results in the same sensation: pleasure, whether the proverbial "spark of joy" or the more complex contentment of, say, finding the right coffin in which to bury a loved one. Advertising's eternal promise is that consumption will bring satisfaction.

It has been said that capitalism can sell anything, other than less. Vincent Stanley, whose role at the Patagonia outdoor clothing company is a strange hybrid of marketeer and philosopher, famously tested that proposition on the busiest shopping day of the year in 2011. Stanley proposed that Patagonia place an unusual advertisement in the *New York Times* on Black Friday, which has become the global start date for the Christmas shopping frenzy. The ad featured an image of Patagonia's top-selling fleece sweater with the heading, "Don't Buy This Jacket." The rest of the advertising copy was equally blunt. "Don't buy what you don't need. Think twice before you buy anything." It spelled out the jackets' environmental costs: to make and ship each one used up enough water to meet the daily needs of forty-five people, and pumped nearly ten kilograms of carbon pollution into the atmosphere, a weight far greater than the jacket itself.

Some of the company's directors saw a real risk that the ad would prove to be a Ratner moment, triggering a drop in Patagonia's sales or even sinking the entire company—one-fifth of retail purchases in the US are made in the Christmas season. They agreed to go ahead with it anyway. "Usually when we make a move like that, we don't plan, we don't have chess moves two or three steps ahead," Stanley said. "We just say, okay, we'll see what happens."

What happened is that Patagonia's sales *went up* over the following months; there wasn't even a drop in sales of the specific jacket that the company had asked customers not to buy. Since then, the company has steadily continued, year upon year, to sell more goods and open more shops, often in locations—the Upper West Side of Manhattan, Gangnam in Seoul, Chamonix in France—that are known for the kind of wealthy recreational shoppers who inspired the company's nickname of Patagucci.

All of this would seem to be jet fuel for the engines of modern cynicism. What could be more ironic than a brand using anti-consumerism as a way to sell more stuff? Yet it might be something else: a glimpse—there's that word again—of what marketing looks like in a lower-consuming world.

Patagonia doesn't advertise a lot. The company does so mainly through its catalogue and website, which, like a lot of sophisticated marketing these days, doesn't sell anything so much as *everything*: an entire lifestyle in which Patagonia products are prominently featured. The Patagonia universe is one of camaraderie and achievement in wild and authentic places, populated by physically fit people who embody words like "soul" and "spirit." You might believe that buying Patagonia will help you become one of them; you might believe it brings you a step closer to that world.

Patagonia also markets through a kind of corporate propaganda of the deed. Most typically, the company attracts attention through its participation in environmental campaigns, but at times it does so through acts of guerrilla advertising. The "Don't Buy This Jacket" ad was one of these, receiving widespread media coverage that Patagonia didn't have to pay a dime for, as was a 2016 campaign in which the company promised to donate 100 percent of the proceeds of its Black Friday sales to environmental campaigns. They expected to do $2.5 million in sales, Stanley told me; instead, they raked in $10 million. "We had some people come in the following week saying, 'We went crazy and bought too much stuff. Can we bring it back?' And we said yes," Stanley said.

At the same time, the brand engages in typical marketing strategies: click on the seven-dollar packet of dehydrated chili-mango slices and you are instantly offered four other products. You can also catch Patagonia in the classic marketing scheme of manufacturing needs you didn't know you had. In 2018, the company launched its "silent down jacket," which eliminated the *swish-swish* sound of fabric brushing against fabric as you move around in a puffy garment. Overnight, ownership of a "noisy" down jacket threatened to become unfashionable and, eventually, an embarrassing sign of old age.

"I sometimes look at the size of our line and the number of things we produce, and I know that there's some tension," said Stanley, whose appreciation of environmental issues was sharpened when he was evacuated from his home during one of the cataclysmic wildfires that have swept across California in recent years, and was later blocked from commuting to Patagonia's Santa Barbara headquarters when torrential rains turned the bare soil, burned down to the minerals, into mudslides. "You know, we're not set up like a state liquor store in the 1950s, with a green wall and metal shelves to make you feel guilty when you're buying. Our stores are beautiful and all the stuff looks great."

There is a name for Patagonia's puzzling approach to advertising. It's called "demarketing," and, according to Catherine Armstrong Soule, a consumer researcher at Western Washington University, it has historically represented a "tiny, tiny, tiny, tiny" fraction of overall advertising. First acknowledged in the 1970s, demarketing involves finding ways to dissuade consumers from consuming too much of a product or service. Examples from that era included Budweiser beer, Kodak's original Instamatic camera, and travel to the island of Bali, all of which met with runaway demand and had to be demarketed.

At the time, people were beginning to recognize that the world's resources were not unlimited. The first scholars to look at demarketing, consumer researchers Philip Kotler and Sidney J. Levy, had the foresight to imagine its application to a world that stops shopping. Marketing, they said, arose during a long period in history when industrial productivity and plentiful resources combined to create an "oversupply" of goods. By the '70s, most businesspeople saw advertising as a fair-weather profession that would be "greatly reduced in a scarcity economy." Yet marketing didn't need to be only and always about increasing demand, the authors wrote in *Harvard Business Review*. Its truer purpose was simply "to adjust the demand to a level and composition that the company can, or wishes to, handle." There was no reason why marketing couldn't encourage what Kotler and Levy called "deconsuming": decreasing demand and consumption.

Recent efforts by a tiny, tiny, tiny number of companies to discourage demand as an act of ecological responsibility have been called "green demarketing." Patagonia's "Don't Buy This Jacket" ad was a pioneering example, and the first to capture Armstrong Soule's attention. A more recent case is REI, an American outdoor goods and services department store, which since 2015 has closed its doors on Black Friday, while also encouraging consumers to spend the busiest shopping day of the year outdoors.

Many people quite reasonably see green demarketing as hypocritical: cognitive dissonance is unavoidable when companies use marketing to both sell and unsell their products. Patagonia didn't expect its "Don't Buy This Jacket" ad to hurt sales, and the company's demarketing has contributed to its steady growth. Similarly, Armstrong Soule once visited an REI store just ahead of its Black Friday closure and was met by staff handing out discount coupons. In effect, they were holding a Black Friday sale— just not on Black Friday.

But there is more to green demarketing than a cynical ploy. It's no surprise that the strategy has been most prominent among outdoor retailers: many outdoorspeople are relatively wealthy but also concerned about the effects of consumption on the planet. A significant part of the outdoor market is made up of what we might call "deconsumers," or people who actively want to reduce their, and the world's, consumption.

Patagonia is arguably the first deconsumer brand with a global profile. They increasingly target a deconsumer market, which they also actively strive to expand by encouraging people to deconsume. In a world of planned obsolescence, or products deliberately designed to stop working, fall apart, or go out of fashion quickly, Patagonia markets its gear as built to last. Besides being durable, many Patagonia goods are deliberately made in classic colours and styles to survive multiple fashion cycles. Through a program called Worn Wear, the company encourages people to use their gear for as long as possible, and frequently promotes photos of Patagonia products looking patched and faded, tattered and torn. If your gear needs repair, they offer that service, and if you're done with it, they will resell or recycle it. Patagonia has remained an endlessly growing corporation in an economy founded on endless growth, but its actions anticipate what doing business might look like in a deconsumer culture.

There is nothing truly discordant about that: a lower-consuming society consumes *fewer* products, not none at all. Reduce global consumption by 25 percent, and there is still trillions of dollars in spending going on. During the Great Recession, most of that spending flowed to bargains and lower-quality goods as households tried to save money without cutting back on shopping, but Patagonia noticed smaller, but to them more significant, trends. Impulse buying and conspicuous consumption slowed in the recession, and some shoppers sought out high-quality, longer-lasting products rather than a quick feel-good fix. The company also observed the strange shift, seen again in the pandemic, toward deconsumer consumer goods.

"The whole outdoor industry benefited from the downturn, because people were no longer going to luxury hotels on vacation—they were going to national parks or going camping close to home," said Stanley. "You'd see your customers coming in and buying tents and sleeping bags and jackets."

It took a lot of marketing to create the modern consumer, and demarketing could accelerate the advance of the deconsumer. In a recent study, Armstrong Soule and other researchers showed Americans from a wide range of backgrounds a photograph of a man in a yellow outdoors jacket who is smiling and flashing the peace sign with his fingers. The man's face is weathered, and his jacket is not only far from new, but also caked with white, pink and bright blue paint. The study effectively asked participants to guess, Who is this man? A person living on the street, too poor to buy a new, undamaged jacket? A financially comfortable weekend mountaineer, hanging on to his jacket for environmental reasons while enjoying its bohemian eccentricity? Something in between?

How the man was perceived depended on subtle signals. Some study participants were shown the original photo, which was taken from Patagonia's marketing materials and showed the jacket with its Patagonia brand and Worn Wear patch visible; they were also told what Patagonia stood for as a company and what the Worn Wear program was all about (hanging on to your aging gear as an act of environmental virtue). Others saw the same photo, with the brand and patch edited out. Those who saw the branding and knew what it meant were much more likely to guess that the man's income and environmental awareness were high. They were then also more likely to consider buying Patagonia products, even at a premium price.

When we know that a person is consuming less as a deliberate choice, and not out of financial need, we attach greater status to that action. It becomes an act of conspicuous deconsumption. "That drives so much of our consumption: I picked this not only because it matches me, but also because I want the world to know about who I am, or who I want to be," said Armstrong Soule. "The idea of giving back some of that to the consumer when they practise anti-consumption—to me, that takes a lot of advertising in a traditional sense."

James Turner is the communications creative who founded Glimpse, the group that plastered the London Tube station with images of cats in order to sell nothing more than the idea that there might be better things to put on urban walls than ads. "We need people who currently work in advertising to reshape the story of consumerism and 'sell' the alternatives to instant gratification with the same energy and ingenuity that they currently apply to consumer products," he said. "The people who are currently in the advertising industry should be the leaders, or at least part of the leadership, for that new movement."

In the same way that much consumer advertising has sold not just products, but a status system that makes us more likely to buy those products, Turner said, demarketing could not only unsell goods or change our relationship with them, but promote a new status system. Could the planet's best advertising minds convince us that the next big thing is volunteering? reconnection to nature? seeking wisdom?

"I have this slightly woolly hope that creativity itself is the next thing," Turner said. He imagines a world in which we form our identities around creative pursuits and self-expression, letting go of the "anchor of brands" to express who we are. It would take, he thinks, plenty of great work by advertising creatives. "The question then is, is there enough capacity in the system to give them all a job?"

Probably not, said Vincent Stanley. During the pandemic, the question of whether Patagonia should grow or not ceased to be philosophical: the company shuttered its warehouses, stores, offices and even its shipping earlier than most. It committed to pay its regular staff through the first months of the crisis, but beyond that, announced that it would furlough many of its workers. "We are shrinking," Stanley said at the time. "Maybe it will be healthier in the long run for the ecosphere. But it's going to hurt like hell for a good long while."

Still, the company planned to continue with a two-pronged approach, both greening their products and figuring how to sell fewer new things. The crisis, after all, had the potential to grow the world's small deconsumer market as people learned how many things they can live without, how many things they don't even miss.

In ordinary times, consumer spending drives advertising, which drives more consumer spending; the two form a feedback loop that perpetually grows the circle. Replacing the message to consume with something like a call for creative expression, or citizenship, or volunteerism doesn't pay for itself in the same way. When people stop shopping, the production of advertising, like the production of other consumer goods, slows down. The clutter and distraction that marketing has made almost ubiquitous in our mental and physical environment gives way to an unfamiliar absence. "And it's better," Stanley said, laughing.

Leonora Oppenheim, a London-based artist and designer, has lived in a muted advertising landscape, the kind we would know in a less consumeristic world, for twenty years. She believes it has made her a different person.

Oppenheim grew up surrounded by the advertising industry. Her father worked in marketing, mainly on behalf of cigarette and tobacco brands. Her first job, at age fifteen, was at an advertising agency. Her second job was with Wolff Olins, a half-century-old global branding agency that has worked with companies such as GE, Google, Microsoft, and Alibaba. Throughout her childhood and coming of age, when most of us simply absorb marketing until we know the globe's brands better than its geography, Oppenheim understood how ads are made, and that their aim is to influence you in particular ways.

That understanding led her into a crisis while she was studying design at the University of London. "I was heading towards a very high end, luxury, experimental design world—interiors and furniture and all sorts of things," she said, sitting in the basement café of an abandoned London schoolhouse that has been converted into artists' studios. "Questions of environmental impact definitely derailed me from that."

She began to resent the mechanisms that push us to buy the goods and services that drive climate change, deforestation, plastic garbage in the oceans, and so much more. "It's like pollution, it feels like visual mental pollution," she said. "Let's say you go to The Gap online and you look for a pair of trousers. It's not just that The Gap will follow you around on your browser for the next week. It's that those pairs of trousers that you've thought you might want—and then decided you didn't want—are stalking you. You're literally being chased through the internet by products that you are trying not to buy. They're trying to wear you down and make you buy them."

In the early 2000s, Oppenheim began to actively avoid advertising. At first she stuck to Britain's advertising-free public television and radio broadcaster, the BBC. As the internet age began in earnest, she was an early adopter of apps that shut out marketing. Later, as ad-free magazines and premium streaming services became available, she bought into them. "The most adverts I see now are while travelling on public transport," she said. "Billboards, buses, posters on the Tube." She tries to avert her eyes.

An obvious result of Oppenheim's ad avoidance is that she pays for a growing list of things that most other people do not. Critics of advertising focus on how clamorously it reminds us to buy this or that; they gloss over how those same advertisements support much of the world's media and its creators, from podcasts and music streaming to social media and news reporting. The coronavirus pandemic revealed the weakness of this model: as people turned to the media for both distraction and information, the advertising that funds it tumbled into freefall. Small, local media, in particular, faced financial collapse just as they were attracting record numbers of readers, listeners or viewers. Oppenheim's self-made world reflects the probable outcomes: we, as consumers, would need to pay a lot more for our information, entertainment and social connection, either directly or through government and not-for-profit agencies. In all probability, that means there would be less of it.

Some product manufacturers have already gone ad-free: the French-Brazilian footwear company Veja, for example, spends nothing on advertising or celebrity brand ambassadors—which the company claims often accounts for 70 percent of the cost of a pair of sneakers—in order to pay better wages to workers and the higher price of organic and sustainably harvested materials. Veja shoes are among the few visibly branded products that Oppenheim is prepared to wear, because she wants to publicly promote their values.

She readily laughs at herself about it all. "What a silly effort," she said. Oppenheim wonders, in a chicken-or-egg way, whether she originally began to avoid advertising out of the desire for a less consumeristic life or because she couldn't afford a consumeristic life and therefore needed to avoid wishing for things she couldn't have. It no longer matters: she is now comfortably settled into her identity as a deconsumer, an anti-consumer.

"The overarching theme is wanting to streamline the kind of information that goes into my brain," Oppenheim said, "wanting to be able to curate it, and to feel—as naive as it may be—that I have some level of control."

Consumer research consistently shows that exposure to what can easily add up to thousands of advertisements a day, most of them telling us that money, possessions and the right image are a path to happiness, success and self-worth, does in fact tend to make us feel worse about ourselves. In cities, especially (where most people now live), the crowds of other consumers and glut of advertising constantly cause us to doubt our social status. In the words of British economist Tim Jackson, we are persuaded to spend money we don't have on things we don't need to create impressions that won't last on people we don't care about.

A person who quits drinking coffee will, if they try a cup later on, recognize just how strong a drug caffeine really is. In the same way, Oppenheim said that when she is exposed to advertising, she can clearly feel the way it plays on our insecurities. In a world with less advertising, she said, people would enjoy greater mental well-being, less pressure to perform ("whatever that means for you in your social peer group"), and probably less depression and fewer suicidal thoughts as they encountered fewer cues to have misgivings about their appearance and self-worth.

At the very least, she said, we won't miss having so many ads around. Before the pandemic, Oppenheim had been struck by the way that more and more people she spoke to were experiencing a stressful sense that time is speeding up, or even that, like in the classic film *Groundhog Day*, they were endlessly repeating the same routine. Many of these people found the eerie stillness of the pandemic disorienting and even frightening. Oppenheim found it familiar. By controlling her mental environment, she had long ago developed a sense of time slowing down, of immersion in a pool of calm that is growing larger rather than smaller.

"I want to be quieter and quieter," she said. "I want to listen more and more to myself."

For two decades, Oppenheim has lived in a curious exile, becoming something of a stranger to the world in which most of the people around her live. Oppenheim didn't simply reject advertising, but ultimately something much larger. She turned her back on materialism itself.

We adapt to not-shopping
more quickly than you think

To know how it *feels* to stop shopping, we might begin with what three decades of research show: that materialistic values are not good for our mental health.

"Materialism is good for the things that it's good for," Tim Kasser, an American psychologist who has studied the subject throughout those thirty years, told me. "If what you care about is status and possessions and economic growth, materialism is great. If what you care about is personal, social and ecological well-being, materialism is not so great."

Materialism has been studied from many angles, all converging on this same conclusion. Its negative effects have been found in children, the elderly and everyone in between. Its downsides prevail among people from a wide range of incomes, education levels, genders, ethnicities and cultural backgrounds, and even among groups in which nearly everyone scores as highly materialistic, such as lawyers, business students and entrepreneurs. In fact, the more materialistic you are, the worse its effects: the drawbacks are strongest among those who place the most value on money and possessions as signs of success, who think that a lot of money and possessions are necessary for happiness, and who put money and possessions ahead of human relationships. The degree to which you are materialist also predicts how self-serving, narcissistic, ungenerous and manipulative you are likely to be. Materialists more frequently have utilitarian attitudes about others (they are "users"), are more likely to have shorter and shallower interpersonal relationships, and are more likely to be lonely. Because materialism discourages empathy, it makes people less likely to volunteer to help others or to care about the environment.

In short, the reason materialism fails to provide lasting comfort, satisfaction or happiness is because that's not its role in the human psyche. It is there to inflame anxieties, stir insecurities, get you out of bed to make your way in the world. "It is not," as Kasser said to me, "nutritive to well-being."

It's one thing for studies to show that materialism makes us unhappy, and another to explain exactly how it does so. The fact that materialism's modus operandi is to make us feel insecure about our wealth and status is only part of the problem. The more important element is that there are only so many hours in a lifetime.

Psychologists cluster the various values we might hold into two main groups. *Extrinsic values* give us satisfaction mainly when they are recognized by others. "Being fashionable" is an example of an extrinsic value; you may take personal satisfaction from your good taste in clothing, but to feel fashionable ultimately requires approving glances, compliments and heart-eyed emojis from people whose opinions matter to you. Extrinsic values put the "conspicuous" in conspicuous consumption, and are the bedrock of advertising and shopping culture. If you sometimes find social media galling, with its currencies of likes, shares, retweets and vote-ups, it is the crass materialism of such systems that you are reacting against.

Intrinsic values satisfy us directly, internally, without much need for outside acknowledgement. "Having close and supportive friends" is an intrinsic value. Others may admire or envy you for the quality of your friendships, but that recognition isn't necessary in order for those friendships to be satisfying. They just *are*. Intrinsic values, too, are frequently deployed in marketing. (Do you love your would-be fiancée enough to give her this diamond ring? Do you care enough about your children to buy a car with these safety features? Do you respect yourself enough to wear an expensive watch?) But such ads are cynical. None of these items are essential to true love, care for your children or self-respect.

"Both intrinsic and extrinsic motives and impulses are basic to what it means to be human—we are conflicted beings," said Kasser. "The question that's really interesting is, when are we which? What are the circumstances in people's lives that conduce them to be more often one way or the other way?"

Even in the world's most materialistic societies, Kasser said, the great majority of people still report that intrinsic values—health, family, friends, striving to be a competent and open-hearted person—are the most important. It's just that materialism is crowding them out. When we pursue extrinsic values, we use up time and energy that could be put toward better ways to satisfy our psychological needs, such as developing an authentic identity all our own, skill in the things we do, and strong relationships with people we care about. We end up too busy showing the world we're winning (or at least not losing) to really succeed at life.

Yet there are aspects of materialism that these theories don't seem to adequately answer. The greatest of them all is why, if shopping not only does not but *cannot* make us happy, we have ended up doing so much of it. Why would so many of us engage in something so clearly not in our best interests?

The explanation for this paradox begins with the fact that materialism research is messier when looked at closely. Yes, materialism is generally bad for everyone, everywhere—but not *that* bad. The effect is small enough that it can be difficult to recognize, even in ourselves. Materialism's negative impact is a broad pattern in society, not a natural law that guarantees that buying some new gadget always and only makes us miserable. There are happy materialists and unhappy nonmaterialists—outliers from the datapoint cluster. In other words, less is more, but not always a lot more. And for a few of us, more really is more, and less is less. It's just that you probably aren't one of these people, even if you think you are.

Materialism is only one of many factors that influence well-being. A consistent finding in happiness research, for example, is that wealthier people report higher well-being. More income doesn't only buy goods and services, it can also provide a person with status, security, opportunities and control over their life. Once essential needs are met, however, the amount of well-being contributed by additional income tends to decline toward the vanishing point. The economist John Maynard Keynes argued that this marks the moment when a society solves its "economic problem": it has provided for those needs "which are absolute in the sense that we feel them whatever the situation of our fellow human beings may be" and begins to indulge those needs "which are relative in the sense that we feel them only if their satisfaction lifts us above, makes us feel superior to, our fellows." (Writing in 1930, Keynes could already see that "needs of the second class" may be insatiable, because the bar of superiority can always be raised, and also that absolute needs aren't restricted to food, clothing and shelter, but could include such necessities as a degree of ease and enjoyment in life.) The challenge for human society, Keynes wrote, would be to recognize when the economic problem had been solved—he predicted, based on long-term economic and demographic trends, that this would occur in many countries by the year 2030. Humankind could then set aside the "money-motive," which he condemned as "a somewhat disgusting morbidity."

A fundamental characteristic of consumer culture is that it muddies and befogs the line at which wealth ceases to improve well-being and begins to detract from it. In recent decades, for example, millions of people in China have enjoyed the benefits of rising incomes as they lifted themselves and their families out of hardship. Now, with relentless status competition, glaring inequality, and a growing generation gap between older materialists and younger people who question the consequences of so much avarice, rising wealth is adding less and less to national happiness. One of the most striking aspects of Chinese consumer culture is the strength of its "green materialism." The nation has become one of the world's leading proponents of an "ecological civilization" in which ever-richer consumer lifestyles will be "greened" through planning and technology—an extraordinary challenge in a nation with nearly 1.5 billion residents.

As much as consumer culture is bad at delivering enduring satisfaction, it is spectacularly good at offering novelties and experiences that are, as the saying goes, fun for a while. Buying the latest earbuds really can bring joy: at their sleek design, the signal they send to others that you are keeping up with technological progress, or just the plain fact that they are *yours*. Even if we recognize—as most of us do, at least some of the time—that the small pleasure of buying something new rarely lasts, consumer culture has made it very, very easy to keep going back for more small pleasures. Line up enough of them, and it becomes a reasonable simulacrum of lasting contentment. It is another of consumerism's ironies that, although it functions like a mental trap, we often think of it as an escape. Consumption is, as one group of researchers put it, "a culturally sanctioned coping strategy"— including to cope with the pressures of consumer capitalism.

Which brings us again to the most straightforward reason that we pursue materialism: powerful forces and structures, largely beyond our control, compel us to do so. As we saw so clearly at the onset of the pandemic, our own livelihoods, everyone else's, and possibly the foundations of civilization itself now seem to depend on our unceasing participation in the earn-and-spend cycle. The world's consumer economy has grown by more than 600 percent since 1960—it is an unimaginably immense machine, but also a frail one, forever on the brink of running out of fuel. And so, on top of a $600-billion advertising industry, we are immersed in increasingly sophisticated physical and digital landscapes that encourage us to behave materialistically. Consumerism is laid out for us before birth, with identities that are easy to put on and markers of success that are well-established, and yet it is not fair to call it a path we all follow. It is many paths, a rich diversity of ways forward, all steering us toward more consumption. If we slow down our shopping, as Peter Victor's models showed, the comptrollers of the economy can rapidly respond with lower prices, cheaper credit, lower taxes, or even bald-faced handouts of "stimulus" money to spend.

All of these influences combine to make it difficult over the long run to pursue intrinsic values instead of extrinsic, materialist ones. "The metaphor I use is bike lanes," said Kasser. "I might want to ride my bike to work every day, but if there's no bike lanes, and all there is are four-lane highways with people driving fifty-five miles an hour, well, I might know how to ride a bike, I might have a bike, but society isn't making it easy for me to ride my bike. In fact, it's actively discouraging me. And there are thousands of ways that manifests itself in consumer culture in regard to intrinsic values *not* being afforded and materialistic values *being* afforded. I have come to believe more and more that there are people out there who want to live their intrinsic values, but they are having trouble doing it."

On the day the world stops shopping, would our values begin to shift? In a conversation on January 30, 2020, Kasser told me that he thought they would. As we turned our backs on materialism and consumer culture, intrinsic values would gain relevance as an alternative set of values for a different way of life.

How quickly would this happen?

"I don't know," Kasser replied.

Later that day, the World Health Organization declared the coronavirus a global emergency. Six weeks after that, the world's response to the disease had evolved into a planetary experiment that explored exactly the question that left Kasser uncertain. The answer turned out to be that the change can happen faster than almost anyone could have imagined.

Consumerism, which had been cruising at record highs, had one last hurrah at the onset of the pandemic. It came in the form of people hoarding household essentials like food and toilet paper, and binge-buying an odd shopping list of prospective quarantine pastimes: cooking and gardening products, jigsaw puzzles and board games, trampolines, webcams, home gym equipment. Among the rich, there was a rush to build backyard swimming pools.

That reaction fit with materialism research, Kasser told me when we spoke again, five months into the crisis. Feelings of insecurity and threat are among the most powerful incitements to shopping and consumerism. One of the few studies on how this applies to a large-scale crisis followed several hundred Icelanders across six months during a severe economic crash that brought the nation close to bankruptcy in 2009. Some of them did respond to the disaster by turning toward intrinsic values. "Before, we wanted to be entrepreneurs. Now we just want to be good people," said one. Most, however, went the other way, becoming more materialistic even though doing so came at a measurable cost to their sense of well-being. This was a case of materialism doing what it is there for: raising the alert level to help us survive when essential needs are under threat. Naturally, insecurity has become a core operating principle of consumer capitalism, built into everything from ads that make us doubt that we're keeping up with the times to the stresses of the credit-and-debt system to the entre-preneurial obsession with "disrupting" comfortingly familiar systems.

Ironically, then, stopping shopping would create the kind of challenges that make us economically insecure, which can lead us to start shopping again. (As you have surely noticed by now, there is a lot of irony, paradox and contradiction in the ways that we consume.) For the purposes of this thought experiment, however, that doesn't happen. Stopping shopping isn't like an ordinary economic crash. What it resembles instead is our retreat into our homes at the height of the pandemic, when we cut ourselves off from many of the everyday encouragements to consume.

Once that happened, millions of people worldwide immediately made a sharp turn toward exactly the pursuits that research had shown improves our well-being: social connection, the deepening of relationships, exposure to nature, personal growth and development, spirituality and mindfulness, and simply the active rejection of materialism. They did so even though they had been forced to stop shopping rather than choosing to do so. The human species appeared to have an instinct for self-care.

When I surveyed my own network of contacts at the height of the global lockdowns, their experiences reflected those that were widely observed. Some, of course, were immersed in the hardships of death, illness, anxiety, joblessness or the loss of a business. Yet many others—often even those facing adversity—were moving swiftly toward a deeper-than-usual engagement with life.

One, a father in the heart of a city of two million people, finally had the time he had always wanted to spend with his young daughters. "There is more laughter in the house than I've ever experienced," he said. A woman in the countryside of southern England, whose family had felt isolated, described a "surreal utopia" in which she was trading potatoes for honey and eggs, had received handmade gifts from her neighbours, and joined with another villager—her polar opposite in political ideology—to turn a local phone booth into a food-sharing hamper. A New York University professor, who said she had purchased nearly all of her meals and even cups of coffee throughout her adult life, was finding satisfaction in fending for herself. "It's not all that hard to make coffee," she declared.

"I am replacing my consumerism with social contact and food," wrote a mall manager from a mid-size city. Nearly everyone, in fact, reported the irony that, in a state of isolation, they were more social than ever, checking in on friends, family and often total strangers, or tending long-neglected relationships over video calls. There were strong currents of self-reflection and personal growth. Reconnection with nature approached the universal: the peculiar perception that there were more birds than usual—at least in part a testament to the fact that we were paying attention to them—was a global phenomenon, as were reports of an "epidemic of kindness."

Just as interesting was the rejection of open materialism. In a memorable early example, public outrage chased the billionaire movie mogul David Geffen off Instagram after he shared images of the mega-yacht he was quarantined on in the Caribbean—precisely the kind of photographic grandstanding that had been the bread-and-butter of social media for years. Women, in particular, expressed relief at their freedom from the image-based expectations of consumer society and the growing list of products that entails: high heels, "shapewear," push-up bras, thong underwear, false lashes, glue-on nails, hair dye; an overlooked but apparently large subgroup of women—those that do not like to shop—made itself known. The *New York Times*, meanwhile, interviewed a male entertainment-industry executive who had once owned 210 shirts, but wore just one for seventy consecutive days of video-call meetings. (No one noticed, he said.) A friend of mine, living in Toronto, wrote that the greatest silver lining of the crisis was a break from the feeling that he had to keep up with the Joneses.

A tall stack of studies predicts that a U-turn away from consumer culture would benefit our well-being. Very few shine a light on how quickly that might happen. One of the most precise, carried out nearly ten years ago by psychologists at McGill University in Montreal, guided a group of students to reflect on various intrinsic values—"devoting time for personal growth and development," "helping your community through volunteer work," and so on—before surveying them for changes in their sense of well-being. Compared to another set of students who were asked to reflect on routine daily activities, those who had turned their minds to intrinsic values felt measurably better about life *immediately*. Such a finding seemed scarcely believable, and yet the pandemic experience confirmed that such changes can take place with remarkable speed. On the day the world stops shopping, it really might be the case that we'd be feeling better about life before breakfast is on the table.

"The thing that intrinsic values have going for them that extrinsic values don't is that they feel good—at least, they feel better," said Kasser. "To me, this upswelling of intrinsic values is reflective of the weights that are normally put on people, which make them behave in extrinsic ways, having been pulled off of them to some degree. Those intrinsic values can emerge more easily."

There was a time when the deeply spiritual wore hair shirts—lined with a bristly animal's pelt—as a prickling reminder that material comforts are not what life is about. Today, any rejection of materialism is often dismissed with the argument that it amounts to "putting on the hair shirt": giving up consumer pleasures for the discomfort of self-denial. In fact, the opposite is true. During the pandemic, we didn't put the hair shirt on. We were finally taking it off.

Things got more complicated.

As the pandemic ground on, the experience changed. Baking bread is a simple, ancient act of self-reliance that is so inherently satisfying that it came to symbolize life in quarantine. Yet almost immediately it also became a competitive marker of status, ambition and accomplishment as social media filled with images of beautiful loaves prepared in beautiful kitchens for beautiful families. Fitness was not only the pursuit of health but of perfect abs to show off to the world, while the sudden outbreak of care for neglected relationships, whether in person or via video calls, turned out to be fraught with emotional challenges, from children unsure how to relate to usually distant fathers to old friends who proved to hold simmering resentments. Many people made promises to themselves to hang on to the good that came out of the crisis: fewer hours at work, a slower pace of life, appreciation for the little things, more time with people they cared about, more time for themselves—in short, a better balance between their extrinsic and intrinsic selves. Instead, as consumer culture was reborn online and commercial life made its cautious return, most of us fell back into familiar patterns.

Even before the pandemic, Kasser had warned me that stopping shopping is a journey that is easier to start than it is to continue. "You might experience some initial well-being benefits from disengaging from consumer culture, but you're going to find that intrinsic values are not all that easy to pursue," he told me. "You may not always have the skills to develop them, succeed at them."

There are several pitfalls. The plainest is that many of us are not very good at behaving intrinsically. In societies sharply focused on extrinsic goals and beliefs, many people are skilled at, say, marketing themselves, but not at developing deeper relationships. They're expert at finding clothes on Amazon to suit their image, but incompetent at growing their own food; they can juggle a schedule packed with activity, but can't sit quietly with themselves for long without anxiety. To shift from what we're proficient at to what we are not can quickly become frustrating. As a result, we are prone to transform intrinsically motivated actions into extrinsically motivated ones, though we may not recognize that's what we are doing. "It kind of poisons it," Kasser said.

The tension between our extrinsic and newly intrinsic selves, like the reemergence of noncommercial time, can feel disorienting. It feels good to arrive at a more intrinsic place within yourself, but where do you go from there? "Intrinsic values are only good for you if you also feel like you are attaining them," Kasser said. "If you're having the experience where you care about intrinsic values, but you're failing to attain them—that's actually bad for your personal well-being."

As the first months of the pandemic passed, the expression of intrinsic values became less and less visible, until the grand global experiment in another way of being seemed to have failed. Kasser saw reason to believe this was not entirely the case. It is the nature of intrinsic values, after all, to be felt inwardly and expressed privately rather than put in the klieg lights for others' applause. Instead of waning, the shift may have been deepening.

In late May 2020, with the first wave of the coronavirus raging around the world, a police officer in Minneapolis knelt on George Floyd's neck until he died, with video cameras rolling. The Black Lives Matter movement soon erupted into a national, and then international, reckoning on racial injustice. It was an unlikely turn of events. The middle of a global pandemic was not a natural moment for millions of protesters to take to the streets. Neither was there any clear reason why the incident should have been anything more than another brief flashpoint: police brutality against black citizens was unfortunately nothing new, videos of similar deaths had circulated multiple times, riots had followed some of them, and even Floyd's desperate words—"I can't breathe"—disturbingly echoed earlier killings. Yet in 2020, Black Lives Matter became perhaps the largest protest movement in American history, and changes seemingly unthinkable only a few weeks earlier came cascading: statues memorializing slave traders toppled; the state flag of Mississippi shed its slave-era symbols; the Washington Redskins football team agreed to change its racist name; and cities as large as Los Angeles and Minneapolis made moves toward a dramatically different approach to policing. Support for the movement climbed more in a two-week period than it had in the preceding two years, rising in every age, education and racial group—all in a nation where divisions in public opinion often seem immovable. "Something," said Kasser, "made people more amenable to those ideas."

Two aspects of psychology could have contributed. One was an effect of noncommercial time. With many people not working, schooling, commuting or consuming, millions had a rare window of freedom to turn their attention to bigger issues. But the widespread shift toward intrinsic values could have played a role as well. Research consistently shows that less materialistic people are also less self-involved and more likely to feel empathy for others. They tend to be less racially and ethnically prejudiced; they are less comfortable with having social domination over those who are different from them.

In other words, part of the reason that more change than usual came out of an otherwise all-too-familiar police killing may have been that a larger percentage of the population interpreted that terrible event with a mindset distinctly unlike the one that usually gets them through the daily work-and-spend grind. A world that stops shopping could move from personal transformation to social upheaval—and the change could begin in a matter of minutes.

We may need to see the ruins to know it's time to build something new

Michael Burawoy has seen an economy die.

Burawoy is a trim, fit-looking man in his early seventies, still with traces of a British accent after decades as a professor at the University of California, Berkeley. On the day I met him, he was dressed in a black tracksuit and matching running shoes, neither of which made him look less of an intellectual. His apartment overlooks both Lake Merritt, locally famous for the necklace of lights that surrounds it, and the formerly notorious downtown of Oakland, now busy with construction sites putting up condos for millennials.

In the spring of 1991, Burawoy had a job drilling holes in planks of wood at Polar Furniture Enterprise in the remote industrial town of Syktyvkar in what was then the Union of Soviet Socialist Republics. It was an unusual position, to say the least. For one, he wasn't good at the job. "My incompetence was transparent," he told me. For another, the Cold War between Russia and the West was at its peak. Some of his Russian colleagues suspected he was a spy, because the truth was too strange to believe. Burawoy was a sociologist engaged in "participant observation," in which the researcher completely immerses himself in the way of life that he is studying. In this case, he was observing the inner workings of a state-run factory that produced wall systems for government housing developments. He had no idea he was witnessing the last days of the Soviet empire.

He had arrived to find Russia in the throes of the "shortage economy" that afflicted the Soviet regime as it struggled to keep pace with the military spending of its Western rivals. Already, officials at Polar Furniture were bartering for everything from rations of sugar and alcohol to placements for employees' children in holiday camps.

"If you went into a shop at that time anywhere in the Soviet Union outside of Moscow, you'd think people were starving," he said. At the same time, people's kitchens were bursting with food. To an outsider, the Russian system looked disastrous, but to those who knew its inner workings, life was comfortable enough. Burawoy fondly remembers the good Russian bread spread with *smetana*, a thick sour cream. The state-run housing blocks were brutalist and dilapidated, but also mostly rent-free, and the Russians he met had made their own apartments warm and welcoming. Polar Furniture operated out of a modern building equipped with advanced technology imported from Germany, and offered good wages, pensions and inexpensive cafeteria meals. People owned toasters, televisions, cars, washing machines. "You wouldn't call them affluent, but they were not poor," Burawoy said. "They had a home, though sometimes it was very crowded. They had security of employment, their children went to reasonable schools. There was very little homelessness."

Burawoy returned to the US in July of 1991; a month later, a failed coup d'état in Moscow threw Russia into chaos, and that December, the once-mighty Soviet Union dissolved. The central government collapsed. Unfortunately, the central government had been in charge of the economy.

"Nobody had seen an economy, in peacetime, descend so rapidly," Burawoy said. It was as if, in a modern capitalist democracy, a failing stock market and banking system had been left to collapse completely. It was as if, in a global consumer economy, the world stopped shopping. Within five years, one-fifth of Russians were living in poverty, the death rate for working-age people had nearly doubled, and Russia's GDP was shrinking toward half its former size. The country became a rare example of declining household affluence so severe that it drove a long and large-scale decrease in material consumption—by fully a quarter across an entire decade.

Burawoy returned to Russia the following summer. By then, many Russians' lifestyles were plummeting into what Burawoy calls "primitive disaccumulation." It was the opposite of a consumer society: instead of accumulating possessions over time, people sold or traded away what they had in exchange for the barest necessities. Streets and markets were soon lined with people displaying belongings for sale in makeshift stalls or on blankets laid on the pavement. Burawoy remembers a Russian student saying, "This is not a free market. This is a flea market."

Burawoy continued to follow the lives of some of his former co-workers. One of them, a woman he identifies only as Marina, had a prelapsarian life that would be familiar to many of us: at forty years of age, she had steady work and was proud of her daughter's excellent marks at school. When the collapse occurred, Polar Furniture managed to hang on—barely—until 1998. By then, wages were often being paid in barter goods. Marina's last payment from the company came in the form of a divan. Her husband, working for the Ministry of Internal Affairs as a carpenter, never knew how he might be paid: with a bus pass, perhaps, or a bag of flour. The worst, Marina told Burawoy, was when he was paid in humanitarian food aid, which she deemed only fit for dogs. An apocryphal story from those days claims that the local schoolteachers were paid in vodka, which did not improve the lessons.

Women tended to fare better than men after the crash, because traditional skills such as cooking and sewing were still in demand and they more often worked in systems such as education and health care that did not collapse completely. Men, meanwhile, were overrepresented in a cruel increase in deaths of despair—from addiction, disease, accidents and suicide. One of the most important means of survival was the *dacha*, a word that roughly translates as "country house" and can mean anything from the large rural estates enjoyed by the wealthy to a garden plot with a scrapwood shack. Prior to the Soviet collapse, working on the dacha had been a pastime much like gardening or cottaging in the West. About a quarter of households had a dacha in 1992. Just one year later, nearly half of them did.

When Burawoy last saw Marina, at the turn of the twenty-first century, her family of four was living in one room of a ramshackle timber cottage, with Marina's sister and niece filling the cabin's second room. They had no running water, and relieved themselves in an outhouse. "It is difficult to comprehend how the six of them can exist together, huddled in this tiny, dark, and dank space," Burawoy wrote at the time. Marina was raising vegetables on her dacha, but many of them were being stolen.

In the end, thieves come for your cabbages: this is what the total failure of an economy looks like. It is a world in which paid employment is scarce, no one can afford to buy much of anything, and people must rely on themselves, their families, and their social networks to survive at a level that is rudimentary by modern standards.

Russia went through this upheaval just thirty years ago. In Western Europe, such a crisis hasn't struck since the Second World War, and the United States has never in its history known an economic disaster this extreme. Its closest approximation is still the Great Depression, when industrial production dropped 62 percent, more than in any other country but Poland. One in four working people wound up jobless. The Depression is remembered today mainly in sepia-tone photographs that look almost charming: hoboes jumping trains; former stockbrokers, still dressed in their suits, selling street-corner apples; "Okies" driving to California out of the Dust Bowl with everything they own strapped to their jalopies. Studs Terkel's *Hard Times* reminds us of the brutal personal stories behind those familiar images: a baby dies of starvation as men, women and children, sometimes fifty or sixty to a boxcar, ride the rails in search of work or government aid. A ruined businessman kills himself so that his wife and kids can collect on his life insurance. Crops of cotton are picked by prison chain gangs made up of black citizens whose only crime is being homeless and jobless. Terkel, who was Jewish, called it "the holocaust known as the Great Depression."

Some modern version of that holocaust would be the inevitable aftermath of stopping shopping, said Aswath Damodaran, a professor of finance at Stern School of Business in New York. The idea that a less consumerist society would be better, he said, stems from the fact that everyone today knows somebody who stepped off the money-in, money-out treadmill, simplified their life, and ended up happier. The paradox is that only so many of us can choose that happiness before it triggers economic catastrophe. "If tomorrow consumerism dropped by 25 percent worldwide, you're going to get a spiralling down where millions are going to lose their jobs," he said. "It would be an incredibly painful adjustment period, where people are going to have to live with a lot less across the board."

Living with less would not be a nostalgic retreat from the age of Walmart and Amazon to the days of mom-and-pop shops, he said. Instead, it would set us on a course for the kind of lifestyle he witnessed growing up in Chennai, a city in southeastern India. Chennai is known today for its rich mix of traditional life and modern comforts, but Damodaran remembers when it had yet to join the global consumer economy. "There were no toy stores. Three restaurants for a city of millions. One bookstore, because who needs books? It's not going to be your nice, attractive Main Street, it's just going to be a collection of stores that sell basic stuff because that's all you can afford to buy, and those are the businesses that can afford to survive.

"There'd be a depression," he said, "and it wouldn't go away."

The Russian situation did not end well. In the end, the former Soviet Union went from an economy almost entirely operated by the central government to an attempted experiment in an almost totally free market. Burawoy calls it Russia's "descent into capitalism." Local mafias, filling the vacuum left behind by the collapse of the state, soon took over the barter economy.

Yet when Michael Burawoy thinks back on the fall of the Soviet empire, the first thing that comes to mind is not struggle or poverty. What is most extraordinary about the collapse, Burawoy said, is that civilization did not, in fact, come to an end. ("We find neither massive starvation nor strikes and food riots, neither the destruction of society nor its explosion," he wrote in the aftermath.) He remembers the dachas especially, where people came together to work; at the height of the Soviet downfall, 92 percent of the nation's potato harvest was coming from dachas and gardens, despite the fact they represented less than 2 percent of Russia's agricultural land. By night, people would enjoy the fruits of their labour, playing cards, debating and drinking. In this extreme economic catastrophe, they really were seized by the strange exhilaration of disaster. "There were endless parties in the dachas, because there was more space there than in the apartments," Burawoy said. "I look back on those years with great fondness. We had very few resources, but we had a good time."

Something of those times seems to have stuck with Burawoy. He prefers to live simply. He doesn't use a cell phone; his apartment is sparsely furnished, mainly with bookshelves; one of the few knick-knacks is a souvenir teddy bear with the old hammer-and-sickle symbol of the Soviet Union emblazoned on its T-shirt. Leaning forward in his hardback chair, Burawoy said that an essential lesson from the Soviet collapse is that tremendous change is possible and people can endure it. They only need to feel that there's a chance at a more hopeful future.

Only when the new Russia began to take shape as one of the world's most unequal, least free, and least democratic nations did people sink into despair, he said. The first months of the collapse may have been wracked with shortages and the loss of familiar comforts, but they were also full of possibility. There was a sense that almost anything they could dream of might be built on the ruins of the old system that had seemed so immutable; what Russians turned toward was consumerism. Today, in many parts of the world, it is an endlessly growing consumer economy that seems inescapable. We feel unable to change course because the only other option appears to be collapse: *there is no alternative.*

"There was hardship, but there was also excitement," Burawoy said. "It was like they'd been let out of prison."

Perhaps ashes and ruins really are what a world without shopping would lead to. At a minimum, we have to accept the fact that what all those voices through history that have called on us to live more simply, to be less materialistic, have been proposing—knowingly or unknowingly—is upheaval and destruction.

Civilization never simply collapses, though. It also, always, immediately begins to resurrect itself. I recall how, in my conversation with Paul Dillinger about how the end of shopping might play out at Levi's, he made the turn to this idea. "There's the initial urgent response and then, once thoughtful people have been talked off their ledges and are coming in from the window, we can start to say, Is this real, how long will it last, why is it here, and what do we want to look like if this is the new reality?" Dillinger said. "There are very scary realities to this disruption. There are a lot of lost jobs. There's also an opportunity to recalibrate consumption to a sustainable level."

That was more than a year before the coronavirus pandemic. The official position of Levi Strauss & Co. at the time was that they would greatly prefer that you not stop shopping. The mantra of the company's CEO, Chip Bergh, was "Build our profitable core, expand for more." Given that Levi's wanted to get bigger, to sell more stuff, allowing Dillinger to speak his mind was an act of unusual corporate courage.

Five months into the pandemic and four months after widespread shutdowns of Levi's stores around the world, I checked in with the company again. By then, much of what Dillinger had predicted about not-shopping as a shock wave that would arc across the globe had proved to be accurate. I wondered if he was right about recalibration, too.

This time, I spoke to Jen Sey, senior vice president and chief marketing officer, from her home in San Francisco. She began, as many corporate leaders do today, by reeling off the ways that the company is making its products less harmful to the environment. Then she said this: "But as we started studying this even more, we realized that simply consuming *less* has the greatest impact. It's great to convince consumers to buy thoughtfully, but really, the biggest impact we can have is to convince them to buy less. And that's kind of a radical notion when you think that, as the marketing leader, my job is to get people to buy more." In that moment, Levi's became the biggest brand yet to publicly acknowledge that consumption itself—including of the company's own products—was the earth's most serious environmental problem. In the autumn of 2020, Levi's began to fold messages about buying fewer but longer-lasting clothes into their marketing, and launched a platform to buy back and resell their products second-hand. "Clothing reuse is far better for the environment than recycling," the company declared. They had plans to make the case for lower consumption more forcefully as time goes on.

What had changed?

"I do think during the quarantine, people came to understand that our actions have consequences—if we drive less, the air clears," Sey said. "You can't avoid the fact anymore that the greatest impact is overconsumption. You can do all you want to greenwash or even to make these modest steps forward in terms of how you make your product. But it won't overcome the impact of overconsumption. It just *won't*. I mean, that's the fact of the matter now."

Even before the pandemic, Sey had sensed that discontent with the fast-fashion model of shopping—what some call *prêt-à-jeter*, or "ready to throw away"—was building to a head; she herself had made a New Year's resolution for 2020 that, other than Levi's products, she would only buy used clothing. Later that January, with the coronavirus beginning to spread beyond the borders of China, she talked to Bergh, Levi's CEO, about the idea that the company should confront overconsumption. He gave it his support. A month later, with Covid-19 beginning to spread on American soil, she raised it at a summit of Levi's leadership. "Some people were like, oh, we can't do *that*," she said. But when lockdowns brought much of the world's shopping to a halt, a business model built around less consumption quickly became more relevant. "It accelerated our thinking on it and our belief in it," Sey said.

The business model that Levi's is looking toward is one in which consumers buy less stuff, most of it higher quality than the typical goods on the market today—an economy of fewer, better things. As a brand narrative, it serves Levi's well, because their main stock in trade is durable products and clothes designed to be worn for years. They have run the numbers, Sey told me, and believe they can sell a message of less and still grow. To do so, their current customers would buy fewer Levi's garments and hang on to them for longer, while the company attracts new clientele who are drifting away from fast fashion and toward deconsumer thinking.

At one level, it's a typical corporate strategy. At another, it's groundbreaking change, and not without risk. Rising out of the sharpest recession ever recorded with a "buy less" message is unconventional, to say the least. As economies reopened during the pandemic, advertisements portrayed shoppers as heroes; the clarion call was for a consumer-driven recovery.

"I think that we're okay sacrificing crazy, outsized growth to chase a buck," Sey said. "I think we want reasonable, long-term, sustainable growth."

The architect John Brinckerhoff Jackson once said there was a "necessity for ruins": we need to see the old world decay in order to step fully into a new one. As we've seen, such changes in perspective are far from rare in economic disasters. It was during the Great Recession that Patagonia saw real potential for a deconsumer market, the Finnish Depression when people felt relief from conspicuous consumption, the pandemic, again, when millions of individuals made a head-spinning shift toward new values. When I spoke to business leaders in Phoenix, Arizona, about the Great Recession, I was stunned to hear that many of them felt the crisis had changed their city for the better. Several pointed out that, prior to the downturn, Phoenix had become "the chain restaurant capital of the world." Then American families cut back on restaurant visits, and boarded-up Olive Gardens, Chili's Grills, and other chain eateries soon joined the empty husks of failed big-box stores. In the void left behind, independently owned neighbourhood restaurants bloomed; a local sense of place began to take root. "Going into the recession we were what I would call a transactional economy," said Mark Stapp, a real estate professor at Arizona State University. "Coming out of the recession we became a transformative economy." Ironically, as Phoenix recovered, it once again attracted the same placeless, faceless commercial enterprises that had failed when the going got tough.

What if that didn't happen? What if deconsumer culture endured? To understand what that society might look like, and how it might work, we need to bring our thought experiment out of the darkness of collapse. We might begin with a humble lightbulb.

III

ADAPTATION

A stronger, not a weaker,
attachment to our things

The lightbulb that has brightened the garage at Fire Department Station 6 in Livermore, California, for the past 120 years will never burn out. Instead, it will "expire." When it does, it certainly won't be thrown out, or even recycled. It will be "laid to rest."

"You have to use the correct terminology," said Tom Bramell, a retired deputy fire chief, with a light laugh. When I spoke to Bramell, who so cuts the figure of a firefighter that he has smoke-coloured eyes and hair, and a permanent hack from smoke inhalation ("I do a bag of cough drops a day"), he had become the Livermore light's leading historian. The bulb has been on almost continuously since 1901; in 2015, it surpassed a million hours in service, making it, according to Guinness World Records, the longest-burning in the world. Viewable online, it has fans around the globe. The bulb has already outlasted multiple webcams.

The parts and materials that made it so durable are something of a mystery, for the straightforward reason that you can't dissect a light that is always on. Here's what is known about the bulb: it was manufactured circa 1900 by Shelby Electric, of Ohio, using a design by the French-American inventor Adolphe Chaillet. It has a carbon filament of about the same human-hair thickness as the ones, typically made of tungsten, that are found in modern bulbs. It was made to be a sixty-watt bulb, though it currently illuminates the Station 6 garage with about the brightness of a nightlight. Shelby bulbs of the same vintage have been studied to gain more insight, but it turned out the company was experimenting with a variety of designs at the time.

The most surprising aspect of the bulb is that it is incandescent, meaning it produces light by electrically heating a filament until it glows white-hot. Fire in a bottle, as they say. This is exactly the same technology still used to produce bulbs with frustratingly short lifespans that you have to buy again and again. Plug in a typical incandescent bulb from the drugstore, and you can expect it to burn for about a thousand hours; if you leave it on full-time, you can expect it to die about forty-two days later.

"We don't build things today to last," Bramell said, surely speaking for almost all of us.

Most people seem to agree that the products we buy today are subject to what the economist Robert Solow, borrowing from an anonymous German friend, called *Das Gesetz der Verschlechtigung aller Dinge*, or the Law of the Deterioration of Everything. But it's important to be sure that this is not nostalgia for an imaginary past. Is it really the case that the products we buy today are worse than they were five, ten or twenty years ago?

"For consumer products, I would say that's definitely true," David Enos, a materials scientist in Albuquerque, New Mexico, told me. Enos, who works at Sandia National Laboratories, the caretakers of America's nuclear stockpile, is a specialist in product durability. His job is to make things that can endure under extreme duress for very long periods of time. He has, for example, explored how to produce containers that can be stored inside a mountain in an atmosphere of pure steam for as long as it takes for nuclear waste to decompose into a harmless substance. "A hundred, thousand, million-type years are the time frames that we're aiming for there," he said.

Earlier in his career, though, Enos had a job working on electrical circuits for ordinary inkjet printers. The machines had twenty-millionths of an inch of gold over their copper traces to prevent them from corroding. "At twenty micro-inches, you're kind of flirting with the cliff, where if you go below that, the durability drops off really rapidly," Enos said. You know what happens then: your printer stops working and you need to buy a new one.

If a company used twenty-five micro-inches of gold over their traces, the printer would be much more reliable, Enos said. The problem then is that most people wouldn't buy it, because the competing printer with just twenty micro-inches of gold would cost less. "We have a mindset now where we buy things as inexpensive as possible," said Enos. "Could we build a phone that would last ten years? No problem. We certainly have the technology to do that. But the costs start going higher and higher. Nobody wants to spend five or ten thousand dollars on a phone and say, hey, this phone's going to last ten years. Most people are like, well, that's great, I don't care. I want a new one after two or three years."

All of that changes on the day the world stops shopping, when the more durable product becomes the common sense choice. If you are trying to buy as few phones or printers as you can in your lifetime, you are prepared to pay more for a phone or printer that lasts. You want to buy fewer, better things.

Unfortunately, we aren't sure how an economy founded on those kinds of products actually works.

The journey from good, long-lasting lightbulbs like the one hanging in the Livermore fire station to the disposable bulbs we know today began in 1924. That year, representatives from the world's largest lighting companies—including such familiar names as Philips, Osram, and General Electric—met in Switzerland to form Phoebus, arguably the first corporate cartel with global reach. At the time, inventors were steadily increasing bulb lifespans, which was creating what one senior member of Phoebus described as a "mire" in sales turnover. Once everyone had filled their home with long-lasting bulbs, hardly anyone needed to buy new ones.

The member companies of Phoebus agreed to depress lamp life to a thousand-hour standard. More than three decades later, in 1960, muckraking journalist Vance Packard popularized the term "planned obsolescence" to describe manufacturers' deliberate efforts to design products so that they are quickly used up, stop working, fall apart, cannot be fixed, or otherwise become stale-dated. The Phoebus cartel's decision to shorten bulb lifespans is considered one of the earliest examples of planned obsolescence at an industrial scale.

Phoebus is easily cast as a conspiracy of big-business evil-doers. It even makes an appearance as such in Thomas Pynchon's novel *Gravity's Rainbow*, in which the shadowy organization sends an agent in asbestos-lined gloves and seven-inch heels to seize die-hard bulbs that burn beyond their thousandth hour of service. "Through no bulb shall the mean operating life be extended," Pynchon writes, turning product standardization into a metaphor for oppression and social conformity. "You can imagine what it would do to the market if *that* started happening."

At the time the thousand-hour bulb was established, however, planned obsolescence was not a secret. Instead, it was openly discussed as a solution to an increasingly serious problem. The Industrial Revolution was making it possible to produce enormous quantities of goods quickly and cheaply. Yet if a factory made a quality product with a long lifespan, before long there would be little demand for what the factory supplied. Economists and businesspeople began to argue that, unless you dealt in coffins, it was bad business and unsound economics to sell a person any product only once. It would enrich society more, they said, to seek a balance between lower quality and more frequent sales. (At the time there was little concern about finite resources or the destruction of the natural world.) By the late 1920s, the repetitive sales model had become so popular that a leading financier declared obsolescence the "new god" of the American business elite.

Advocates for shorter product lifespans could be found across the political spectrum. Giles Slade, in his book *Made to Break*, traces the term "planned obsolescence" to its roots. The earliest reference he found was in a 1932 pamphlet, "Ending the Depression through Planned Obsolescence," that promoted short-lived products as beneficial to the working class. In 1936, a similarly themed essay in the magazine *Printers' Ink* declared durable products "outmoded" and warned, "If Merchandise Does Not Wear Out Faster, Factories Will Be Idle, People Unemployed."

This Depression-era argument, which one business writer of the time summed up as a "sound and genuine philosophy in free spending and wasting," became another crucial part of the modern consumer economy. We wouldn't buy a product once; we would buy it again and again throughout our lives. We would shop and reshop. Repetitive consumption is now built into almost everything we buy, and obsolescence has become, as Slade puts it, "a touchstone of the American consciousness."

Thirty years ago, a new technology emerged that threatened to challenge planned obsolescence. It was the kind of product we would want in a deconsumer society: long-lasting, energy efficient, better in every way than what it was designed to replace. It came in the form of a lightbulb.

The first light-emitting diode was demonstrated at a GE facility in Syracuse, New York, in 1962, but it wasn't until the 1990s that LEDs could produce white light more efficiently than incandescent bulbs. They are a genuinely revolutionary technology, so much so that their widespread adoption is considered an important step toward slowing climate change.

The bulbs have legendary durability. The basic building block of LED technology is the semiconductor, which easily can be made to last. Bulbs that promise a 50,000-hour lifespan are not uncommon—forget to turn one off and it will burn for nearly six years. Hardware store LED bulbs more often offer a still-impressive 25,000-hour lifespan. In a typical American household, each light is turned on for an average of just 1.6 hours daily. Under normal conditions, then, a thoroughly ordinary LED lamp would do its job for forty-two years.

By 2019, the sale of LED lamps was a booming business that also seemed to be a sign that the deconsumer story didn't have to end in collapse. It could also spark an age of "good growth," as businesses created quality products to replace the throwaway stuff of the past. Grow the good, shrink the bad.

LEDs also showed, however, that good growth wouldn't last forever. The lighting industry has a term, "socket saturation," that describes the point at which most of the world's short-lived incandescent bulbs have been unscrewed from their sockets and replaced by durable LEDs. At that point, in theory at least, the world stops shopping for lightbulbs. What happens to the lighting industry when everyone's bulbs last half a lifetime? As Fabian Hoelzenbein, a London-based lighting market analyst, put it, "That's the billion-dollar question."

Toward the end of the 2010s, "socket saturation" seemed to be just around the corner. It never arrived, though, because LEDs were assimilated by consumer culture. We've already seen one way that this occurred: we took the money LEDs saved us and used it to buy a lot more lights. Then, in the same way that long-lasting incandescent bulbs were soon followed by short-lived incandescent bulbs in the 1920s, long-lasting LEDs were followed by short-lived LEDs. A profusion of new manufacturers, most of them in Asia, rapidly drove down cost and quality. A durable technology was turning into a disposable one.

"You can buy bulbs on eBay that are of such low quality that, when you screw them in, you can actually get a shock," Hoelzenbein told me. He'd heard reports from China of people buying bargain LED lightbulbs by the kilogram, knowing some would last and others might not work at all.

Some governments put in place minimum lifespan standards for LED bulbs in order to hang on to the benefits of their durability. Even so, another way to sell more bulbs emerged, and that was to build LEDs into goods still subject to planned obsolescence. A "smart" lighting industry emerged, with products that, for example, gradually brighten your bedroom when it's time to wake up or set off explosions of light as you play your video games. Light fixtures became a locus for the internet of things, connecting to speakers, security systems and other devices. In other words, LED lighting underwent "gadgetization," making it susceptible to the constant upgrades familiar from phones, tablets and other digital products. "We're not inventing this consumer behaviour. It's what technology companies do," Betty Noonan, a spokesperson for Cree, an American company specializing in LEDs, told me. "I have replaced more damned flat-panel TVs in my home, just because they got thinner and brighter, than I care to even tell you."

In a world that stops shopping, on the other hand, we wouldn't buy more LED bulbs with the savings from energy efficiency, and we'd prefer long-lasting bulbs over short-lived ones. We would be far more skeptical of the need for digital upgrades. As a result, we would come face to face with the question, unanswered since the early twentieth century, of how to manage a society founded on good, long-lasting stuff.

"My starting point is, get the economics right," said Tim Cooper, a design professor who heads the sustainable consumption research group at Nottingham Trent University, and has been researching product durability for nearly thirty years. We tend to think of the consumer economy as highly complex, and in many ways it is: a baffling system where cotton grown on one continent may be spun into fibre on another and made into a T-shirt on yet another; a contradictory place where investors can move their money around the globe at the speed of an algorithm but most workers cannot freely cross a single national border in search of work. Yet the basic operating principle of that economy is straightforward. Goods and services are produced for consumption, nearly all of which is carried out by or on behalf of individual consumers. ("We don't export products to aliens on Mars," as one economist said to me.) The economy expands with a growing population, but most of all through an ever-expanding array of new products and experiences, which we consume at a faster and faster rate. The most important contributor to that faster pace of consumption is the decreasing lifespans of the things we buy.

A world without shopping, Cooper said, is still a consumer economy, but one grounded in quality rather than quantity, meaning products will be well made and designed for longer lifespans. Since better goods typically require more work and better materials to produce, prices will be considerably higher, making up for at least some of the lost earnings caused by the drop in the overall number of products sold. That also means that, in a deliberate transition to a market of fewer, better things, many more people would remain employed than is the case when consumption slows down in a severe recession. Meanwhile, a much larger part of a deconsumer economy would be driven by what happens during a long-lasting product's lifetime, when it may require maintenance, repair or upgrading, or be rented, shared or resold. It would be a "radical, systemic change," Cooper said. Could a deconsumer economy be the same size as a consumer economy? The answer to that question depends on human ingenuity, Cooper said. But he suspects that, at least initially, it would slow economic growth.

"What drives the throwaway culture? Well, often people want to have the newest and the latest," Cooper said. "But there *are* people who want to have the oldest and the best."

The idea that durability would be at the core of a lower-consuming culture dates back at least to 1982, when the Organization for Economic Co-operation and Development urged governments to promote longer product lifespans as a way to slow the avalanche of garbage piling up in the world's landfills. Obviously enough, that didn't happen. It was only as 2020 approached that Cooper saw action being taken on durability at the national level. In 2015, France made planned obsolescence illegal, defining the practice as the deliberate reduction of a product's lifespan in order to increase its replacement rate, with steep fines and even jail time a possibility. When, in 2018, Sweden cut in half its sales tax on repairs, it was making a pioneering attempt to address carbon emissions by reducing consumption, rather than "greening" it. By 2021, the entire European Union was preparing to embed a "right to repair"—better access to the tools, parts and information needed to fix products—in its consumer policies, with a further goal to provide shoppers with labels indicating how long a product should last.

Durability is especially important to the sharing economy. Sharing goods was initially promoted as an action that reduced consumption by its very nature—common sense tells us that if people share, say, a car or an electric slow cooker, then each of them does not need to own one. The sharing economy proved to be much more complicated than that, most famously in the case of ride-hailing schemes, which, rather than inspiring people to reject car ownership, led many to take more trips using services like Uber and fewer by foot, bicycle or public transit. In many places, ride-hailing made traffic worse, not better. But durability affected sharing in an even more basic way: unless vehicles were specifically designed to withstand the constant wear and tear of sharing, they broke down faster.

Even the simplest forms of sharing are undermined by planned obsolescence, said Julie Smith, who for years headed America's oldest tool-lending library, in Columbus, Ohio. "We don't feel that *anything* we're buying now beats the quality of the older stuff we inherited," Smith told me. "It's just not as good of stuff. The metal's not the same kind of metal. You know, a shovel can be sharpened, but not if it isn't made of something you can sharpen."

There are two kinds of durability, and making better stuff addresses only one of them. The other is within ourselves: the durability of our relationships to things.

Our landfills are already full of durable products slowly being crushed by accumulating layers of additional durable goods. Each lamellation of discarded lampshades, side tables, bicycles, keyboards, sweaters, hot tubs, gaming consoles, toilets, children's toys and so on, many of them perfectly functional, represents a problem not with the physical lifetimes of things but with our lack of desire to hang on to them.

For decades now, consumer culture has been defined by novelty and newness. Still, there remain a few things we love as much or more as they age. Leather jackets, cast-iron pans, blue jeans, Turkish rugs, vintage watches, the faces of the actors Benicio Del Toro and Isabelle Huppert— time inscribes itself on these things in ways that we admire. To make sense of a world that stops shopping, we'd need to enlarge this appreciation, shake it out of its long slumber.

More than a thousand years ago, the Japanese practice of *wabi-sabi* emerged. The term is difficult to translate, but evokes both thoughtful melancholy and the passage of time—the way you might feel walking among ruins. At its most familiar, wabi-sabi celebrates that which is faded, patinaed, simple, modest. It's captured most clearly in *kintsugi*, the five-hundred-year-old craft of repairing, say, a dropped and shattered ceramic bowl, not by concealing the cracks, but by highlighting them with golden or silver lacquer. The result is a luminous tracery that makes the broken object as appealing, or more so, than when it was unblemished.

Like almost everything else, the concept has been swallowed up by consumer culture. Books on wabi-sabi design praise it as "the ultimate in sophistication." Gone is the wind-tossed allure of a field in winter; in its place are spotlessly clean, uncluttered houses decorated with choice antiques, the kind of homes that it is difficult to imagine a child living in. But wabi-sabi can be much more demanding than that, embracing the tarnished and stained, eroded and dirty, even the ugly, badly made or incomplete. It isn't a look or a style, but an attitude that finds beauty in the imperfect.

In a world that consumes less, the things you own are going to get older. More of them will look used and worn, because you won't replace them as often. That could easily feel depressing. In fact, one explanation for our current obsession with newness is that it keeps us from thinking about aging and death. Wabi-sabi is the adaptation that frees us from having to experience it that way.

The architect Adolf Loos, making an argument against flawlessly styled homes way back at the turn of the twentieth century, said that products become truly our own only when they have history and stories behind them. Among the most memorable belongings in the household Loos grew up in was a table he described as a crazy jumble of wood adorned with dreadful ornaments. "But it was our table, *ours!*" Loos said. When things are not built to last, or we replace them once they no longer look new or in fashion, we lose the opportunity to form such a force of connection.

Wabi-sabi is the mindset that gives the past a life in the present, but it can also be a vision of the future. Passing through Amsterdam, I visited the offices of Fairphone, a company that offers mobile phones that are built to last. The phones are modular, meaning they are easy to disassemble: they showed me how a broken screen could be replaced, or an older camera upgraded to a new one, in under a minute. Fairphone also offers software and security support far longer than the major phone manufacturers. Many of their customers are people who found the rapid replacement cycle of mobile phones wasteful. But they discovered a different kind of deconsumer, too. As it turns out, many people who trade in their phones for the latest model do so with ambivalent feelings. They have formed an attachment to the device itself—its nicks, scratches and dents, the way it feels in their hand—and don't want to give it up. Fairphone offers these customers what they are looking for: their old machine, able to do new tricks.

A worn, dusty, weathered and jury-rigged future—it's one of the most popular aesthetics in science fiction. Giant holograms above dingy streets in *Blade Runner 2049*, Neo's tattered sweatshirt with the holes along the neckline in *The Matrix*, and the enduring appeal of steampunk, with its mashup of whalebone crinolines and quantum computing, zeppelins and space travel, are all wabi-sabi. So is the *Star Wars* universe, with its spacecraft that resemble the beater cars of the 1970s, its grimy bars, its heroes dressed in patched and threadbare kimonos, a style that dates back a thousand years. The animated film *WALL-E* is set on a ghost-town Earth that still somehow feels more like our home than the shining space colonies humans have moved to. "It's the beauty of decay," the film's cinematographer, Jeremy Lasky, once said, "like when you go into old buildings that have been abandoned."

We could, in a world that stops shopping, build things not only to last, but to age gracefully. First, though, we'd have a more challenging task: to bring a wabi-sabi eye to the stuff that already surrounds us, all those perfect-looking artifacts of an age of beautiful garbage. Lamps that barely hold their bulbs, barstools standing on shaky legs, beds that creak and fail. How long could we make them last? Could we finally love them? The first symbol of a wabi-sabi future might not be a charming tote bag that has replaced our plastic bags, but a plastic bag that has been patched so it can last a little longer.

Fast fashion cannot rule but
it may not have to die

ast fashion is the opposite of a world in which we buy better but
less. It is the utmost example of selling more and worse.

That there was something we could call fashion, and that it
changed over time and you ought to keep up with it, is dated by historians
at least as far back as the 1300s. Yet centuries passed before ready-made
garments bought in shops replaced homemade or tailored clothing. Only
a hundred years ago, it was ordinary for men to be "married and buried"
in the same suit, or for women to wear hand-me-downs from their mothers
and grandmothers. Only in the mid 1960s did scholars begin to remark on
the accelerating fastness of fashion cycles driven by mass production and
mass media.

We didn't demand fast fashion. Even the first detailed account of the
fashion industry, written by the German historical economist Werner Sombart
in 1902, dismissed the myth that fashion follows the tastes of consumers and
not the other way around. "The driving force in the creation of more recent
fashion is altogether much more the capitalist entrepreneur," wrote Sombart.
"What the Parisian coquette and the Prince of Wales contribute is no more
than a kind of mediating assistance." This is just as true today of the social-
media influencer and the hip-hop celebrity when compared to an industry that

chooses the year's colours and hemlines so far in advance that either they are exceptional readers of the consumer mind or, as Sombart understood, they hold most of the power to decide what style will be.

If we did not ask for fast fashion, we did take to it with enthusiasm. The number of garments sold each year has approximately doubled in just the last fifteen years. The number now exceeds one hundred billion, at about fifteen articles of clothing per year per person on the planet. Not that clothing purchases are distributed evenly, of course. Despite soaring sales in countries like Brazil, China, India and Mexico, consumers in richer nations not only buy far more clothing but continue to increase the number of clothes purchases they make.

The clothes themselves are mostly garbage-in-waiting. Speaking to ordinary young adults in the US, Britain and Australia, the *New York Times* had little difficulty finding young women who felt that they should rarely be seen outside the house in the same outfit. "If I'm only going to wear something once or twice, I'm going to want to buy the cheapest possible," said a sixteen-year-old in Wilmslow, England, who shops online every day. A feedback loop has been engaged, in which lower prices encourage shoppers to cycle through clothes more quickly, which drives companies to make clothes that won't hold up to more than a few wears. The lifespan of clothes has decreased more sharply in the twenty-first century than ever before.

If the proliferation of clothes advertised as "green," "sustainable" or "organic" has convinced you that these problems are getting better, rest assured that is not the case. Based on pre-pandemic trends, the industry will be three times larger in 2050. There's no reason to imagine that fashion can't get any faster, either: a recent survey by the global consulting firm McKinsey & Company found that the number-one priority of fashion industry executives was speeding up the cycle. With fashion's speed and cheapness today, social norms are quickly shifting toward attire that looks like it has just come from the shop. We are losing tolerance for any sign that our clothing has been lived in.

In a major report in 2017, the UK-based Ellen MacArthur Foundation identified "increasing the average number of times clothes are worn" as perhaps the best way to reduce the environmental impact of the clothing industry. Doubling the use of our clothes would, for example, cut the garment trade's climate pollution by nearly half. Shutting down worldwide clothing production for a year would be equal to grounding all international flights and stopping all maritime shipping for the same time period.

Yet once again we land on the horns of a dilemma, because millions of people earn their livelihoods making those clothes. Most of those workers are in poorer countries that are highly dependent on the industry. The greatest clothing producer is China. The second-greatest is Bangladesh, a nation with a population half the size of America's in a space not quite the size of Iowa. In Bangladesh, over a third of manufacturing jobs and nearly 85 percent of exports come from the apparel industry. In a country where one-fifth of residents live below the national poverty line, the garment industry provides jobs to more than four million people. Six out of ten of them are women.

Just as the coronavirus began to creep across the globe, I reached out to factory owners in Bangladesh. Abdullah al Maher replied to me as if he had been waiting for my call. Maher is CEO of Fakir Fashion, a knitwear manufacturer for major brands such as H&M, Zara, Pull & Bear, C&A, Esprit, Gina Tricot and Tom Tailor. Maher told me that Fakir Fashion's towering factory on a narrow road in Narayanganj, a town just east of the capital city of Dhaka, employs more than 12,000 people. During peaks in the fashion cycle, the company manufactures a mind-boggling 200,000 articles of clothing *every day*—and they are adding more production lines. Fakir Fashion and its workers would seem to be utterly dependent on shopping as we know it today.

Suppose that shopping stopped, I said to Maher. Suppose that consumers worldwide suddenly paid heed to those critics who say we should buy fewer clothes as a way to lessen the impact of the industry. What would happen?

Maher paused. When he spoke, it was with the tone of one sharing a secret. "You know," he began, "it wouldn't be so bad."

Fakir Fashion is owned and operated by the Fakir family, which takes its name from the Muslim tradition of fakirs, who live lives of spiritual devotion without the distraction of possessions. Changing times made that an improbable career. "They're not supposed to go into industry, they're supposed to go into the jungle and preach to the animals," Maher said, laughing. "But then they realized, you had to have money to do that."

Clothes-making has a long—and brutally ironic—history in Bangladesh. For centuries, the area around Dhaka was renowned for the quality of its handwoven silk and cotton textiles. A length of the finest fabrics, given names like "running water" or "woven air," could take two weavers a year to produce, working only when there was enough humidity to keep the fine threads from breaking.

Cotton was arguably the first product of the global consumer age. In the mid 1600s, most clothing in the West was dull, because wool and linen did not dye easily, and silk was expensive. By the end of that century, millions of imported chintzes—brightly dyed and printed lengths of cotton cloth from what is now India and Bangladesh—brought colourful fashions to the upper classes and ultimately the public at large, first in England and then across Europe. With this "clothing revolution," as the historian Frank Trentmann puts it, familiar patterns of modern consumption took off: affordable fashions, more rapid changes in look, faster turnover of clothes. Consumer culture often accelerates in this manner: a spark of real delight that goes on to burn wildly out of control.

In the eighteenth century, the trade with Europe underwent a reversal. Much of Europe banned basic cottons from South Asia in order to build competing industries. With the Industrial Revolution, which began in the textiles trade, Britain began to take over the market with even cheaper, more abundant fabrics and clothes. They advanced with the power of empire. Bangladesh would not be a major producer of clothing again until the late 1970s. Since then, the country that once made the world's finest textiles has become synonymous with the cheapest and fastest of fashions.

Yousuf Ali Fakir, the grandfather of the current generation of the Fakir family, made the family's first turn toward textiles through the trade in jute, a rough textile that is spun into rope, twine and sackcloth. His sons became pioneers in Bangladesh's ready-made-garment industry in the 1980s. In 2009, three brothers of the current generation—Fakir Badruzzaman, Fakir

Kamruzzaman Nahid, and Fakir Wahiduzzaman Riyead—founded Fakir Fashion with the goal of making it one of the world's largest knitwear factories, but also a model of social and environmental responsibility. Little more than a decade later, Maher said, the company has learned a hard lesson. "Nobody pays for that," he said. "Nobody gives a shit about it."

Maher is a lively, quick-smiling man, even as he shares his unconcealed disgust with the fashion industry. It's a subject he knows from wide personal experience: he has worked in almost every aspect of apparel, including years as the Bangladesh manager for Sears. He recalls, early in his career, meeting an American corporate vice president who arrived on a first-class flight, stayed at Dhaka's best hotel, and complained about the quality of the bottled water. "Right behind the hotel there was a slum built on a marsh, with houses on bamboo poles, where people drinking from the lakes and rivers were going off to the same factories he would be asking later that day to cut their prices," Maher said. He remembers thinking back to his university years, when he had studied Charles Dickens's tales of Victorian-era inequality and injustice. "The stories are the same."

Over the past twenty years, Maher watched that pattern play out again and again as major clothing brands made demands on suppliers in Bangladesh to lower their prices while also completing orders faster and constantly improving their workplace and environmental standards. Fakir Fashion has implemented certified projects to treat its wastewater, harvest rainwater, use more solar power, provide meals and child care for workers, hire workers with disabilities, build schools in the local area and more. They have been unable to pass on any of the expense of these improvements to apparel brands or consumers, who continue to want more for less.

There's an old saying: if something's too cheap, somebody else is paying. Maher's workers earn $120 to $140 per month to work six days a week—low wages not only globally, but by Bangladesh's standards—to do jobs that are made more stressful with each acceleration of the fast-fashion cycle. Outside the factory gates, those workers endure the environmental consequences of a nation cutting corners to keep its industries competitive. The air in Narayanganj, once known as the "Dandy of the East," is typically an ocherous grey-brown and sometimes makes foreign visitors nauseous—the city is one of those where blue skies appeared like a miracle during the coronavirus lockdowns. Bangladesh is one of the nations hardest hit by climate change, although carbon emissions per person there are radically lower than in richer nations. (About twenty-five times lower than in Germany or Japan, for example, and roughly forty times lower than in the US or Canada.) Most of Bangladesh is situated on enormous, low-lying river deltas that drain the Himalayas, making the country vulnerable to faster glacial melting, more frequent and powerful cyclones, and rising sea levels. Chittagong, the city where Maher went to university, now undergoes widespread flooding—as much as 60 percent of the city—with every high tide throughout much of the year. "Tides go up and down in their homes," said Maher. "It's becoming Venice, but nobody is coming to visit this Venice. No one wants to come and die in the city's shitty, dirty water."

Yet what bothers Maher most is a less tangible harm: the insult of seeing the clothes his company makes sell for prices that show just how little they are valued. "Generation Z and millennials are really demanding ethical products," he said. "But when you buy a fast-fashion T-shirt for four dollars, or two dollars, you never ask, 'How could this shirt have landed in Berlin or London or Montreal for this price? How does the cotton get grown, ginned, spun, woven, dyed, printed, sewn, packed, shipped, all for four dollars?' You've never realized how many lives you are touching, all because *your* payment doesn't pay for their wages."

I asked Maher what kind of price increase would make a difference. The first sum that came to his mind was surprising: two cents—an amount so small that in many countries it's rounded up or down to the nearest bit of pocket change. If he was able to pass along two cents more per garment made in his factory, it would be the equivalent of two extra days' pay each month per worker (a raise of 7 to 8 percent). Alternatively, the two-cent increase could allow Fakir Fashion to produce fewer articles of clothing— they could make clothing better, or simply at a less harried pace—without anyone losing their job or any income. Imagine what might be accomplished if shoppers were willing to pay an extra dime.

Remarkably, the same fast-fashion forces that embitter Maher at the low end of the apparel market also stymie those who are trying to make clothes for a deconsumer economy. On the other side of the globe, breathing in the clean sea air of Providence, Rhode Island, Amanda Rinderle and her husband, Jonas Clark, sell dress shirts of such high quality that they can be worn for ten years or more. Unfortunately, they have to compete with the system that Maher knows so well.

When Rinderle and Clark came up with the concept for their Tuckerman & Co. brand in 2013, they had hoped to use American-grown organic cotton, milled in America, to produce long-lasting, made-in-America shirts. Because the apparel industry is overwhelmingly devoted to rapid-fire production of cheap and disposable products, however, everything Tuckerman wanted to do was a challenge.

To make a durable dress shirt, you need cotton with a long "staple," or fibre length, which makes for finer, stronger thread. Plenty of cotton is grown in the United States, but there is so little demand for both organic cotton—about 1 percent of the market—and long-staple cotton that Tuckerman had to draw on a global supply chain. It took five hundred phone calls to find a single mill that was both able to make fabric to Tuckerman's standards and willing to switch between conventional and organic cotton stocks to deal with their orders. That mill was the Albini Group, a fifth-generation family business in northern Italy. "The only place we can really get the fabric is probably the best fabric manufacturer in the world," Rinderle, who is Tuckerman's CEO, told me.

Organic interfacing—the material that gives collars and cuffs their structure—was available from less than a handful of companies worldwide; Tuckerman settled on one in Germany. Durable buttons made with corozo, a renewable vegetable ivory, turned up in Panama. They were able, at least, to manufacture the finished product in America; they were being made by Gambert Shirts in Newark, New Jersey. The end result was shirts that cost $195 each. Walmart, meanwhile, offers dress shirts for $15. Many of the clothes it sells are made in Bangladesh.

A well-made shirt offers value across its lifespan: wear a Tuckerman once a week for five years, and it has cost you about seventy-five cents per week, a better deal than if you bought a $60-dollar shirt and disposed of it after one year, and much better than a $15-dollar shirt thrown out after ten wears. Still, many households either cannot or refuse to pay $195 up front for a shirt. It is a fact that consumers worldwide have benefited financially from faster fashion. In countries like the UK and US, the proportion of the household budget spent on clothing has dropped from about 15 percent at the dawn of the twentieth century to 5 percent or less today. According to the US Bureau of Labor Statistics, we've used the savings mainly to pay for rising housing costs and for what they call "non-necessities": everything from weekend getaways to all the just-plain-stuff that fills homes and storage units.

"We are self-conscious about our price point," Rinderle said. She'd like to get the shirts down to one hundred dollars, which will only happen if Tuckerman & Co. becomes more like the fashion industry it was intended to defy: they can have the shirts made by lower-paid workers overseas using fewer organic and renewable materials. "It could potentially be tough to produce 100 percent of what we make here and be price competitive, as much as it pains me to say that."

When the coronavirus struck, the effects of a stop to shopping for clothes were quickly made real. As Paul Dillinger at Levi's had predicted, the industry began to fall apart: more than a million garment workers were furloughed in Bangladesh alone. According to Worker Rights Consortium, an industry watchdog, most leading brands refused to pay even for orders that were in production or ready to ship, until public outcry pressured them to do so.

I spoke to Maher again as the first lockdowns began to lift around the globe. I wondered: Having witnessed the harm to his country from a world that had stopped shopping, was he still so hungry to see the garment industry change? In the rising morning heat of the last weeks before the monsoon, Maher was as fiercely cheerful as ever. "Bringing in fast fashion to your country, you are also harming your country," he said.

The greatest danger for the garment trade is not a slowdown in shopping, Maher said, but a failure to find a way to slow down shopping. In a world in which billions of people already have enough apparel, the only way to keep them buying is to generate unnecessary demand. The way to create unnecessary demand is to accelerate fashion trends. The way to accelerate fashion trends is to make clothes cheap enough to buy more and more often. And the only way to make clothes that cheap is to cut corners on quality, working conditions, wages or environmental standards—the disaster of everyday life that Bangladesh has been living for years.

A transition to a world that consumes less clothing would be painful for Bangladesh. Even if the nation's garment industry made fewer, better clothes that sold for higher prices, Maher doubted that the six thousand factories in the country could keep as many people employed as they do today. "Maybe there should be four thousand factories, or three thousand," he said. But they would provide living wages, pollute and waste less, and compete on quality and efficiency, rather than greed and speed. "There'll be no rat race then," Maher said. "There'll be a real race."

If fast fashion must fall in a world without shopping, that doesn't mean it would disappear completely. Already, there are hints of what it could become.

Trove, when I visited its global headquarters, was as stereotypical a start-up as you could care to find. It is stationed in a small industrial park wedged between an artificial lagoon and the Bayshore Freeway in the outer orbit of San Francisco. Actual vultures sometimes circled overhead. Andy Ruben, Trove's founder, seemed to know every employee on the warehouse floor by name—though in American bizspeak, we weren't in a warehouse. We were in a Fulfillment Center.

For ten years, Ruben was a wunderkind executive at Walmart—in his own words, the "belly of the beast" of consumer culture. As a trailbreaker in sustainability in the world's largest retailer, he saw how difficult it was to change the way we consume. He promoted energy-efficient lightbulbs, only to watch the number of bulbs in the typical American home nearly double from thirty-five to more than sixty. He saw that you could offer a long-lasting power drill instead of a made-to-break power drill, but that did not address the inherent wastefulness of having millions of American households own drills, many of them hardly ever put to use. "It was always three steps forward, sometimes two back, sometimes four," he told me.

He left Walmart with a specific goal: to reduce new product purchasing by 25 percent. He wanted the world to stop one-quarter of its shopping.

His current business, Trove, works behind the scenes. "If you cut through everything I've learned, again and again it's *friction*. If things are too hard, they don't work," Ruben said. The company's clients, such as Nordstrom, Levi's, Patagonia, REI, and women's clothing company Eileen Fisher, work with Trove to build systems that make it easy for customers to bring back products they no longer want. These are shipped to Trove for inspection, cleaning and repair, and go back on sale at a discount through the brands' websites and stores.

Despite a lot of hype, the second-hand apparel market remains small: less than 10 percent overall, and that's including clothing rental. Still, it's a thirty-billion-dollar business, and growing—it was one of the industries that increased sales during the pandemic. Reselling clothes is not a new concept, of course. What is new is this: there's nothing "used" or "second-hand" feeling about the goods passing through Trove. The warehouse does not have that thrift-store smell. It's another lesson in today's consumer culture: clothes now pass through our lives so fleetingly that the difference between second-hand and new is often vanishingly thin.

The brands Trove works with have high standards: Eileen Fisher, for example, would only resell clothes that were in "perfect condition," without a hint of visible stains, holes or other signs of wear. That was more than half of what they were getting back. Many of the products that come to Trove still have their shop tags—to call them "used" is actually a misnomer. America's closets and basements, like armoires and attics around the globe, have become an enormous storehouse of unused and unloved things—a planet-spanning Unfulfillment Center.

Trove now moves hundreds of thousands of items a year ("It's not nothing anymore," Ruben said), but this business model, too, is undermined by consumer culture. Since resold items are generally cheaper, they allow some people to simply buy more stuff, while people who bring back goods for resale often get a gift card to spend on new things. Still, Ruben estimates that at least 70 percent of sales truly replace the purchase of a new product with a resold one. As evidence, he points to the fact that Patagonia expects 10 percent or more of their revenue to come from second-hand sales by 2023. Since used goods sell for lower prices, the company needs to sell a lot of them to take that big a bite out of overall sales. That likely means that, just a few years from now, one in five products that Patagonia ships will have been sold for a second—or third, or fourth—time.

The goal, say resale advocates, is to make consumption *flow*, bringing items into our lives when we need them and out when we no longer do. Historically, this is far from uncommon. In Renaissance Italy, even very wealthy people constantly moved clothing in and out of pawn according to changing needs and incomes, and the most stylish clothes were considered suspect, since they would lose their long-term value the moment trends shifted. (The tradition never faded completely, and pawning goods for small loans underwent a revival in Italy during the pandemic.) Karl Marx, during his struggling-young-economist years, rented his suits, while in the seventeenth and eighteenth centuries, many shops sold both new and second-hand goods. Even as late as the 1970s, hand-me-down clothing, toys and furniture were ordinary even in affluent families. Today, the circulation of goods is a natural fit for consumers whose lives have grown cluttered with stuff, who travel and move a lot, and who frequently live in urban apartments rather than sprawling suburban or country homes.

Flow is not free of environmental costs. Resale adds a bunch more shipping, handling and other logistics to the lifetime of a product, but it replaces—at least in theory—the entire raw-material and manufacturing supply chain that brings us new things. It's often described as a system of access, rather than ownership, though in Trove's particular model, you really would own each thing—perhaps for a day, perhaps for a lifetime. Other models include rental, subscription to a pool of items, or sharing networks. Together, they make a counterintuitive promise: we can use up far fewer resources while also acquiring and disposing of products as quickly, or more quickly, than ever before. "There would be fewer products, but we'd have products coming in and out of our lives all the time," Ruben said. He smiled—a little slyly. "If we can get into a flow of items, I think we could be consuming a lot *more*."

Cyndi Rhoades sees another way that fast fashion could linger beyond the day the world stops shopping. Wildly red-haired, looking every bit like the music video and documentary filmmaker she once was, Rhoades is the founder of Worn Again Technologies, a UK-based business that has found a way to dissolve—yes, *dissolve*—your unwanted clothing and reformulate it into raw materials that can be spun once more into clothes. The process is akin to a perpetual motion machine: toss an old T-shirt into one end of the process and a new one comes out the other.

Worn Again's current mission began in 2011 with a chance meeting between Rhoades and a chemical scientist named Adam Walker. It turned out that Walker, who is now the company's chief scientist, had designed software that allows you to punch in the material you want to isolate and then generate a list of solvents that might do the job. Rhoades asked him about textile recycling. "He went into the lab, conducted a little laptop experiment, and came back with, 'Here's your polyester, here's your cellulose from cotton,'" Rhoades said. The whole project had taken three months. "We thought, great, it's all done. We thought we had discovered the holy grail."

Instead, it took nearly a decade to sort out how the process could work at larger scales. The concept, though, remains simple. The emerging textile reprocessing industry that Worn Again is a part of needs a feedstock of fabrics made of cotton or polyester or a blend of the two (it can include up to 10 percent other materials, such as buttons or the elastic fibres that make stretch pants stretchy). About 80 percent of all clothing meets these conditions, meaning that each year more than forty million tonnes of potential feedstock is produced—an embarrassment of riches.

You place these clothes in a solvent that dissolves the polyester, and then—this takes some serious chemical engineering—reseparate the solvent and the polyester. At that point, you have the raw material to produce a pure polyester pellet that is ready to turn into fibre, the same as if it had been made from oil. Cotton goes through a similar process, except that it doesn't end up being cotton in the end. Instead, you extract the basic chemical building block of cotton, which is cellulose. The final product looks and behaves quite a bit like cotton and can be used to make textiles similar to viscose, lyocell and Tencel, which are already made into clothes in factories around the world. The rest of the materials that go into our garments—other fabrics, dyes, finishes and so on—come out as waste, but on average so far, almost 90 percent less waste than throwing out clothes entirely.

If you have heard about circular design or the circular economy, this is the kind of circle they're talking about: a cycle in which products are constantly reused or recycled into new products without ever ending up as waste. Currently, not much of the economy is circular, and it isn't becoming more circular, either. (The nonprofit organization Circle Economy began tracking the numbers in 2018, when 9.1 percent of the economy was circular. By 2020, the number had dropped to 8.6 percent, and the amount of materials consumed by the global economy was higher than ever.) In the garment trade right now, only about 1 percent of discarded clothing is recycled into other clothing, and a further 12 percent is turned into lower-quality goods like mattress stuffing and wiping cloths. From the perspective of circular economy companies like Worn Again, a hundred billion dollars' worth of raw materials each year are ending up as waste.

In February 2020, Worn Again opened a pilot research and development facility in Redcar, England, putting them one step away from a trial-size version of a clothes reprocessing plant. The company has a vision of forty operating plants by 2040, with the first factories opening in Western Europe and the United States, in part because of those regions' efficient waste collection systems, but also because consumer culture itself is the feedstock. Large numbers of wealthy consumers, throwing out their stuff, are to clothing recycling what the cotton field and oil refinery are to today's apparel industry.

Stopping shopping would seem to threaten that feedstock: every shirt or pair of jeans that isn't purchased is one less garment that can be recycled. Rhoades is unconcerned. Even if clothing sales were cut in half worldwide, it would still leave twenty million tonnes of new garments in production each year that meet the clothing reprocessing industry's standards. If all of them became raw materials for Worn Again, it would be enough to supply four hundred of their factories.

There's more. A company like Worn Again could theoretically mine the world's closets and landfills, which are bulging with clothing and fabrics.

"We actually have enough end-of-use textiles already in existence to supply our annual demand, so we wouldn't have to drill for oil or grow cotton again," Rhoades said. There's enough that deconsumer culture might still be able to offer a little fast fashion—something bright and clever, something constantly changing and then recycled, to add flair to our durable pants and classic jackets.

"It would enable that, for those that want to live that path," said Rhoades. "We're not all going to be shopping the same."

The real threat to the promise of a circular economy is, once again, the sheer scale of consumption. Could the circular economy provide an adequate wardrobe for all of the world's nearly 8 billion people? Rhoades thinks it could. Could it supply us all with the fast-fashion lifestyle of the world's richest consumers? No. If you need more and more clothes—if demand for clothing perpetually grows—then the circle itself has to expand, like a black hole that sucks in energy and resources. A circle that never stops growing, or a flow of goods that always gets wider and faster, eventually runs up against the same problems as a perpetually growing consumer economy.

Which raises a more philosophical question: Does a circular economy, or a circulating one, amount to an end to shopping as we know it? Each changes the things we acquire and how we acquire them. Neither asks that we make much change to the have-it-all, more-of-everything mindset, or questions whether consumption should be so central to our lives in the first place. But there are businesses that do—businesses that still remember a time long before anyone spoke of consumer culture.

Business plays the long, long, long, long game

There is a business concept called the "four mores" that could stand as the motto of modern consumer capitalism. Because it sounds greedy and underhanded, however, it's rarely mentioned outside business schools. The four mores are as follows: sell more things, to more people, more often, for more money. To do so is to achieve the ultimate in perpetual profits, sales and growth.

Mitsuharu Kurokawa was puzzled by notions like these when he moved from Japan to the US to complete a business degree. He remembers a scenario posited by one of his professors there. Suppose a customer wanted seven hundred units of your company's product, but your factory was designed to make batches of five hundred. What would you do? The correct answer, his professor said, was to make one thousand units, provided a profit could still be made if seven hundred units were delivered to the customer and three hundred scrapped as waste.

"I just don't think it makes sense, is what I was thinking," Kurokawa told me, sipping a cup of matcha. "We never try to overproduce. We also try not to underproduce. We try to be very efficient."

Kurokawa's perspective on business takes an unusually long view. Currently in his thirties, he is in line, as his father's only son, to become the eighteenth member of his family to lead Toraya, a Japanese confectionery company. The firm has existed since at least the 1600s, making it about 420 years old. Toraya is a tortoise in a world of fruit flies, Methuselah among the tweens. The average lifespan of even the biggest companies on the stock market has fallen from sixty-seven years in the 1920s to fifteen years today. The average for businesses as a whole is now just ten years.

Almost every company likes to believe that their brand is beloved enough and strong enough to survive the end of shopping—that their particular business is made to last. Toraya's claim is more credible. When the coronavirus struck in 2020, it was only the latest in a list of storms the company has weathered. Toraya burned down to its signboard in 1788, when a fire razed nearly fifteen hundred city blocks in Kyoto, which was then Japan's capital. Later came the two-year period when the Japanese royal family—Toraya's best customer, at times accounting for half of their sales—fell on hard times and failed to pay their bills. When Japan's capital shifted to Tokyo in 1869, Toraya shifted its headquarters as well (in an age before motorized transport), and then moved six more times as Tokyo expanded to become the world's largest city. Toraya survived the 1923 Great Kanto Earthquake, which also spawned a tsunami, a blaze that devoured nearly half the city, and a hellish fire tornado as tall as a twenty-storey building. One hundred and forty thousand people died, but the quake did not stop Toraya from launching a delivery service the following year. Then their factory was devastated during the American incendiary bombing raids on Tokyo during the Second World War, which reduced to ashes an area nearly ten times larger than was destroyed by the atomic bombs dropped on Hiroshima and Nagasaki later in the war. "If your factory is blown up, it's very difficult," Kurokawa said. Toraya has known disaster, and through it all has remained a family business dedicated to making beautiful little treats.

"Since I was born, I was totally surrounded by sweets," Kurokawa said, sitting in a Toraya tea room in the upscale Tokyo district of Roppongi. All around him, well-dressed Tokyoites eat a pastry that looks to Western eyes like a cocktail wiener folded into pale pink sponge cake, all wrapped in a wet leaf. In fact, it is an infinitely smooth cylinder of sweetened red adzuki bean paste tucked within a slice of steamed and pounded rice-flour cake;

the leaf really is a leaf, from a cherry tree, and has soaked in brine for a year. The confection—a perfect balance of sweet, salty and savoury flavours—is called *sakura mochi*, and it celebrates cherry-blossom season, which has arrived unnervingly early this year. "You don't have to eat the leaf," Kurokawa told me. It was delicious.

The treats that Toraya produces are called *wagashi*, and they are intended to engage all the senses—even hearing, because the confections' names are chosen to call serene images to mind: Journey through the Clouds, Breeze from Awa, Sarashina Autumn Moon. Among the most popular is a small loaf of firm, dark jelly called Night Plum. When the loaf is sliced, round cross-sections of whole white adzuki beans are revealed; they are meant to evoke "the glimmer of white plum blossoms in the dark night and their drifting scents."

Unfortunately, foreigners often mistake Toraya's products for soap. The most popular wagashi, called *yokan*, are translucent rectangular bars, and many of the other treats have the bright, floral look that the West associates with bath time. In 1980, Kurokawa's grandfather decided that France was the place to start bringing Toraya to the world outside Japan. He sensed that the French, with their sophisticated appreciation of cuisine, would "get" wagashi. He opened a Toraya shop in Paris, a block from the Place de la Concorde, and his instincts proved correct. The French did "get" wagashi—it just took a while.

"I heard that for maybe ten or fifteen years we definitely didn't have many customers," said Kurokawa. "If you are not thinking about the long term, then you would close the store maybe in one year. But our goal was to let people from other cultures know our culture, and to create even better sweets by getting the French influence. So we decided to keep it, and after thirty years we were able to turn it into a sort-of-profitable operation."

Thirty years to turn a profit. Three times the average lifespan of a business today.

Economic diversity is like biological or cultural diversity: a storehouse of ways of being. A sudden shift in circumstances and today's dominant players may swiftly fall, as forms better suited to the new conditions rise from where they've been waiting in the shadows. In a natural system, a force like climate change could trigger a shift. In an economy, the end of shopping certainly would.

One way of doing business has dominated our recent understanding of the economy, and that is the pursuit of profit-driven growth by large corporations. Toraya, on the other hand, is an example of a long-standing family-operated business, sometimes referred to as a "henokien." The term was coined in 1981 by Gérard Glotin, then the head of Marie Brizard, a family business that debuted an anisette liqueur company in 1755 in France. Glotin derived the word, which he applied to family companies that have existed for two centuries or more, from the biblical character Henok (a.k.a. Enoch), who in some Christian traditions is said to have lived 365 years on Earth. Then, in a feat not even equalled by Jesus, Henok ascended to heaven *without ever actually dying*.

Family businesses have an overlooked history. Only recently have they begun to attract focused study. What researchers have found is that, wherever you go in the world, family firms will likely make up about 70 percent of all companies and 60 percent of the workforce—they've been called the "hidden champions" of the economy. They are the mom-and-pop shops, independent restaurants, salons, locksmiths, contractors, freelancers, the offices of doctors, lawyers and accountants. They probably fix your teeth, repair your shoes, dry-clean your suits, care for your kids, do your landscaping, bake your favourite pizza, run your favourite bar or café. They were hard-hit by the Covid-19 crisis, but were also more likely to be the kind of beloved local businesses that neighbours rallied to save.

Not all family companies are small. Across major stock indices in the US and Europe, family firms represent one-third of businesses. Whether a large corporation with shareholders to please is any different when it's controlled by a family is the stuff of perennial debate. But family firms that are privately owned and are not listed on the stock markets do tend to behave differently. This is especially true of those that have endured for centuries.

Consider the question of profit. "I can't say we don't look for profits—of course we look for profits," said Kurokawa. "But if profits or sales were our first priority, we could do so much more. There are so many things I can think of that I would do to cut costs, like not making the sweets by hand or closing down operations that are not profitable."

Toraya does use machines and automation in its factories, but also maintains a hand-production division. The company's view is that not one of Toraya's three thousand different wagashi recipes was invented by a machine. Until artificial intelligence advances to the sophistication and creativity of a master wagashi-maker, machines will simply repeat the tasks they were programmed to do. Automation is innovation frozen in time.

Today, Toraya has eighty shops and cafés, nearly a thousand employees, and about two hundred million dollars each year in sales—the same as they did ten years ago. In 2001, Kurokawa's father set down Toraya's vision for the entire twenty-first century. He did not list profit maximization as a priority. Instead, he went with the following: maximum satisfaction for the customer, reinforcing the Japanese lifestyle and culture, social responsibility, and providing employees with rewarding lives. The company is an example of what author Bill McKibben calls "deep economy," in which business is integrated into community and culture. Many businesses now glibly refer to their customers as their "community"; again, in Toraya's case, the claim has a bit more heft.

The very mindset of Toraya is not his family's to decide alone, Kurokawa said. There is the Japanese imperial household to consider, whose relationship with Toraya extends through the long history of the company. There are also the three families who are recognized as having the highest level of traditional tea-ceremony mastery, all of whom order from Toraya. Two hundred seventy farmers in the Gunma mountains are contracted to grow Toraya's white adzuki beans, which have been cultivated in those fields long enough to be recognized as genetically distinct. Fathers and sons work together in Toraya's factories; an octogenarian calligrapher still contributes to their packaging designs, just like his father did, and his daughter may continue the lineage. "That kind of intergenerational relationship—there are a lot of them for us," Kurokawa told me. The absolute highest priority for Toraya is continuity. The past and future are of central importance to henokiens, encouraging a long view that, in turn, produces a distinctly different way of doing business. After hundreds of years, no one wants to be the one who leads the company into ruin.

For one, long-lived family companies tend to offer goods and services that have what economists—echoing the field of psychology—call "intrinsic" value: they are functional or beautiful or traditional or delightful, but above all, they are timeless. On the list of recognized henokiens are winemakers, jewellers, bell-founders, soy sauce brewers, foresters, publishers, cleaning-product manufacturers. Beretta, the firearms maker (fifteen hundred new weapons each day), is a member.

Taking the long view also appears to encourage better social and environmental practices: again, it's not an abstraction to family business owners that their actions today create the world that their children and grandchildren will live in. Pride plays a role, too. "Many family firms are named after the family, so it's the family reputation which is always at stake," said Lise Møller, a strategic adviser on family enterprise at Institut Européen d'Administration des Affaires (INSEAD), one of the world's leading business schools, based in Fontainebleau, France. As a general rule, old family firms are conservative. They tend to do well in economic downturns, in part because they have historical experience to draw on, but also because they have no need to focus on making short-term profits to please shareholders.

An especially crucial way that a henokien approach makes sense for a world that stops shopping is that many of them do not focus on expansion. Asked where on the list of priorities he would put growth, Kurokawa is bemused. In the same way that an apolitical person is not concerned with politics one way or another, Toraya is "agrowth." If growth is an outcome of the company's pursuit of its values, so be it. If not, that's fine too. Growth can even be seen as a warning sign that a company is putting those values at risk. Among traditional sweets-makers in Japan, for example, there is informal agreement that it is improper to take over another confectioners' market share except under extraordinary circumstances, such as when a competitor—if you can call it that—goes out of business.

Indifference to growth is heresy among Western capitalists. Yet no-growth business makes up a huge part of the economy already. No one expects their local family-run restaurant to endlessly enlarge. That same model is common among the longest-lived businesses, said Tetsuya O'Hara, a product innovation consultant who has worked with Gap Inc. and Patagonia. O'Hara did his MBA in California, and graduated with what he called "old school" business values: "how you take market share, how to grow as quickly as possible, how you can cut back your costs, how you can raise your retail prices." But his own family has been making a textile finishing agent in Kyoto for almost a century, and growing up he had been introduced to other long-standing companies. Japan is the world's hotbed for them, with nearly thirty-five thousand companies that are more than a century old, and dozens that have endured more than five hundred years.

O'Hara speaks regularly at universities and business schools, and for a time he tried propounding the model of long-lived companies. American students, he said, were especially uninterested. "They are interested in short-term returns. They love growth, and how you can make money quickly," he said. "It's the culture. The United States doesn't have such a long history, and particularly in California, the state still has gold-rush culture. People are still chasing the gold."

There are a few reasons why Japan might have produced so many corporations with a deep-time view of business. For one, the country has been beset throughout its history by terrible earthquakes, fires, tsunamis, recessions and wars. Instead of endless growth, it has been a culture of rise and fall, its people renowned as *gamanzuyoi*, or "steadfastly patient."

Then there is the fact that, until the late nineteenth century, Japan passed 250 years in isolation under a policy of *sakoku*, or "closed country." Throughout that time, the economy grew very slowly, with most new wealth spent on practical improvements like better housing and clean water systems. Shops and restaurants became widespread and consumer goods like fans and combs gained popularity, but homes remained mostly unadorned and possessions few in number. Consumer historian Frank Trentmann calls it a "culture of simple comfort" that might have given the Japanese a higher quality of life than Europeans at that time.

Simple comfort also made environmental sense. A nation that almost entirely closes its borders is left to survive on its own resources: it becomes Earth in miniature. To the Japanese under sakoku, the idea that natural resources are finite was much more tangible than it is for a modern consumer whose bananas come from Ecuador, their smartphone from China, and their T-shirt from Bangladesh. When you can walk east to west across Japan's largest island, Honshu, in a matter of days, it's hardly surprising that you might develop an ethic that considers it madness to throw out three hundred units of a product to fulfill an order for seven hundred.

Does Kurokawa feel that deep-time thinking in business is *better* than short-term thinking? He is an even-minded person, and I admit that I expected him to reply that both are important. Instead he said, "Of course."

He offered one more history lesson: in 1915, Tokyo decided to commemorate their recently deceased emperor with a Shinto shrine and sacred forest. At the time, the area they selected was marshy farmland on the outskirts of the city.

The foresters planned out the project in stages, beginning with a hundred thousand young trees that would be planted around the few existing pines. Over a hundred years, a broad-leaf woods of oak, chinquapin and camphor trees would rise to become an untended forest. No one involved in the planning would live to see the final outcome.

Today the mature forest covers a slow-rising hill alongside Harajuku subway station. It's a green respite, where a sense of calm prevails and there's clean air for your lungs—and it is surrounded to the horizon on every side by the megalopolis of Tokyo. Kurokawa became speechless with awe at the brilliance of the deep-time vision.

"If you don't think in that way," he said at last, "what kind of passion do you have for human life?"

People often imagine that long-standing businesses must be dull, unchanging institutions—stuck in their ways. It is a maxim of corporate culture that if you're not growing, you're dying. We've come to assume that, because we live in a global economy that produces a lot of both growth and innovation, we can't have one without the other.

Henokiens function in precisely the opposite way to this widespread misimpression. Much of the reason they're rare is that it takes constant innovation to survive the seismic shifts of history. Sometimes, that means reinvention upon reinvention, such as the Van Eeghen company of the Netherlands, which was founded in 1662 to trade in wool, wine, salt and other basic goods, then went on to found a bank, buy and sell American real estate, build locks and canals, grow tobacco and cotton, return to shipping, and finally, after the Second World War, to deal in spices, dehydrated foods, and now in health supplements.

Lise Møller said that—despite all the rhetoric around agility and disruption in business today—she would expect henokiens to adapt to a world without shopping *more* quickly than conventional, growth-driven companies. Even long-standing firms with a "do one thing well" approach, like Toraya, are accustomed to constant evolution in business models and shifts in consumer tastes. Kurokawa said that everything Toraya makes tastes different now than it did even a few years ago; they ceaselessly breed new adzuki beans to keep pace with climate change, and have recently found a new market for their yokan as emergency supplies for this age of disasters (nuclear accidents, typhoons, tsunamis, pandemics). Toraya's motto is, "Tradition is continuous innovation." The translation into French is more insistent still: "Tradition is a succession of revolutions."

We think we live in an age of unprecedented innovation, but it's more accurate to say that it's an age of *easy* innovation, said Kris De Decker, a technology journalist. Cheap energy, most of it powered by oil, made it possible to mine resources and produce products at exceptional speed. "We pretend as if energy will last forever and that it has no downsides. From the moment you are within a limitation, you need to innovate to improve your life," he told me. "And then it gets really interesting."

In 2007, De Decker was writing about tech for major European newspapers while losing faith in its ability to solve the world's great problems, climate change foremost among them. He started *Low-Tech Magazine*, mostly as a platform to challenge the high-tech-will-fix-everything mentality. "Then one evening," De Decker said, "my girlfriend was reading a book and she was like, 'Do you know about the optical telegraph?'"

He did not know about the optical telegraph. He began researching, and took his first step into what he calls "this whole world that we forgot"—the history of innovation without high technology.

An optical telegraph, it turned out, was a system of towers placed just within eyesight of each other (through a telescope), in order to communicate messages visually. Each tower looked something like an old-time windmill whose blades had been damaged by a storm: two signalling arms dangled from a single, long cross-arm. Using levers to toggle the various arms, a telegrapher could communicate signals—each coded to a letter, number, word or phrase—to be relayed down the line. It was a faster, smarter version of smoke signals. A fifteen-character message could travel down the first complete optical telegraph line, which stretched 230 kilometres from Paris to the town of Lille, in half an hour. Each individual signal moved at 1,380 kilometres per hour, which, as De Decker calculated, is faster than most passenger planes.

That was in 1791. Before long, the technology doubled in speed. The network from Lyon, France, to Venice, Italy, could transmit a typical message across 650 kilometres in a single hour. The optical telegraph was invented half a century ahead of the electrical telegraph and nearly two hundred years before the first email.

What struck De Decker was not that that the optical telegraph was somehow better than modern communications tech—it clearly is not—but that it was a marvel of innovation that worked within limits that are extremely important today. In this case, the technology achieved rapid, accurate, long-distance communication (at least by day, and when there was no fog) with an ecological footprint restricted to small amounts of timber and quarried stone—and without the need for either electricity or fossil fuels. "As history shows, people were very able to keep improving the human condition and society," De Decker said. "We could have taken a completely different path in the twentieth century."

Traditional economists have long claimed that innovation is driven by the profit motive, but that, too, does not appear to be the way that it actually works. Eric von Hippel, an economist at the Massachusetts Institute of Technology, led research in several countries that found that many innovations don't even originate within businesses, but rather among everyday people, who often share their ideas freely. Von Hippel gives the example of an amateur bike-builder who creates a new design for a mountain bike, then rides it around town, posts images of it online, even encourages others hobbyists to copy the design or improve on it. The inventor takes satisfaction not from making money, but from creating something useful and gaining standing in the community. Similarly, scientists themselves tend to invent the scientific instruments that are most important to the advancement of science, often profiting little or not at all from their inventions.

Thousands of examples conflict with the idea that innovation depends on a desire for money and growth. Perhaps the most famous case is the American moon landing in 1969, much more the result of Cold War rivalry and exploratory zeal than a race to profit from outer space. Another is email, which programmer Ray Tomlinson invented as a side project while working on ARPANET, a government-funded precursor to the internet. "Our sponsor, the Department of Defense, never said anything about wanting email. My boss didn't say anything about email," Tomlinson said later. "It just seemed like an interesting thing to do with a computer and a network." It was the polar opposite of the modern start-up trying to create the next fleeting app to attract a billion dollars in investment.

If recent history's consumption disasters have been marked by a lack of innovation, it's because we, as societies, tend to sit them out, waiting for the consumer-driven recovery. A permanent slowdown in consumption, on the other hand, is more likely to trigger an eruption of inventiveness than its sudden end. "We have to rethink *everything*," said De Decker. "There's a need for a lot of innovation there, but innovation with another meaning."

For years now, De Decker has run a personal experiment in low-tech living—a lower-consuming lifestyle, including largely stopping shopping. He understands that in the eyes of most other people this makes him, as he put it, a "die-hard idiot." Originally from Belgium, De Decker now rents a home with no heating system near Barcelona ("I now have this thermal underwear fixation," he said), does not own a car, has an old push-button Nokia cell phone and a 2006-model laptop, travels frequently in his work but never by airplane, and runs a version of his website on solar power. These choices, combined with his knowledge of past solutions to problems that we still face today, help him see what might need to change in order for society to consume less. An example: "I notice very clearly that the whole railway network in Europe is disintegrating." To reach many destinations on Europe's high-speed train network today, De Decker said, often costs more money and burns more energy than it did to travel by rail a century ago. Most surprisingly, it can also waste more time. Because many night trains have been cut, large distances once covered while asleep must instead be traversed during waking hours. In fact, apply this "perceived time" approach, and it sometimes takes more useful hours in the day to travel to the airport, wait, fly and finally make it to your destination than it did to travel by night train in the past. (Another forgotten innovation is the train ferry—a ferry designed to load rail cars. "They were very common," said De Decker. "There's even a book about train ferries. I have it.") The philosopher Ivan Illich made a similar point when he said that a person on a bicycle is always saving more time than one driving a car, because the cyclist spends so much less time earning the money needed to own and operate their mode of transportation.

A world without shopping—think of it as a leaner, more efficient consumer culture—might also tilt toward innovation that is more often genuinely useful. Through the clamour of business media, we've gotten used to thinking of innovation as good in and of itself. In fact, a cursory glance at the world around us reveals innovations that are undeniably good (say, eyeglasses), undeniably bad (digital identity theft), and, most common of all, have a mix of upsides and downsides (smartphones). In the throes of the Great Recession, former US Federal Reserve chair Paul Volcker surveyed the new financial products, such as mortgage-backed securities, that had brought the global economy to its knees. "Were they wonderful innovations that we want to create more of?" he said. Then he added this: "The most important financial innovation that I have seen in the past twenty years is the automatic teller machine. That really helps people." It's said that his speech received thunderous applause.

Could we lose 25 percent of innovations—fewer new candy bars, late-night-TV inventions, dubious investments, new cuts and colours of clothing, viral Christmas gifts, fads and trends—without suffering?

"I think 90 percent of them," said De Decker.

Houshi, a *ryokan*, or traditional Japanese inn, is the oldest continuously operating family business in the world—the henokien of all henokiens. It was founded at the site of an *onsen*, or hot spring, over thirteen hundred years ago, in the calendar year 718. That's nearly eight centuries before Christopher Columbus found his way to the Americas. It's decades before the Vikings had even begun to sack the British Isles. In Mexico, the Maya civilization was just peaking. The complete Quran was not even a century old, *Beowulf* a century away. It is easy to imagine that, at Houshi, you will steep in ancient waters and sleep beneath beams cut from trees larger than any that still stand, the wood black and sacred with age. Fifty generations will haunt your dreams.

It isn't quite like that. Houshi is a place where a more timeless approach to business collided with an evanescent one. The clash left its mark, the way a scar is new growth on old skin.

Houshi is in Awazu, a town just two hundred kilometres from Tokyo as the raven flies but far enough off the beaten path that it takes nearly four hours to get there. Long before the coronavirus pandemic made end-of-days imagery familiar worldwide, Awazu was undergoing a slow-motion apocalypse.

Abandoned houses—some slumping with age, others forsaken recently enough to still be filled with belongings—dot the narrow streets. They make for a grim first impression, but they're practically cheerful compared to the decaying hotels. Arranged along the green hem of Mount Haku, the huge buildings loom with puckering plaster, rusted balconies, fallen tiles. Towers wear cloaks of vines, looking more like crags peeping out from the forest than any kind of human habitation. Everywhere, there is the eerie cast of things too new to look so old.

Houshi is a welcome sight. A four-century-old cedar stands sentry outside, and the inn's paint is fresh white against dark wood and tile. Staff, each in a colourful kimono (the Japanese robe is so classic that the word translates as "thing to wear"), greet guests and politely guide baffled foreigners through the etiquette of footwear, dining and public bathing. (Do not hang up your towel or set it down on the floor. Instead, fold it into a neat rectangle and place it on top of your head like a duchess's fascinator.) From nearly anywhere in the building, tall windows gaze on a courtyard garden of stone, forest and water.

The current overseer of the inn is Zengoro Houshi, now in his eighties. As he knelt to serve tea and wagashi, he spoke of the ancient hot spring that fills the inn's baths in the kind of loving tones usually reserved for living things. But his voice was tinged with regret. "The Zengoro name has now continued for forty-six generations," he said. "I am probably of the generation that has achieved the least."

As the story goes, a great Buddhist teacher came to this area centuries ago, called by Mount Haku itself. After he arrived, a voice told him where he could find a hot spring with the power to heal. As pilgrims began to make their way to Awazu in the hope of being cured of their ailments, the teacher left the waters to the stewardship of the original Zengoro, who was the adopted son of an apprentice. From then on, the hot spring and its lodging were continuously passed down from father to eldest son, Zengoro to Zengoro to Zengoro. There were the usual earthquakes, floods and typhoons, but the community of Awazu would simply make repairs and carry on. It remained a quiet, slow-changing corner of the world.

Then came the "Japanese miracle." In the final years of the 1980s, encouraged by financial deregulation and low interest rates, Japan's already booming economy went berserk. The frenzy of speculation is remembered as "the bubble," in much the same way as people worldwide still recall "the Depression." At its height, the total value of real estate in Japan, which is 5 percent of the size of the United States, was twice as high as all American properties combined.

Awazu was transformed into a popular resort town, overrun by suddenly wealthy Japanese with money and stress to burn. Hotels filled as quickly as they could be flung up, and Zengoro recalls parties every day with businessmen and their hired geishas and "hostesses"—women, often foreigners, who were paid to be pretty and pleasant companions. He was told that no one wanted to see old, black wood anymore. They wanted steel and colour and glass.

Economists have nostrums for what happened next: "There is no such thing as a one-way bet," for example, or "Things that can't go on forever, don't." Japan's overheated economy peaked on December 29, 1989. A long decline began that in some ways has never ended.

"Luckily, I kept this entrance and one wooden building. But there were older, valuable buildings I took down, which I should not have. I made the decision alone, and now I regret it every day," Zengoro told me. "From now on, we should not change according to the changes in society but based on our own set of values."

With the historical structures replaced by a more modern edifice, there is not much at Houshi now to remind visitors that the inn first opened its doors a hundred years before gunpowder was invented. The clearest hint of antiquity is a guest house made of Japanese cypress without the use of a single nail; it stands in the garden—seeming almost to have sprung from the soil—and has hosted Japanese royalty. Otherwise, Houshi feels as though it were decades rather than centuries old: modern and a little wilted. A room that used to be set aside for Zen meditation now has five glowing fast-food and drink machines.

The family has also been stung by personal tragedy. The eldest son who was meant to inherit the business—the forty-seventh Zengoro—died young. Several years ago, the remaining daughter, Hisae, returned to Awazu and began to learn the business.

Zengoro is hard on himself, very hard. Walking the halls of the inn, he looks like a man who carries an actual great weight on his back, a burden that he is afraid to put down for even a moment. What he can't see is his success. As a global society, we long ago made a bet that the future would always be built on rising wealth and perpetual growth, always the new and never the old. All around Awazu, that contradiction in terms—a future never built to last—is gradually falling down in decay. Houshi is still standing.

If we're no longer consumers,
what are we instead?

A few years ago, in autumn, a young woman named Zoe Hallel saw that a shop was going to open near her home in the London suburb of Dagenham. She was curious about it, as she was curious about anything new in the neighbourhood—because she desperately wanted her life to change.

"I was so isolated, I never socialized," Hallel said. "There's people you pass on the street for years and years, and you can live here and recognize people for ages, and unless you have a reason to talk, you just pass each other and never say hello."

Hallel understood that she was hoping against hope. She had no reason, really, to think that a shop would make a difference to her. Although they dominate public space in cities and towns, shops are not typically social places, and, if you don't have the money to spend in them, even cafés and pubs might as well be blank walls. For all its frantic activity, consumer culture is frequently atomized and private—crowds of people who are together alone.

Twenty-five years old at the time, and with a young daughter, Hallel faced more than just the modern world's familiar absence of neighbourliness. For close to a decade she had struggled with agoraphobia, a type of anxiety that overwhelmed her with fear if she tried to walk more than about a block from the house she and her child lived in with her parents. Even this was an improvement on the five years she had spent almost entirely in her bedroom.

Soon a name appeared in red vinyl lettering in the shop window: Every One Every Day. Hallel had been trying to walk to a pedestrian crossing that would lead her to the new attraction, but had yet to make it. Her heart would pound, and before long she spiralled into panic. Then one day the shop was finally open. There were chairs out front, the kind you'd see on a beach.

That weekend, Hallel's mother came home with a newsletter issued by Every One Every Day. It turned out the place didn't sell anything. Instead, the flyer was full of things to do: lessons in making squash soup, a birdhouse-painting workshop, dance classes. Everything was free. "I felt I had so much energy wasting," Hallel said, "and then all of a sudden you've got all these things to learn, and I just didn't want to miss a day of anything."

She made it through the door of the shop. It changed her life.

Because our primary role in society today is as consumers, it is natural to predict that, if we stop consuming, we will become something else. Critics of consumer culture have tended to go further, arguing that this next thing will inevitably be nobler: we'll be more neighbourly, more responsible, more philosophical, more spiritual.

Jon Alexander thinks this is a dangerous assumption.

Alexander, formerly a London advertising creative, is a founder of the New Citizenship Project, an organization dedicated to finding a new role we can play when we give up on being consumers. One of his favourite quotations, which he recited to me rapid-fire from memory on the banks of the Thames in London, is from Lawrence of Arabia's memoir of the First World War:

The morning freshness of the world-to-be intoxicated us. We were wrought up with ideas inexpressible and vaporous, but to be fought for. . . . Yet when we achieved and the new world dawned, the old men came out again and took our victory to remake in the likeness of the former world they knew.

Leading up to the First World War, Alexander said, most people on Earth were first and foremost *subjects*, or individuals who owed allegiance to god, ruler or country. At the war's end, a question hung over the smouldering ruins: to restart society as it had been, or build a different society? It was the same question that was widely asked when the coronavirus pandemic shut down the world—and it had the same answer. "There was a really fascinating moment of failure to step into a new world," Alexander said.

It took another world war to put the global order on a different path. Out of the Second World War came truly new ideas and institutions like the Universal Declaration of Human Rights and the World Bank, and a dramatic expansion of public services. The new society would be a consumer society, with GDP growth as the principal measure of its success. And there was an updated role for the individual. "We went from consuming to being consumers. It had been one identity among many, but then it became *the* identity," said Alexander.

Every One Every Day proposes a different possibility: that we can become, first and foremost, *participants*. More than a decade ago, a British social activist named Tessy Britton began to compile examples from around the world of a new kind of community project: people getting together, usually without much money or bureaucracy involved, to learn, share or make something. Filling a vacant plot of land with allotment gardens, for example, or setting up a free space for bike repairs. Britton saw more in these efforts than the latest trend in middle-class Pollyannaism. For one, she recognized that these projects often bring together people from different religions, ethnicities, social classes and so on, which had proved difficult to achieve with other approaches. For another, she began to realize that, while any single project of this type touched only a small number of people, if you put enough of them in one place, you'd end up with a radically more participatory way of life. "In this vision I imagine there would hardly be any time to do any 'proper work,'" she wrote in 2010. "We would be so busy growing, making, cooking, chatting, learning, teaching."

Seven years later, as CEO of the Participatory City Foundation, Britton oversaw the opening of two Every One Every Day shops in the Borough of Barking and Dagenham—beachheads of participation. By 2022, the target is to have five shops, a warehouse filled with tools and machines for creative production, as many as fifty "mini-hubs" led by local residents, and hundreds of free or low-cost activities in a borough of two hundred thousand people.

Barking and Dagenham is not an obvious choice for the world's largest experiment in "participatory culture." An hour on the Tube from central London, the borough's starting point was a volunteering rate half the national average. Unemployment, at 11 percent, was more than double the nation-wide figure at the time. Name your indicator—teenage pregnancy, life expectancy, children in poverty, crime, annual income, childhood obesity—and it's worse than usual in Barking and Dagenham.

Dagenham, the more distant of the two suburbs, is London's poorest address. Working class here mainly means low-paying service jobs. To a foreigner, the British term "high street"—the main shopping street in any town or neighbourhood—sounds rather grand. That is not the case with Dagenham's high street. There are no fashion chains or alluring window displays here, just basic services and take-away restaurants and a handful of family businesses like Stardust Linen and Harrolds Discount Jewellers. It's the kind of place where you might see a man pay for his groceries with coins dug out of a wallet that is otherwise empty of banknotes or credit cards; duck under an awning to take shelter from a typical London cloudburst and people clutch their bags and veer away from the sudden movement.

Yet in Every One Every Day's first eight months, more than two thousand people got involved in seventy projects across nearly forty locations, and the numbers have climbed steeply ever since. Suddenly, people in Dagenham were getting together to cook batches of take-home meals, spruce up public spaces, sell their own crafts at a pop-up shop, turn roads into temporary playgrounds, or learn to make films or write spoken-word poetry. Locals were offering free lessons in how to make cocktails, do yoga, braid hair, make soap. A "listening barber" provided half-price haircuts for children who practised reading aloud while they were in the chair. The foundation had planned a thousand-square-metre "makerspace"—a warehouse full of equipment ranging from a 3-D printer to a metalworking drill press to an industrial kitchen. They ended up opening one more than three times that size, next door to an evangelical mega-church.

But statistics do not capture Every One Every Day's impact. For that, you need people like Zoe Hallel, who seemed so confident when I met her that it was a shock to learn that just a few months earlier she had been living in near-total isolation. Hallel was taking the Every One Every Day concept seriously: she was in the shop every day. One of her new friends was Yetunde Dabiri, whose daughter, Daniella, is close in age to Hallel's daughter, Mia. The two mothers and their children live two minutes' walk from each other but had never met until Dabiri stopped by the shop. "I was welcomed, and then we had a cup of tea, chatted—and since then I've been attached to this place," Dabiri told me. To see Dabiri, Hallel, and their daughters walking down Church Elm Lane, a black woman and her white friend, a white girl and her black friend, may not be extraordinary in some places, but Dagenham is a community where white nationalists held a dozen local council seats only a decade ago. Their Nazi-like emblems can still be seen in the borough, often as brazenly as on the T-shirt of a passerby.

I asked Dagenham participants how they spent their free time before Every One Every Day. I expected to hear that they had gone shopping, gotten their nails done, hung out at pubs and coffee shops, took the kids to the amusement park, went daytripping or to the cinema. Instead, what I heard again and again was, "I did nothing."

"I've lived in this borough for fourteen years," said Dabiri, "and what I've done is gone to work and drive back home and stay indoors. Even weekends, when I don't work, I get in the house on Friday evening; next time I come out of my house is Sunday morning when I'm going to church. And it's just me and Daniella. She is always asking, 'Mommy, where are we going?' And I'm like, 'Nowhere.'"

It turned out that Barking and Dagenham actually had perfect conditions for participatory culture in at least one important way. If our primary role in consumer society is to work and spend, then quite a few people in Dagenham are excluded. Many do not have steady work, are retired with limited income, or are unemployed; many more don't earn enough on the job to have extra money to spend once the bills are paid. The borough is a stark reminder that when you don't have the means to consume in consumer culture, there isn't a lot else to do.

It isn't easy to leave behind one social role and adopt a new one. Before it launched Every One Every Day, the Participatory City Foundation sat down to review what it had learned from its years of groundwork. They found that the single biggest barrier to getting people to participate was the "novelty of participation culture." People didn't know what participation was, how it worked, how to do it. It wasn't "culturally normal."

We can stop shopping, but the consumer mindset lingers on. "It's pretty heavily embedded in us," said Nat Defriend, deputy chief executive of Every One Every Day. "I don't think it's our nature, but it's certainly in our culture. It's an important driver of the way that human societies and communities are set up, and certainly of economic relations."

Defriend is a former parole officer—he looks like a kindlier Jason Statham—who grew tired of the top-down, after-the-fact problem-solving methods of the criminal justice and social welfare systems. A participatory culture, he thought, would provide more people with a sense of community, purpose and opportunity from childhood onward, preventing social problems before they began. It wouldn't just *happen*, however. It had to be built.

Every One Every Day is supported by two pillars. The first is an infrastructure of participation: everything from the shops and warehouse to safety plans and communications. The second pillar is a team trained to help people adapt to their new roles as participants. The goal is what the organization calls a "full participatory ecology," in which every person in Barking and Dagenham will have twenty opportunities *each day* to participate in a free activity with their neighbours, without ever needing to travel more than fifteen minutes' walk from home.

"What's the grand term? A 'paradigm shift,'" Defriend said. Every One Every Day operates in the consumerist world—one of its goals is to generate a hundred new businesses in Barking and Dagenham within five years—but also outside of it. A lot of sharing goes on, but Defriend does not consider it a "sharing economy," because that term has been hijacked by for-profit businesses like ride-hailing and home rental. In Barking and Dagenham, sharing is often as simple and immediate as a group of women drawing lines on the floor of a workspace to mark out an area where they can take turns caring for each other's children. It's a clear example of how, in a place where consumer culture is somewhere between absent and dysfunctional, participants' quality of life could dramatically improve without money changing hands, without economic growth.

Jon Alexander argues that the same tools that have made participatory culture easier—social media, instant communications, user-friendly digital platforms—could also be used to involve us in larger decisions facing society. "Why is participation as a citizen allowed to be so deeply dull and so heavy and 'worthy'?" he said. An existing example of how this wider role as citizens might work is jury duty. In a jury trial, people from various walks of life are gathered, develop in-depth and often complicated knowledge of a situation, and then are asked to work together to decide how best to apply the law. The same could be done around issues like action on climate change, how schools educate children, what we want from our media, and how tax dollars are spent.

"What we are today is consumers who vote. What I think we could become is citizens who consume," said Alexander. "I think that changes the things that we do—it dials some of them up and it dials some of them down."

One of the most important things it dials up is what Zoe Hallel discovered: social connection. To spend time in the Dagenham shop is to fully appreciate how isolated many of us are and, in all likelihood, to recognize some of that loneliness in yourself. There are daily small incidents that seem ordinary but feel profoundly moving as you realize how uncommon they actually are. A woman in late middle age, an immigrant, described seeing a group of "hoodies" coming toward her; she had been about to cross the street in fear when she recognized the young men from a community potluck—they smiled and greeted her as they passed. Another woman, a senior, came into the shop to ask if the weekly Tea and Tech session would help her husband learn to use his smartphone. Yes, she was told, they could help with that. The woman was delighted—her husband had owned the phone for *two years* without knowing how to use it. A not-quite-teenage girl, dropping into the Dagenham shop for the first time, learned there was a chicken coop in the backyard. "You have *chickens?*" she said, as though she had just been told that Prince Harry was offering polo lessons in the garden. A minute later she was stroking the feathers on a hen's back for the first time in her life, a look of disbelief on her face.

"It's very hard work, but it's very rewarding work—*ridiculously* rewarding work," said Carley Stubbins, who moved to Barking and Dagenham when a personal emergency forced her to relocate at short notice. A friend who once lived in the area warned her that he had slept with a knife under his pillow. "I had hideous views and impressions of the place," Stubbins said.

She soon discovered Every One Every Day, attended session after session, and finally ended up working in the Dagenham shop. She was keeping a journal, she told me, filled with "magical things"—moments when she had witnessed strangers bonding or people discovering their own potential. On her Christmas holiday that year she went to Spain, where she had a revelation. "I'm in love with the borough," she said. "On the flight home I was champing at the bit to get back to my crummy little house in Dagenham."

Dagenham makes an unlikely utopia, but it's easy to start seeing it as exactly that. As they say about London weather, though, stick around awhile. Late on a spring afternoon, when a drenching rain had dragged enough clouds down from the sky that the sun could finally peek through, AJ Haastrup, a project designer with Every One Every Day, set out with a local schoolgirl to plant some trees on a neglected stretch of roadside. I joined them.

We had just arrived at the site with our apple and pear tree saplings, digging tools and wheelbarrow when a well-muscled man emerged from behind the wall of a row house development. "You're not planting those *here* are you?" he said. Haastrup replied that yes, that was the plan, and that he had permission from the borough council to do so. "You don't plant them next to fucking *houses!*" the man said.

The angry man saw nothing but problems. The roots of the trees would damage the buildings. In the spring, the apple and pear blossoms would fall and rot, and in the fall the leaves would do the same. He had seen enough in his life to know that some do-good fruit-picking project would never last, and in a year or two he'd be looking at a shaggy mess of unpruned trees while rotting fruit stunk up the block.

"That's the old rhetoric," Haastrup said to me as we retreated from the scene. There was more work to be done in the neighbourhood before it would accept the trees. "I am *so* used to it," Haastrup sighed, and seemed to be speaking from all his years in Barking and Dagenham—it might be important to note here that Haastrup is young and black, while the angry man was white and middle-aged.

From its inception, Every One Every Day was intended *not* to be utopian. It was created with an acceptance that any new role we fill as human beings will contain its own frustrations, daily hassles, unfairnesses and conflicts, but most of all, that we will have to learn how to do it. Like consumer culture, participatory culture is a permanent work-in-progress.

One afternoon in the Dagenham shop, a group went in a matter of moments from exchanging teasing jokes to a clash over whether one of those jokes had crossed the line into racism. A woman named Zenab stormed out of the shop. A few minutes later she returned, calm and composed.

Zenab (she does not go by a last name) emigrated as a child from Kenya to Britain, where she grew up in a low-income housing estate in Barking. She had recently moved to Dagenham, but had struggled to make new friends until, one day, she saw an Every One Every Day shop being set up. She had no idea what it could be. When it opened, her daughter sat in one of the beach chairs out front. "That was the start of it," Zenab said.

Zenab has a bold consumer identity: a typical outfit might be black boots, white jeans, and a white shag coat with matching hat. But her new role as a participant has plainly given her a larger life. She and her children are involved in everything.

"I think this should be permanent. This is something that is needed in the whole of London. Even maybe outside," she said. "The experience in the shops is so good that I'm even struggling to keep myself out of the shops. If I'm not in the Barking shop, I'm in Dagenham. If I'm not in Dagenham, I'm in Barking."

Sometimes there is conflict, she said, but that, too, is part of life in a community. And besides, on this afternoon, she had work to do. A few minutes later she was teaching a small group of people—different ethnicities, ages, classes, genders—how to make urojo, a Kenyan soup that she has made her own after learning the basics over the phone from her mother, who was living in Glasgow. Zenab wanted everyone to participate.

ZENAB'S UROJO

3 cassava roots (or sweet potatoes), cut into ½-inch slices
3 small red onions, diced
3 sweet bell peppers, diced
4 tomatoes, diced
1 Tbsp vegetable oil
2 Tbsp amchoor powder (or 3 to 4 unripe mangoes)
1 tsp turmeric
salt

Boil the cassava approximately 30 minutes or until soft. Sauté onions and peppers on medium heat in a large saucepan for about 5 minutes. Add the tomatoes (and mangoes, if using), salt the mixture to taste, and cook until the tomatoes break down and the mixture begins to stick to the pan. Add just enough water that the mixture no longer sticks, then simmer until it just begins to stick again. Drain the cassava and add it to the sauté. Add enough water to just cover the mixture. Taste for salt and add more if needed. Stir in the amchoor powder (available where global or Indian ingredients are sold) and turmeric. Cook until the soup thickens, then cook another 10 minutes at a bare simmer. The soup should have a thick, stew-like texture. Enjoy.

15.

We are still consuming way too much
(part one: inconspicuous consumption)

When you turn on the air conditioner, are you shopping?

It was this question, as I sank deeper into the day the world stops shopping, that led me to realize that my thought experiment might need to expand its reach. The blurry border between the consuming we actively do through our choices and the consuming we do as the background to everyday life—eating, doing the laundry, heating and cooling our homes, driving to and from work—had become impossible to ignore.

Some even say that, when it comes to climate change and other environmental crises, to stop shopping misses the point. Buying less stuff almost never turns up on lists of the best ways to green your lifestyle, which focus instead on energy efficiency, how much meat we eat, the size of our homes, and how much we drive or fly. This is partly a problem with how things are counted. The impacts of shopping are often underestimated, because they're distributed across categories: apparel, electronics, appliances and so on—sometimes even "miscellaneous." In a recent study of greenhouse gas emissions related to consumption in nearly a hundred major cities around the world, these categories, taken together, rival food and private transport. And while most of the natural resources being used in the world's rising economies go into infrastructure like roads and housing, in the richest, most technologically advanced societies, it really is the overall glut of consumer goods that has the highest impact—and this is the lifestyle that much of the rest of the globe aspires to.

At the same time, to focus only on the consumption that we think of as consumerism misses a lot of consuming. And as we will see in the peculiar case of the air conditioner, where one kind of consumption ends and the other begins is often only a question of time and the stories we tell ourselves about what normal life ought to look like.

The weather in New York on August 27, 1936, was good, which for Willis Carrier meant it was bad. He would have much preferred the kind of summer day when New Yorkers' minds fog and shirts stick to their backs in a sweltering fug. Instead, the temperature was 22 degrees Celsius, a perfect day to be outside. Carrier, meanwhile, was in WABC radio's Manhattan studio to explain that only "indoor weather" could raise humans to their highest potential.

"The air-conditioned life of the future will be something like this," he said. "The average businessman will rise, pleasantly refreshed, having slept in an air-conditioned room. He will travel in an air-conditioned train and toil in an air-conditioned office, store, or factory—and dine in an air-conditioned restaurant. In fact, the only time he will know anything about heat waves or arctic air blasts will be when he exposes himself to the natural discomforts of out-of-doors."

It's unlikely that Carrier, now remembered as the father of modern air conditioning, truly believed in the science-fiction future he was describing. At the time, only a tiny fraction of homes in the US, and virtually none anywhere else on Earth, featured air conditioners. More than a decade later, in 1948, his own company's researchers still estimated that the US market for residential air conditioning was only 312,000 well-to-do households, mainly in the sultry Gulf Coast states and summer-seared Wheat Belt. (On the day of Carrier's WABC interview, it was 41 degrees in Kansas City, then in the throes of Dust Bowl drought.) The company classified

Washington, DC—famously built on a malarial swamp, and considered a tropical outpost by early British diplomats—as a zone of only occasional climatic discomfort. Summertime cooling for homes in northern cities like New York or Chicago, Carrier's team figured, was the realm of "extreme luxury."

The challenge of getting air conditioners into American homes wasn't technological. By the time Carrier was dreaming of a fully air-conditioned future, machines were blasting cold air into plenty of factories, department stores, cinemas and government buildings. The real difficulty was that most people saw air conditioners as a costly solution to not much of a problem.

People were accustomed to dealing with heat and cold, and they didn't give up those customs easily. In hotter places, they lived in homes designed to provide cross breezes, with windows that opened—detailed guidelines for natural ventilation reach back to Marcus Vitruvius's *Ten Books on Architecture*, published during the Roman Empire. For shade they used covered verandas, overhanging eaves and canopies of trees, while their thick stone, brick or clay walls mimicked the cool of caves. In Japan, many houses had removable walls; in the tropics, they might have no walls at all. The Arab world developed the courtyard garden—with its shadows, plants and fountains—as the hot-climate answer to the hearth fire of colder places.

In the United States, which today is far and away the air-conditioning capital of the world, people used to take to porch swings and gazebos. Louisiana was famous for oversized ceiling fans; the desert Southwest had its "swamp coolers" that could chill the air by 20 degrees or more through evaporation; New Yorkers slept on their fire escapes or blew fans across trays of ice cubes.

There are limits. At around 35 degrees, air reaches the temperature of human blood, and even a breeze begins to feel like hot breath. At temperatures beyond this point, culture provided solutions. The Spanish world took—in many places still takes—its siesta, eating, drinking and resting through the day's worst heat. Elsewhere, people migrated, the way they still do in parts of Europe, to spend the height of summer in the mountains or at the beach; American husbands became "summer bachelors" as their wives and kids left for more pleasant climes while they stayed behind to work in sweltering cities. Japan confronted its hot, humid climate with mindfulness. Households would hang wind chimes outside and paintings of mountain streams inside, the first to draw attention to the slightest breeze, the second to help them think cool thoughts.

Most of all, people *enjoyed* the weather, despite its extremes. In 1971, Michel Cabanac, a French-Canadian scientist, published the results of a study that explored this mystery. Cabanac's test subjects each sat in a bath while they dipped one hand into a separate container of water. If the bathwater was uncomfortably cold, and they dipped their hand into hot water, even to the point of being slightly painful to the touch, they reported the sensation as pleasant. The same was true if the bathwater was uncomfortably hot and the container's water cold. If the bathwater and container water were both too hot, or both too cold, test subjects reported the opposite—it was unpleasant. If both the bath and the container water were comfortable, the experience was neither pleasant nor unpleasant. It was neutral.

As with a lot of the best science, the findings had a commonsensical quality: a hot bath or a cold shower, like a chocolate bar or a glass of water, can be either very pleasant or deeply unpleasant, depending on circumstances. But why, exactly? Cabanac concluded that the roots of pleasure are not to be found in comfort, but in discomfort, because pleasure was relief from discomfort. He called the effect *alliesthesia*, which translates roughly from Latin as "change sensation." Build up the fire in a chilly house in the morning, and the relief from the cold feels especially good. Beer never tastes better than when it's a respite from a hot and humid day.

When air conditioning hit the market, the shift to climate-controlled living was a choice between discomfort relieved by many small pleasures or comfort that was always the same. Not surprisingly, it met with widespread indifference and resistance. Since it couldn't be sold as a necessity, it first had to advance as a luxury. When arguably the first mechanical air-conditioning system was set up in New York in 1902, it didn't bring comfort to the women and immigrants working in stifling basement and loft manufactories (the word "sweatshop" has American roots); instead, it cooled the stock exchange. But even among the rich, sales were slow.

Air-con finally began to take off in the 1950s, but it was less a case of the market supplying consumer demand than of the market demanding a supply of consumers. Since the 1930s, utility companies that sold electricity had promoted the electrical gadgets of the day, from irons to toasters to refrigerators. Air conditioners joined the list. A series of heat waves helped, as did the fact that it was an era when human progress was equated with new technologies; studies found that whenever an air conditioner appeared in a neighbourhood, protruding from a window, others soon sprouted like mushrooms. AC was being conspicuously consumed—it had become a Veblen good.

By 1957, air conditioning began to be included in house prices, marking the point where it first made the shift from a gadget we shopped for to part of the background of everyday life. That same year, one of the co-founders of the Carrier Corporation, Logan Lewis, wrote a pamphlet for the company's staff to remind them that the success of air conditioning was hard won and had never been inevitable—the technology remained all but absent from European homes. Its advance, he warned, should not be considered irreversible.

Air conditioning, as we know it now, involves a lot of consumption—it uses more electricity than any other activity in US households, followed closely by heating—but has nothing to do with shopping. It has become a part of what is sometimes called invisible or inconspicuous consumption— consumption we carry out because that's the way things are done, the way the system is designed. We cannot achieve a lower-consuming society without confronting it.

"I'm not interested in the activity of shopping," said Elizabeth Shove, a sociologist at Lancaster University in northwest England, where the River Lune unfurls from the hills they call the Pennines. "I'm much more interested in infrastructures and institutions and technologies. They define the meaning of normality, which we then all follow."

For decades now, Shove has thought and written about ways that we end up consuming without feeling like that's what we're doing. Washing our clothes, owning a refrigerator, driving to the grocery store if you happen to live in the suburbs. "Normal" life turns out to be riddled with changing expectations, patterns and constructions that can greatly increase our personal consumption. Many of them, Shove found, relate to the "three Cs"—comfort, cleanliness and convenience. Home heating and cooling are examples of shifting standards in comfort. Clothes washing and drying machines, and their promoters, transformed the meaning of cleanliness. The appliances had the potential to help housewives do the laundry in far less time, freeing them to enjoy more leisure; instead, women ended up doing the wash more often. (People in the United Kingdom wash their clothes five times more frequently than they did a century ago, which is still less often than Americans wash theirs—and Americans wash bigger loads in bigger machines.) Through a recent shift in ideas of convenience, food delivery, coordinated by digital connectivity, has heaped courier trips to the home on top of drives to grocery stores and restaurants.

Think back on changes you've seen in your lifetime, and dozens of examples will likely come to mind—many of them beginning with a new consumer product or service on the market. Also from the realm of cleanliness was the twenty-first century's near-total takeover of bar soap by liquid soap dispensed from disposable plastic bottles. As the first winter of the coronavirus pandemic set in, a new standard in comfort seemed to be emerging: there was a rush on patio heaters and fire pits, most of them powered by fossil fuels. We increasingly heat and cool not only the indoors, but the outside world as well.

These new norms often become more consumptive over time. Consider the notion of "room temperature." A century ago, there was no such thing. Air-conditioning standards, including an ideal room temperature, were first developed around 1920 as engineers faced a public rebellion in favour of windows that opened to let in fresh air—a movement that gained so much traction that some schools began to keep their windows open down to near freezing, popping the kids into padded bags to keep them warm if necessary. For air-con promoters, finding an air temperature that most people found "neutral" or "acceptable" was a way to pit science against citizens' surprisingly strong attachment to natural weather in all its tempestuous variety. "When no town could deliver an ideal climate," writes historian Gail Cooper in her book *Air-Conditioning America*, "all towns became potential markets for air conditioning."

In European countries such as the UK and the Netherlands, room temperatures of 13 to 15 degrees were once considered normal. In the US, the standard for winter comfort rose from 18 degrees in 1923 to 24.6 degrees in 1986. The trend has been creeping upward for decades. Room temperature in the workplace normally resides around 22 degrees today. Above this, air conditioning kicks in; below it, on comes the heating.

"The idea of a normal comfort temperature was a spectacular achievement, and requires huge amounts of resources to maintain it," said Shove. The first "brownout"—a partial failure in the energy supply—due to a spike in air-conditioner use took place during an August hot spell in New York in 1948. With the power that a typical American household uses on air-con today, a typical European household could meet well over half of its total electricity needs. But air-conditioning use is increasing in Europe, too, and soaring in China, India and elsewhere around the world.

It is another bitter irony of our times: air conditioning warms the climate, and a warmer climate makes us use more air conditioning. As René Dubos, who popularized the phrase "think globally, act locally," once wrote, "The state of adaptedness to the world today may be incompatible with survival in the world of tomorrow."

As our adaptations become norms, the ability even to discuss changing them becomes difficult. During the 1973 oil crunch, Richard Nixon, who, let us recall again, was a Republican president, had the following to say about an air-conditioned America:

How many of you can remember when it was very unusual to have a home air conditioned? And yet this is very common in almost all parts of the nation. As a result, the average American will consume as much energy in the next seven days as most other people in the world will consume in an entire year. We have only 6 percent of the world's people in America, but we consume over 30 percent of all the energy in the world. Now our growing demands have bumped up against the limits of available supply.

Nixon then proposed a plan for reducing energy consumption that only a radical environmentalist would propose today: changing the country's consumer norms, overnight. It is unimaginable that a current US president would dare to make such a statement. Nixon wanted the number of airline flights cut back by more than 10 percent, the kind of measure that has since only been tolerated during crises like 9/11 and the pandemic. He called for lower speed limits, curbing "unnecessary" lighting, greater use of mass transit and carpooling. Most of all, he focused on temperature control. Winter was fast approaching, and Nixon asked Americans to lower their thermostats in order to achieve a national average of 20 degrees (68 degrees Fahrenheit). This would reduce the use of heating oil by 15 percent. "Incidentally," said Nixon, turning avuncular, "my doctor tells me that in a temperature of 66 to 68 degrees you're really more healthy than when it's 75 to 78—if that's any comfort."

When we change the way we consume, we change ourselves, sometimes to a surprising degree. A number of years ago, Wouter van Marken Lichtenbelt was invited to a meeting in Eindhoven, the Netherlands, with the kind of experts—architects, engineers, urban planners and so on—who design the artificial "environment" that most of us now live in. Van Marken Lichtenbelt, a researcher in nutrition and movement sciences at Maastricht University, was surprised to learn that these other professionals felt that an important part of their job was to provide an indoor climate that the average person would find comfortable. "I thought, What a strange idea," he told me.

Van Marken Lichtenbelt's usual professional circle is more specialized: people who research how the human body heats and cools itself and how that relates to metabolism and health. In that milieu, it has been common knowledge for some time that there is no such thing as an average comfort level. "One man's breeze is another man's draft," as the old saying goes. Women tend to prefer higher temperatures than men, and most elders like it warmer than working-age adults. A comfortable "room temperature" in tropical countries often leans as high as 30 degrees Celsius, far higher than in temperate climates. (Even the term "temperate" is debatable; temperate to whom?) Someone typing at a desk wants warmer surroundings than a cleaner who is constantly in motion, big people usually prefer cooler air than lean and little ones, and then there are the temperature-preference tendencies of those who are ill, pregnant, undergoing menopause, or simply wearing lighter or heavier clothing.

Van Marken Lichtenbelt spoke up. Instead of pursuing some fixed ideal of average comfort, why not allow the indoor climate to vary with the time of day and the seasons? It would, he declared, be better for our health. "And then I thought, Health? We never looked at health." He decided that's what he would do. Van Marken Lichtenbelt and his colleagues began to test the health effects of mild exposure to cold—and soon made a discovery about the human body.

The studies resembled those carried out by Cabanac when he was researching pleasure. In one experiment, for example, participants reclined on a temperature-controlled water mattress in an air-conditioned tent. Starting at a typical room temperature of 22.3 degrees, they then faced gradual cooling until they began to shiver. At that point, the temperature was raised just to the point where the shivering stopped, and the test subjects remained in a chilly-but-not-shivering state for two mildly uncomfortable hours.

The studies provided some of the first clear evidence that adult humans, like many mammals, have not only white fat but also brown fat—a tissue that uses nutrients and white fat as fuel to produce body heat. (We never have much brown fat.) When van Marken Lichtenbelt and his colleagues exposed people to mild cold, they found that a condition called "non-shivering thermogenesis" ensued: the test subjects' bodies went to work at staying warm.

Non-shivering thermogenesis doesn't need brutally cold temperatures to kick in; it churned along nicely at 14 to 16 degrees for lean, lightly clothed people, and was active even at 19 degrees. What's more, van Marken Lichtenbelt and others have found that most of us readily adapt to temperatures considerably cooler or warmer than is usual in air-conditioned and heated buildings and homes. Yet we spend more and more time in what scientists call a "thermoneutral" condition—we live at temperatures that feel comfortable.

"Comfort and health may be related but they are not synonyms," said van Marken Lichtenbelt. He and other researchers have concluded that the epidemic of "metabolic syndrome" in the rich world—a slowdown in metabolism that can result in weight gain, type 2 diabetes, weakening of the immune system, and other health problems—is driven not only by diet and physical activity, but also by temperature exposure. As a third pillar of metabolic health, we should put up with more heat and cold in our lives, at least enough to make our bodies have to work to keep us warm or cool.

That's easier said than done. Shove has shown that shifts in our ideas of what constitutes a normal way of life tend to be ratchet- or corkscrew-like processes that demand more and more energy and resources; once they move forward into our expectations, regulations and the built environment, they are difficult to reverse. It is especially difficult to change them through our actions as individuals. "It's not a personal issue," said Shove. "These standards are completely worldwide, and we're caught up in them whether we like it or not. And so it's not really a matter of individually how many jumpers you're wearing or anything like that. If you come into work the temperature is set somewhere else, so you overheat if you're dressed for cold conditions. I'm basically *anti* the whole attitude-behaviour-choice kind of thing."

Even in our private lives, it's hard to go by different norms. You might decide to let your own home's temperature drift with the natural climate. You will adapt. Your living quarters will not, however, be a pleasant place for any unadapted visitors who are used to watching TV while wearing a T-shirt, whatever the season. They will find your home suffocatingly hot in summer. In midwinter, they will find it unbearably cold, and may consider your offer of a sweater—or worse yet, a pair of thermal long underwear—strange and unhygienic.

Many energy and environmental policies aim to meet narrow standards of comfort more efficiently, which misses the point, said Shove. "It's the overly narrow view of comfort that's the big environmental issue, not the efficiency with which it's met." In recent decades, efforts to green consumption have dramatically boosted the energy efficiency of heating and cooling technologies, and the buildings they heat and cool. Consider, though, that we could have made similarly great strides—in an instant—simply by turning our thermostats up or down a couple of degrees and adapting.

"Technology is part of the discussion, but it might be clothing technology and not heating technology," said Shove. She points to Japan's national *kuuru bizu*, or "cool biz," program, which encourages workplaces to leave the air conditioning off until indoor temperatures climb to 28 degrees. At the same time, a public relations campaign has shifted social expectations around summer businesswear from suits and ties to light pants and even Hawaiian-style shirts. The program has reduced carbon emissions by millions of tonnes. (The tie industry initially lost millions in business, but it has begun to market summer-weight ties.)

"What people take to be normal is immensely malleable. Since there are no fixed measures of comfort, cleanliness, or convenience, it is perfectly possible that future concepts will be *less* environmentally demanding than those of today," Shove once wrote.

A world without shopping, it seems, is only a beginning. We don't buy the goods and services we unconsciously consume; we buy into them. But suppose we did stop "shopping" for air conditioning, reducing our usage by at least 50 percent in the richer countries. We'd save enormous amounts of energy. What else would happen?

"We're still working on how important it is, but we should really take it seriously," van Marken Lichtenbelt said. Based on what we now know about the health effects of temperature, the day the world stops air conditioning will lead to fewer cases of type 2 diabetes, fewer people catching colds and flus, and probably less obesity, too. Just as importantly, there might also be an end to what some have called "thermal boredom"—the tiresome sameness of the indoor environment. "We always think in terms of comfort," he said. "But why not think in terms of pleasure?"

Van Marken Lichtenbelt himself lives in an old farmhouse in Maastricht where he keeps the thermostat dialed down and has no air conditioning. In the winter, he and his family spend much of their time together in the kitchen, which, along with a traditional stove to huddle around, has modern heated flooring. Most of the year, however, van Marken Lichtenbelt prefers the cool morning air that pours in through the open window of his home office: it makes him feel fully alert and alive. He then enjoys the rising warmth of the day. "Sometimes it's a bit chilly," he admitted, "but then I think, well, it's good for me."

We are still consuming way too much
(part two: money)

T here is another, even more thorny challenge to actually achieving deconsumer culture, and it is that old troublemaker, money. How to think about it, what to do with it, what it will or won't be good for, who will have the most of it.

Let us start with that last point: how to be rich in a world that stops shopping. The slowdown in consumption is obviously dramatic in the homes of the well-to-do, who consume by far the most on Earth and would need to scale down their lifestyles much more than everyone else. As they would surely soon discover, however, richness is surprisingly adaptable.

Edith Wharton was America's great chronicler of New York's turn-of-the-twentieth-century rich; she was born Edith Newbold Jones, and some scholars believe it was her own relatives who inspired the phrase "keeping up with the Joneses." The lifestyle of elites in those times could certainly be lavish: in 1897, one family's gala—intended to imitate the extravagance of the same French royalty who, a century earlier, had their heads cut off by revolutionaries—was decorated with so many orchids, lilies and other flowers that New York's greenhouses could not supply enough and more had to be shipped in from elsewhere. In today's currency, such parties would be valued in the millions.

Yet it was also in many ways a modest standard of living compared to today's. In a scene from Wharton's novel *The Age of Innocence*, Miss Sophy Jackson, one of the grandes dames of New York high society, recalls what upper-class women had worn to that year's opening night at the opera. "The extravagance in dress—" she manages to say, before falling speechless. Finding strength to carry on, she explains her shock at recognizing only a single dress from the previous year's premiere. Everyone else was wearing something new. "In my youth," Miss Jackson says, "it was considered vulgar to dress in the newest fashions."

Wharton tells of another woman, renowned for her love of luxury, who placed an annual order for twelve dresses; when the *New York Times* interviewed "ultra-fast" fashion shoppers in Generation Z, they found even middle-class young women—the kind with after-school jobs or attending third-tier universities—who were buying eighty to two hundred fashion items a year. Then, of course, there is the plain fact that the very rich of the nineteenth-century Gilded Age lived largely without electricity and modern plumbing, drove horse-drawn carriages instead of cars, and travelled overseas, by ship, perhaps once a year. Their houses were often no bigger than those of ordinary suburbanites today.

In other words, the state of being rich is a strange one. The struggle of the poor to overcome basic material deprivation is not so different today than it was a century ago. Wealth, on the other hand, has nothing to do with any fixed condition of luxury or comfort, and everything to do with luxury and comfort in comparison to everybody else at a given time. Is there a place for the wealthy in a world that stops shopping? The history of richness says yes.

Archetypes of consumerism among the rich can be traced back at least as far as Renaissance Italy, when trade expanded in Europe and globally and people from almost all walks of life became shoppers. Isabella d'Este, a young noble in the city of Mantua in the sixteenth century, demanded "the latest novelties," described her lust for things as "insatiable" and the goods she longed for as "more dear to us the faster we can have them." Once, she asked that a family friend who was visiting France bring her the finest black fabric available to humanity. "If it is only as good as those which I see other people wear, I had rather be without it," she pouted.

Yet for the most part, personal indulgence was considered suspect in the Renaissance. Wealth was to be enjoyed quietly, behind closed doors, and had to be justified in the eyes of both God and the restless masses by spending money to build public works, fund armies, sponsor a feast or—especially—erect a church. "A richly decorated chapel," notes the historian Frank Trentmann, "was very different from, say, a modern Ferrari." In China's early consumer culture, connoisseurship was shown through ownership of antiques, or skill at writing poems or playing the zither, rather than through wealth alone. Anti-materialist, anti-consumerist and arguably even anti-capitalist values have been readily embraced by the well-to-do in the past, said Clifton Hood, a historian at Hobart and William Smith Colleges on Seneca Lake in New York who is one of the few scholars of America's rich. ("To study a topic is not necessarily to glorify it," he said firmly.) Through much of the eighteenth and nineteenth centuries, for example, the wealthy in the US were divided over the core value that we now associate with the rich: the open pursuit of making a lot of money. "In the United States, the upper class was always interested in differentiating itself from the middle class," Hood told me. "A lot of that involved thinking of themselves as being more genteel, more special, more refined, more art-loving, generally more knowledgeable and more sophisticated."

To be upper class in that era demanded not only wealth but conformity with demanding standards of speech, education, hygiene, etiquette, dress and conduct. Members of high society were expected to contribute, or at least appear to contribute, to the advancement of knowledge, public welfare or science. It was common among them to be proficient at painting, writing, needlework or some similar craft, and to be conversant in languages other than English. They defined themselves by these qualities to such an extent that, in censuses of the day, some described their occupation only as "gentleman."

"To be upper class meant not to be earning a living, or not to be *eager* about earning a living," said Hood. "It's 180 degrees removed from where we are now, where upper-middle-class people not only work longer and harder, but boast about it."

The early American blue bloods took inspiration from Europe's aristocrats and nobility. Already wealthy, they looked down on those who needed to make money, even as self-made merchants, traders and business people became richer than they were. Their anti-materialism certainly wasn't motivated by environmental responsibility or ideals of simple living—it was a form of snobbery used to maintain their status and privilege. Yet their way of life points to the different forms that richness can take.

When Thorstein Veblen mocked the late nineteenth-century rich, he aimed much of his ire at their privilege to enjoy leisure and leave unpleasant work to lower classes. While he argued that conspicuously wasteful spending was one way the rich make their status known, this didn't have to involve endlessly consuming more—the same purpose could be served by buying expensive goods that are no more useful than cheaper ones. We hear echoes of Veblen's derision today when sceptics of a buy-less-buy-better economy scorn that idea as "pay more, get less."

"The rich only select from the heap what is most precious and agreeable. They consume little more than the poor," wrote the economist Adam Smith a century earlier. While this was surely an exaggeration, it is certainly true that the standards of food, clothing, entertainment, sanitation and travel enjoyed by Britain's upper class would seem lacking to even the average person in a rich country today. Smith, too, had reservations about materialism. The pursuit of wealth for wealth's sake, he said, resulted in "fatigue of body" and "uneasiness of mind," and he appears to have admired the Greek philosopher Diogenes the Cynic, who, as the story goes, was once approached on the streets by Alexander the Great and offered anything he wanted. Diogenes replied that what he wanted was for Alexander to step aside, so that his shadow would stop blocking Diogenes's enjoyment of the sun.

American culture eventually came to celebrate even the crassest money-making and conspicuous consumption, and to elevate businesspeople and entrepreneurs to the status of heroes. Still, for much of the twentieth century, consumption by the rich was suppressed. With economic recessions, war and social unrest coming to the fore in the 1930s and 1940s, and again in the 1960s and 1970s, the rich pursued more modest and private lives, at times even selling off their mansions in the Hamptons and Newport to do so.

As one longtime New York realtor once said of conspicuous wealth, "It was considered un-American." The rich were also, as they likely would be in a lower-consuming economy, simply less rich. According to the Urban-Brookings Tax Policy Center, for the fifty years following the Great Depression, the tax rate on the highest income bracket averaged 80 percent, redistributing much of the richest Americans' wealth. Beginning in the 1980s with the advent of politicians like Ronald Reagan in the US and Margaret Thatcher in the UK, and with growth increasingly seen as the be-all and end-all of economics, far less was asked of the wealthy. The comparable tax figure for 2020 was 37 percent.

"If you went to prestigious country clubs thirty, forty, fifty years ago or more, you would not see the latest golf duds, you would see people wearing old Brooks Brothers or Paul Stuart khakis, because they don't really have anything to prove," said Hood. "They establish their bona fides in other ways." In a world that stops shopping, it isn't hard to imagine that richness would soon be reinvented, perhaps through a return to snobbish standards of taste and etiquette, the use of servants, freedom not to work, ostentatious philanthropy or simply political power. The rich could still be richer than the rest of us in comforts and possessions. It's not as though the rooms of their mega-mansions would somehow be emptied. They are already full, to bursting.

Yet from the moment the shopping stops, another problem with money arises: when it isn't spent, it accumulates. What to do with all that unspent money becomes a conundrum not only for the rich, but for the rest of us, too.

In 1998, the Japanese government launched a program called Top Runner with the fairly hum-drum goal of raising energy-efficiency standards for major home appliances. The campaign was a success: less than a decade later, the newest refrigerators, air conditioners and televisions were operating on up to 70 percent less energy. It appeared to be a win for "green consumption." Common sense suggested that, since the appliances were more efficient, electricity use in Japanese households must have gone down.

Not so. It went up and up.

Nozomu Inoue and Shigeru Matsumoto, two researchers at Aoyama Gakuin University in the heart of Tokyo, decided to investigate. As they began to examine the data, the mystery only deepened. Besides more energy-efficient appliances, there were two other major reasons that electricity use should have been declining: for one, Japan's population had been shrinking throughout the five-year period; for another, a sluggish economy had meant that the typical household was losing income. The reason people were using more electricity, Inoue and Matsumoto concluded, is that when Japanese consumers saw that the Top Runner appliances saved them money, they chose to spend that money on more and bigger appliances. People were adding a second or third television or air conditioner to their homes, and upgrading to the largest refrigerators on the market. "The effectiveness of green consumption," wrote Inoue and Matsumoto, "is lost."

The two researchers compared what they observed to the "Jevons paradox," named for William Stanley Jevons, an economist who studied why the use of coal in nineteenth-century Britain was rising at a rate that threatened to deplete the supply and cast the nation into a dark age. In 1865, Jevons drew a counterintuitive conclusion: as people found new ways to burn coal more efficiently, they were using more coal. Instead of using less coal to achieve the same results, a complicated interplay of product prices, consumer demand and higher profits was putting coal to more and more uses.

Jevons was an admirer of growth and technological progress, but as an economist, he called it as he saw it. He didn't see any solution to the problem, either, other than to suppose that our appetite for consumption either wouldn't prove to be bottomless, or would be ever more difficult to satisfy. "We cannot, indeed, always be doubling the length of our railways, the magnitude of our ships, and bridges, and factories," he wrote. "In every kind of enterprise we shall no doubt meet a natural limit of convenience." A century and a half later, global consumption of nearly everything continues to increase—including coal, though demand may be flattening at last.

Stopping shopping appears to finally offer an escape from the Jevons paradox. If, in a deconsuming world, we invent a television that is three times more energy efficient, then we will not use the money we save to shop for extra televisions, each one bigger than the less efficient one we used to have. Instead, the gain in efficiency actually pays off: we end up with the same number of TVs, but use up less energy watching them.

Except that, said David Font Vivanco, an environmental scientist based in Barcelona, money remains a trickster. Font Vivanco studies "rebound effects," which are the often unforeseen consequences that arise from changes in technology and social behavior. The Jevons paradox and Japan's Top Runner program involved rebound effects linked to advances in energy efficiency. But buying less stuff, period, has rebound effects of its own.

"The way I like to think about it is rather simple," Font Vivanco told me. "If you have some economic savings, then you're going to spend them. You have a certain amount of money and it will go somewhere that will cause an impact." Rebound researchers call this problem "respending." If you stop shopping, you save money. If you then spend that same amount of money on things that you may not think of as consumerism, such as video-streaming services or outdoor adventures or physiotherapy or air conditioning—then the environmental impact of your lifestyle can easily stay the same or even worsen.

Here is a rule of thumb: if you are spending more money, then you are probably increasing the environmental impact of your lifestyle, and if you are spending less money, then you are probably decreasing it. Wherever it flows, money makes its mark. In the United States, every dollar spent translates, on average, into about 0.25 kilograms of greenhouse gas emissions; spend a hundred dollars, and your contribution to the economy will produce about twenty-five kilograms of carbon pollution. But in another of money's strange twists, although Americans are the world's biggest consumers per capita, an average dollar spent in a poorer country has *worse* consequences for the climate. For the planet as a whole, every hundred dollars spent produces forty kilograms of climate pollution—60 percent more than the same money spent in the United States. That's because, in many places, people put most of their money toward basic, energy-intensive goods like food, gasoline and electricity, while in the US they might spend it on a savings bond or an app or a brand-name sweater. Wealthier countries also tend to produce goods using cleaner technologies. Ironically, it would be "greener" for a poor person in India to buy an iPhone than to spend the same amount of money on the food and electricity they actually need.

Suppose, then, that you respend your money on investments. Unfortunately, the companies you invest in produce goods and services for the consumer economy. If you save your money in the bank, the only difference is that the bank invests it for you. (Savings and investment are two more key ways in which the affluent are more likely to increase their environmental impact.) In either case, you are simply postponing your consumption until a later date. Savers, for example, are often planning a big-ticket purchase, such as a trip overseas. "If you're travelling around taking airplanes, that's not going to work, right?" said Font Vivanco. "If you enrol in some art classes, then maybe, yes." Then again, you might go to your art classes by car, or rent a studio to practise your craft in, or feel tempted to fly to Arles, France, on a guided tour to paint the same scenes that Van Gogh painted. "This idea that services are better than products, it doesn't make much sense. Services have a footprint," said Font Vivanco. The services we use, the experiences we have, contribute to the dollar-by-dollar impact of our consumption.

Rebounds occur in three main ways. There are direct rebounds, in which, say, the invention of more efficient TVs leads to the sale of additional televisions. There are indirect effects, in which people spend the savings from their more efficient televisions on other goods and services. Finally, there are mysterious and poorly understood "economy-wide" or "transformational effects." An example might be the way that improving the efficiency of televisions makes them cheaper, which makes people buy more of them, which changes the norm from one in which families watch a single TV together to one in which everyone watches their own show on their own TV, which encourages the creation of more narrowly targeted television programming and advertising, by which point the consumer economy as a whole is growing in about a dozen different directions. Overall, this has been the pattern of recent history at a global scale: an environmental impact that is far greater than the sum of its cleaner, greener parts. When rebound effects take us to a worse place than where we began, it's called "backfire." We have created a backfire economy, a backfire culture.

Rebound effects are weird all the way down. According to Elisabeth Dütschke, who studies how the public responds to technological change in energy systems, some rebounds can be driven by "moral licensing," or our tendency to use good behaviour to justify bad behaviour. Picture a person who adopts a vegan diet (because meat production results in a lot of carbon pollution), then feels justified taking more trips by airplane. A study in Germany found that the adoption of fuel-efficient cars resulted in people driving more; fuel-efficiency may also give people a sense of permission to buy larger, more powerful or more luxurious cars, Dütschke said. Similarly, Norwegians who bought electric cars then became more likely to use their car to run an errand than were drivers of gas-powered vehicles. In fact, as electric car ownership has increased, so have reports of a wide range of wasteful uses, from owners preheating them in the winter to leaving their air conditioners running to keep their dogs comfortable while they go shopping. Because of rebounds, Dütschke said, even people who make deliberate efforts to "go green" typically make less of a difference than they imagine, no difference at all, or even worsen their impact on the environment.

While research into the human behaviours that cause rebounds is still nascent, it appears that a fraction of the population—probably a small fraction—really does reap the full benefits of switching to greener lifestyles and technologies. When this group buys a more fuel-efficient vehicle, for example, they also change their behaviour and drive the new car less often. This has been called "sufficiency behaviour"—arrival at a sense of *enoughness*. Sometimes, sufficiency leads to "spillover," which is the opposite of backfire. In a spillover, people who choose to go green in one facet of their lives end up making further green choices. They drive less, then start eating vegetarian meals, too. They stop shopping, and then are inspired to also turn down the thermostat in winter and wash their clothes less often. What's more, they generally do not feel that these actions sacrifice their quality of life. "The sufficiency idea is that you voluntarily cut back and are still happy," Dütschke said. No one yet knows what makes some people embrace sufficiency when so many others do not.

A study led by sufficiency researcher Maren Ingrid Kropfeld looked at four kinds of people who resist mainstream consumer habits to see how effective they were at reducing their environmental impact. The groups were environmentally conscious consumers, who try to live green lifestyles; frugals, who take pleasure in saving money; tightwads, who hate spending money; and voluntary simplifiers, who actively choose to consume less. The simplifiers had far and away the most success at reducing their impact. In fact, they were nearly twice as effective as the second-place group, the tightwads. Frugals didn't lessen their impact at all, and neither did green consumers—reflecting, at a personal scale, the broader failure of green consumption to make a difference across recent decades. The authors of the study concluded that perhaps people who live with less, rather than those who live green, should be our role models for living more lightly on the earth.

Yet even the simplest-seeming solutions to consumerism, such as buying fewer, better things, involve rebounds. If you pay a higher price for a well-made pair of shoes instead of a poorly made pair, you might guess that this counteracts the rebound effect: by using up more money to get the same consumer good, you're left with less money to spend on other consumables. But the money you spend on your quality new shoes is redistributed, paying the wages of workers, salaries of managers, fees of suppliers and so on. It gets respent. You could take this year's clothes budget, use it to pay a tutor to teach you a new language, and thereby reduce your ecological footprint—but then it depends, doesn't it, on how your tutor spends that income.

The list of ways to spend money without rebounding is short. You could start by purchasing products that will reduce more harmful forms of consumption, such as camping gear to replace the flights you will no longer take on your holidays. You could eliminate your debts, perhaps giving you that feeling of financial security that psychologists have shown tends to lower people's materialism. You could donate to causes that directly reduce consumption—such as libraries—or protect land and water from resource exploitation. You might, as an act of fairness, give money to agencies that help people meet their basic needs, directly offsetting their much-needed rise in consumption with a decrease in your own.

You might demand a higher tax rate from your government so that it could accomplish similar goals.

Or you can just avoid accumulating cash, most obviously by working less. "If you reduce your income, you can make sure you reduce your consumption," Dütschke said. She once did exactly that, cutting back her paid hours as a rebound-effects researcher. She found she continued to work the same number of hours ("I always find it all so interesting"), but she did have less to spend. Then she realized that her employer was probably using the money it saved on her salary to pay somebody else.

At the end of the eighteenth century, Thomas Malthus famously recognized the threat that a rising population posed to limited food supplies, and argued that the solution to this problem was the perpetual growth of human productivity. Ever since, the central idea of economics has been that we live in a world of scarce resources. More recently, though, some thinkers have argued that our greatest challenges come not from a lack of resources but from their abundance—and they always have.

The French philosopher Georges Bataille was among the first to describe the problem of surplus wealth, in 1949. "It is not necessity but its contrary, 'luxury,' that presents living matter and mankind with their fundamental problems," he wrote. Up to a point, a society can absorb wealth by improving its standard of living. Ultimately, however, it begins to accumulate in troublesome places. The horrific violence of the First World War and Second World War, Bataille argued, resulted from nations growing wealthy enough to engage in dangerous arms races. He called the excess wealth that made it possible "the accursed share."

"It must be spent, willingly or not, gloriously or catastrophically," said Bataille. Many older cultures understood this—"if only in the darkest region of consciousness"—and deliberately destroyed wealth from time to time. They squandered it in festivals and sacrificed it to gods. Fortunes were buried with the dead, as in ancient Egypt, or poured into glorious public buildings and monuments, as in Renaissance Italy; even now, some Maya villages in Central America have a "levelling mechanism" by which anyone who begins to gather for themselves a lot of land or money is awarded, by their community, the honour of sponsoring the year's great feasts, at the end of which they are highly esteemed—and no longer rich. Such practices are so widespread in space and time that anthropologists have argued that the deliberate destruction of wealth is one key way in which the "human ecosystem" differs from the natural one.

Our own times are not an exception to the rule. In the early twentieth century, the West debated what to do with the new power of industry to produce extraordinary wealth—more goods than we could possibly use. The answer we found was to make products that destroy themselves: planned obsolescence. Consumerism itself can be compared to an endless festival that quickly and constantly turns abundance into waste. We have, in fact, turned the destruction of affluence into our economic engine, with the problematic result that doing so creates ever more affluence. We see surplus wealth pooling in historic quantities in the hands of a few; we see this imbalance driving up the cost of living worldwide; we see it in overheated and speculation-driven investment and real-estate markets. When we fail to destroy wealth in a planned and orderly manner, we tend to do so involuntarily. The word we use for this is telling: a "correction" in the economy. The world's millionaires and billionaires alone lost $2.6 trillion—written in full to better feel its magnitude, that's 2,600,000,000,000 dollars—in the Great Recession, with repercussions for people in all walks of life. Then growth could begin again. As Bataille said, "It is necessary to dissipate a substantial portion of energy produced, sending it up in smoke."

The choice of words is an interesting one. When David Font Vivanco takes his thinking on rebounds out to the furthest limit, he finds just one sure way to deal with all the wealth that accumulates when we stop shopping.

"You just burn the money," he said. "That's the most straightforward solution—just have the basic stuff and forget about luxuries. Burn the money."

IV

TRANSFORMATION

We finally, actually, save the whales

The whales have been waiting a long time to be saved. It was first supposed to have happened after 1859, when Edwin Drake, a prospector working in Titusville, Pennsylvania, bored through twenty-one metres of dirt and bedrock and launched the era of underground oil drilling, also known as the modern industrial age. Two years later, a cartoon in *Vanity Fair* magazine showed gaily-dressed sperm whales popping champagne corks and dancing under a banner reading "Oils Well That Ends Well." The gist was that petroleum products would replace all the consumer uses that whale oil was being put to (making soap, lubricating the gears of industrial machinery, lighting the world with lamps and candles). The bloody business of whaling would come to an end.

Instead, we were soon using petroleum to kill more whales than ever. The new fossil fuel powered the construction of whaling fleets, made it possible to drive the boats farther and faster, and allowed huge factory ships to process whale oil and freeze whale meat without needing to return to shore. Oil and gas were even used to run compressors that could inflate like balloons those whales that otherwise sank after death, expanding the variety of species that could be hunted. For several decades, despite the steady invention of products that really did replace whale oil with petroleum, whalers slaughtered an average of a hundred whales a day. Once we've started to consume a thing, we rarely choose to deconsume it.

Then the whales were saved again. In 1986, most of the world's whaling nations agreed to bring large-scale industrial whaling to an end. By that point, most species were considered "commercially extinct," or so few in number that it cost more to find and kill them than they would earn when brought to market. Some, such as the blue whale, the world's largest living animal, were almost completely wiped out. But at last, the population of whales began to rise rather than fall.

Before long, though, there were worrying signs that we might be killing the great leviathans in an entirely new way. As one whale researcher put it, "We're not actually going out and sticking them with a piece of steel anymore. We're just ruining their lives."

Striking evidence of this fresh assault emerged when the 9/11 attacks led to a short, unexpected experiment in what happens to the wild world when consumer culture comes to a grinding halt—a prelude to what we witnessed across months during the pandemic. Overnight, the skies emptied of airplanes. Marine traffic, too, nearly vanished. One boat that remained on the water was crewed by a group of marine biologists. They were in the Bay of Fundy, on the east coast of Canada just north of the US border, and they were collecting the feces of North Atlantic right whales in order to test them for stress hormones.

There are only about 450 North Atlantic right whales left on Earth. Some of us tend to imagine that critically endangered species are evolution's snowflakes: unique expressions of life's diversity, but not tough enough to handle a changing world. It's hard to make this case with right whales. They evolved at least four million years ago, twice as deep in time as our own early ancestors. An adult may weigh more than seventy tonnes, with about the same dimensions as the kind of recreational vehicle that is equipped with two washrooms and a walk-in closet. They can live a hundred years and maybe many more—few have the opportunity to find out.

Right whales take their name from having been the "right" whale to hunt, because of the high value of their blubber and baleen, and they had already been driven to rarity by the time of the American Revolution. Yet they do not die easily. The intentional killing of right whales was banned in 1935, but in March that year, it took a group of fishermen—apparently not up to speed on international law—six hours, seven hand-thrown harpoons, and 150 rifle rounds to kill a ten-metre calf off Fort Lauderdale, Florida. If right whales are threatened with extinction, it's not due to a lack of grit. It's because their home, which spans three thousand kilometres of coastline from southern Canada to northern Florida, is next door to one of the richest and busiest consumer societies on Earth. More than a decade ago, right whales had already been nicknamed "the urban whale."

The researchers that were studying right whales in the days after 9/11 were from the New England Aquarium, in Boston. The aquarium keeps a digital map of North America's eastern seaboard, showing shipping traffic, fishing traffic, undersea pipelines and cables, and so on, and it is as crowded with lines as a map of Manhattan. There are signs that whales may feel at least as harried by busyness as we do: in Iceland, for example, they appear to spend more time in waters where whaling ships occasionally show up to hunt and kill them than they do in the near-shore protected zone where they're constantly followed by whale-watching boats. North Atlantic right whales are exposed to all the effluvia of civilization—their blood is polluted with an alphabet soup of chemicals (DDT, PCBs, PAHs and so on), oil and gas, flame retardants, pharmaceuticals, pesticides. Their food supply—mainly flea-like plankton called copepods—has become unpredictable as the climate changes due to the buzz of human activity. Whales sleep differently than we do (they put one hemisphere of their brain to sleep at a time), and yet we can bet that a noisy, busy, polluted ocean is a more challenging place to sleep than the quiet ocean that used to be, the ocean that some whales are old enough to remember.

Scientists describe these impacts as "sublethal," meaning that none of them is likely to cause death on its own. Yet Rosalind Rolland, a senior scientist at New England Aquarium, points to a stark contrast between North Atlantic right whales and southern right whales, a closely related species that lives at the very fringe of global consumer culture. Rolland once travelled to the Auckland Islands, five hundred kilometres from New Zealand in the direction of Antarctica, to see these southern cousins.

"They were fat, they were happy, they had no skin lesions, they were curious. It was dealing with a completely different animal," she said.

The worst of these sublethal effects is noise. In 1992, marine acoustics scientist Chris Clark, now retired as a graduate professor of Cornell University, was selected as the US Navy's marine mammal scientist. Using the navy's underwater listening posts, he was able to tune in to singing fin whales—second only to the blue whale in size—across a patch of sea larger than Oregon. In a data visualization he later created, the singing whales wink on and off, hot spots that appear, spread their sonic glow, and fade. Then enormous flares ripple across the entire space. That's the acoustic imprint of a seismic air gun, used to probe for oil and gas deposits under the sea floor. "This was an epiphany," Clark said. He had witnessed the way that human-made sounds could overwhelm, at enormous scales, whales' ability to hear and be heard in the ocean.

Clark calls day-to-day life for North Atlantic right whales "acoustic hell." In waters buzzing with human activity, the chance of two whales hearing each other—to find a mate, to keep track of a calf, to announce the discovery of food, or for the simple pleasure of another's company—is about one-tenth of what it was a century ago. Boat noise is sometimes so loud and constant that the whales give up and go silent, something they are only otherwise known to do during powerful storms. "Humans can't comprehend the magnitude of the insult that we pour into the ocean," Clark told me. The main source of all that noise is the propellers and engines of commercial shipping vessels, the ones that bring us all that stuff. Besieged by sublethal impacts, the health of North Atlantic right whales has visibly worsened. They are thinner than they were three decades ago, more heavily infested with whale lice, and more marked by lesions and scars; the females give birth to fewer calves. The animals' welfare may now be so poor, their suffering so serious, that sublethal impacts have turned lethal.

Ships can kill these whales outright, too: a leading cause of death for the animals is "ship strike," or being run over by boats. Every time we hit the Buy Now button for a product shipped from overseas, the risk posed to whales increases. Marine traffic on North America's east coast is some of the heaviest on Earth, supplying the world's greatest shoppers. But shipping in general is so heavy today that some have begun to call shipping routes "marine roads." The roads have their own air pollution. Although ships are one of the most energy-efficient ways we can transport the world's merchandise, they also move 80 percent of it, meaning there are now so many cargo vessels, getting bigger all the time, that they account for 2.5 percent of global greenhouse gas emissions. Ships currently carry well over ten billion tonnes in material goods each year—more than a tonne for every one of us, although, as always, some get a lot more than others.

The North Atlantic right whale and southern resident killer whale, which is found in the Pacific border waters between Canada and the United States, are two populations threatened with near-term extinction simply by the growing intensity of the consumer economy; without a change in that intensity, other species will surely be added to the list. On the day the world stops shopping, we might finally, truly, save the whales.

All of which brings us back to those New England Aquarium researchers out on the Bay of Fundy in the days after 9/11. When the data came back on how much stress hormone was in the whales' feces that they had collected during that eerily quiet time, they found anxiety levels lower by far than under "normal" conditions. In the absence of the usual shipping traffic, the fishing boats, the pleasure craft, the power yachts, all the hubbub of modern maritime life, the whales were apparently enjoying a sea of calm. Even the scientists were struck by how clearly they could hear whale calls through their equipment. It was as though they'd been standing beside a freeway that had fallen silent, and could suddenly hear the birds singing. It was the sound of whales in a world of *less*.

The end of shopping is a new dawn for wild things. Recessions and depressions—whatever their cause, whether market speculators or a pandemic virus—have always been good for nonhuman life, slowing the creep of bulldozers, the pollution of rivers, the mines that turn mountains into holes in the ground. There is more darkness for nightingales and dung beetles; more silence for whales to sing in; far less risk that another gemstone strip mine will shrink a little further the range of rare species like the Malagasy rainbow frog, more colourful than any jewel and found in a few Madagascar canyons and nowhere else on Earth.

Alan Friedlander is another person who didn't have to wait for the pandemic to witness how nature changes when throngs of people disappear. He could do so once a week in Hanauma Bay, a small protected area on the outskirts of Honolulu, Hawaii. The clamshell cove, actually a flooded volcanic crater, is one of the most heavily visited coral reefs on the planet. A million people a year—about three thousand a day—come to snorkel and swim and play in the waters here, but on Tuesdays it closes to the public. That's when scientists like Friedlander, a marine biologist at the University of Hawai'i, do research there.

"It's like a different place," said Friedlander. Sea turtles, usually spooked out to deeper water, graze algae near the shore. Endangered Hawaiian monk seals, with their shy-smiling faces, might make an appearance or even haul up on the beach. "This big school of bonefish often shows up in ankle-deep water. I mean, that would be their preferred habitat if there were no people around," said Friedlander. Bonefish are long, slender ghosts in the shallows, drawing traceries on the surface with their tails. "I always have the question, where are they the other six days a week?"

When the coronavirus crisis struck, tourism to Hawaii slowed to a trickle. Suddenly, every day, everywhere, was a lot more like a Tuesday at Hanauma Bay. At the time, Friedlander was carrying out research in two other marine protected areas: Molokini, an almost completely submerged volcanic crater in the wind-ripped channel between the islands of Maui and the Big Island; and Pupukea, a rugged coastline on the north shore of Oahu where the force of the waves has been known to drag large boulders off the shore and into the deeps. Both, in ordinary times, are very human places.

Molokini is a small marine conservation area, just over thirty hectares in size, or about one-tenth the size of Central Park in Manhattan. On any typical morning, two dozen commercial tour boats disgorge a thousand snorkelling visitors into the water to explore a reef sheltered by a crescent of crater's edge that stands above the surface. "You can basically jump from boat to boat and not hit the water out there on a busy day," Friedlander told me. "It's effectively a semi-enclosed, large swimming pool." Pupukea, meanwhile, is just across the Kamehameha Highway from a shopping centre, includes two major swimming and diving areas, and has been so hard hit by fishing that many locals consider it "fished out." Finding a parking spot is a perennial problem.

When tour operators and even boat-launching ramps were shut down in the pandemic, Friedlander witnessed a dramatic change at Molokini. About a thousand barred jacks moved onto the reef. To see the huge school—each silver-blue fish the size of a serving platter—would be a snorkeller's delight, but Friedlander had never recorded them in the preserve during more crowded times. He soon discovered that a similar thing was happening at Pupukea: a gigantic school of fish had shown up, this time Hawaiian flagtails, silvery and perch-like, with tails that look like they've been dipped in ashes. "There's a big ball of them right next to shore," said Friedlander, "which is kind of rare—because they're delicious."

We may not think of ourselves as being at war with nature, but one sign that we are is that when the human world retreats, the natural world advances. The change happens quickest in the oceans, because so many living things there move so freely: they sense when we are gone and swim in to fill the space. During the pandemic, the first signs of rewilding often appeared in suddenly empty waters: fish and jellyfish in the calm, clear canals of Venice; river dolphins alongside the ghats—huge riverside stairways for bathers—of Kolkata, India, for the first time in three decades; crocodiles surfing the waves at a popular beach in Mexico. But the same principles, Friedlander said, apply to the land as well. Release the steady pressure of human activity, and the wild beasts return, grow in number, express their most natural behaviours—including the urge to explore. With Chicago under a shelter-in-place order, a coyote made an early morning tour through an empty downtown, running past shops for Cartier, Gucci and Louis Vuitton. In northern India, elephants retook an ancient travel corridor they had abandoned years earlier as humans encroached; one stopped to climb the stairs of a small temple.

We don't need to disappear entirely to provide relief to the natural world. In Molokini, for example, Friedlander and his colleagues found a "magic number" of tour boats that seemed to prevent snorkelling tourists from displacing the big schools of fish. That number was twelve boats—about half the usual activity.

"We think we understand ecosystems and know how to effectively manage them, but we really don't," Friedlander said. "Nature does a much better job of managing itself than we ever could. You just have let it do so. You know, give it enough space to breathe."

So much of what we do to other species through our consumption is unintentional. A study of land clearing in Australia examined what happens, for example, when we replace wild habitat with another auto mall or vacation housing complex (the rise of second-home ownership has been one of the fastest-growing consumer trends of the twenty-first century), or those sprawling, nameless data centres and shipping warehouses that are springing up everywhere in the age of online shopping. Maybe you imagined that the animals simply packed their bags and made a fresh start somewhere new. I regret to inform you this is not the case. "The clear scientific consensus is that most, and in some cases all, of the individuals present at a site will die as a consequence of that vegetation being removed, either immediately or in a period of days to months afterwards," the researchers write.

They lay out the suffering in detail that, again, I am sorry to bring to your attention: animals are crushed, impaled or lacerated. Some are buried alive. They endure internal bleeding, broken bones, spinal damage, eye injuries, head injuries. Limbs are lost, and "degloving"—partial skinning, alive—occurs. Those that flee their homes (many are surprisingly reluctant to do so) are often run over on nearby roads, entangled in fences, die of exposure, or make easy prey for predators. You don't really want to hear this, but tree-dwelling species may cower in their holes up to the moment they pass through the sawmill or the wood-chipping machine. You don't really want to hear that koalas may starve when land is cleared—"an issue that has surprisingly not generated much discussion," said the study's authors. By their estimate, fifty million mammals, birds and reptiles ultimately die each year due to land-clearing in two Australian states alone.

We consume wildlife. Even the species we eat are often bound up more in questions of our identities and status than our bodily hunger. A case in point: the manumea, an unusual bird found only in the South Pacific island nation of Samoa.

In Samoa's jungles, dozens of pyramid-like structures stand overgrown by vines and trees. The mysterious edifices are not small: they are often wider than a basketball court and at least as tall as a one-storey building, with rounded lobes stemming off a central platform. Known as "star mounds," they were used, at least at times, to hunt pigeons. One of these was the manumea, a big, dark-blue-green and chestnut bird with bizarre, tooth-like serrations on its sunset-coloured beak. Since it is one of the closest living relatives to the extinct dodo, the manumea is sometimes referred to as the "little dodo."

When the ancestors of today's Samoans arrived by boat three thousand years ago, the islands were home only to creatures that could swim, fly or drift to their shores. Pigeons, including the manumea, were some of the largest and tastiest wildlife available. Under Samoa's strongly hierarchical social system, hunting them became a chiefly sport, in the same way that deer hunting in England was once the preserve of British aristocrats. When a village hosted a pigeon hunt, invited Samoan chiefs, or *matai*, are thought to have been assigned to the lobes on the star mound, and would then compete to capture the most wild pigeons, using long-handled nets. It was a ritual, a spectator sport, a reason for communities to gather and feast. The pigeon hunts disappeared rapidly under the influence of European missionaries in the early nineteenth century, yet the practice didn't end, so much as it was reinvented.

In 2014, Samoa's statistics bureau wrapped up a survey of what Samoans were eating and drinking. Rebecca Stirnemann, a biologist from New Zealand, saw an opportunity to sort out who, exactly, was eating pigeons. By that point, many people thought that pigeon, no longer restricted to the chiefs, had become mainly a food for poorer people, carrying out what is known as subsistence hunting—hunting to put dinner on the table.

Stirnemann wanted to be sure, because by then the manumea had joined the unfortunate ranks of the world's rarest birds. Only about two hundred, and possibly far fewer than that, remain.

Stirnemann found that Samoans were collectively eating more pigeon than anyone had anticipated. But the poor weren't eating the most: nearly 45 percent had been eaten in the homes of the nation's richest 10 percent of people. Expand that to the wealthiest 40 percent of households, and the share of pigeons being eaten climbed to a stunning 80 percent. "We were all surprised by the results," said Stirnemann. "People didn't realize they were having such a big impact on the population of pigeons, let alone manumea. And they also didn't realize who it was who was predominantly eating them."

The status and cultural meaning attached to consuming pigeon in Samoa had never gone away. While no one was deliberately hunting manumea any-more, they were still being killed accidentally by hunters gunning for pigeons, many of which are sold or given as gifts of respect to people such as chiefs, politicians and church leaders. How often a Samoan eats pigeon seemed to correlate with their wealth, power and status—even though the well-to-do of Samoa are a far cry from the global millionaire and billionaire elite. "It's not like wealthy-with-swimming-pools wealthy. It would just be your richer people in the average population," Stirnemann said.

This was not the way consumer culture was supposed to progress. For decades, experts had predicted that people raised out of poverty would stop hunting wild animals for food and medicine and instead do their shopping at the grocery store and pharmacy, the way people do in wealth-ier countries. Economic development, the idea went, would save the world's wildlife. Instead, a growing body of research shows that, as the need to eat wild creatures as food abates, those animals are transformed into consumer commodities.

Research from the Brazilian Amazon showed that as people there left behind rural life for the cities, *more* wildlife was being eaten, not less. Poorer households were still hunting wild animals to feed themselves, but also selling them to richer people. When it came to threatened and "prestige" species—including one kind of monkey, a large rodent called the lowland paca, and a fish that can weigh as much as a German shepherd—the wealthy were the greatest consumers. In Peru's rainforest cities, some of the heaviest buyers of wild meat proved to be visiting military personnel, industry executives and tourists. In Vietnam, rhinoceros horn is still used as medicine, but the illness might best be described as "affluenza": almost 80 percent of users were treating hangovers or other symptoms of modern excess, in some cases mixing the powdered horn directly into wine to make a cocktail described in news articles as "the alcoholic drink of million-aires." By the time the coronavirus first passed to humans in China, most likely through an unknown wild animal, wild meat had become mainly a delicacy and other animal products, like fur and traditional medicine, were luxuries; the trade had sharply increased, rather than decreased, with the nation's rising wealth.

CITES, the treaty body that oversees the Convention on International Trade in Endangered Species of Wild Fauna and Flora, picked up on the trend. "We are seeing a disturbing shift in demand for some species from health to wealth," the organization announced in 2014. Threatened species were being eaten as a flash of conspicuous consumption by businessmen bonding on drunken sprees, by wealthy families honouring visitors, by urbanites hoping to reconnect with their rural roots.

Much of the reason that people in the West assumed that, as poorer countries developed, fewer wild animals would be eaten, is because they believe that is what happened in their own cultures. But in the late nineteenth and early twentieth centuries, commercial "market hunters" were still supply-ing mainly upper-class Americans with wild delicacies like diamondback terrapin and canvasback duck even as—especially as—those species' popu-lations were decimated. Throughout the Western nations, the trade only slowed with the advent of strictly enforced conservation laws. Even then, consumption of the wild didn't disappear. The US and UK are major importers of wildlife products; a study of eBay found that the United States is the end destination for two-thirds of the traffic in protected species.

Even legal wild foods reflect a shift to "elite consumption." A 2018 study by an international team of fisheries scientists looked at where fish caught on the high seas—outside any nation's jurisdiction—were going to market. Conservationists were concerned that the high seas were being overfished; fishery defenders replied that the catch was helping to feed the world's hungry. In the end, the researchers found that most of the high-seas fishery was feeding upscale consumers in places such as the United States, the European Union and Japan. Several species were used almost entirely as feed for fish farms or pets (again, mainly in rich nations), while others were turned into "nutraceuticals" aimed not at combatting hunger or disease, but at optimizing the performance of already healthy people—to make us, as we say today, "better than well." The coronavirus outbreak, too, made plain that most of the wild things still eaten in the rich world are consumer goods much more than they are food. When restaurants, hotels and resorts all closed, demand for seafood crashed—it has mainly become a luxury that we rarely eat at home. The types of tuna most in demand for sushi were expected to enjoy a brief pandemic population boom. Their biggest predator—us—had disappeared overnight.

"All of us are consumers of wildlife in one way or another," Rosaleen Duffy, a political ecologist at the University of Sheffield, told me. "We eat wildlife, we wear it as clothing and accessories, we consume it as medicine, and we buy ornaments made from it."

A world that stops shopping consumes far less of almost all of these things, and in return we get back some of what the pandemic showed us we miss much more than we knew. Everyone enjoyed the clear blue skies and the fresher air in our lungs; we all seemed to thrill at every sign of a natural world reborn. We were also reminded that we often crowd ourselves as much as we do the wildlife. To see images of Venice, Rome, the Louvre, the Sphinx, the Taj Mahal, and the ruins of Machu Picchu, all without the usual mobs of visitors, was to remember what makes them wonders of the world—and to see what would be restored if we pursued fewer, better experiences. The fish at Molokini in Hawaii weren't the only ones who preferred the reef with half as many boats; surveys show that's what tourists want, too.

If the world's travellers wandered less often, then the natural world around us would grow more and more spectacular, Friedlander said. People who did come to Molokini would witness something truly worth the journey, with more and larger fish and a greater richness of species. The behaviour of the reef's creatures would change, too, and it might change quickly. On a visit a matter of weeks after the pandemic shutdowns began, Friedlander said he was buzzed by manta rays, and two bottlenose dolphins came close to check him out. "I don't think they would have done that if there were hordes of people in the water," he said.

There's a continuum. On a reef where humans hunt fish, they are naturally skittish and fearful. On a reef where they're not hunted but are exposed to people all the time, many disappear; the rest become blasé. A reef where a human is neither a threat nor a constant presence is best of all. It's there that nonhuman life is neither fearful nor indifferent, but *curious*. In a lower-consuming world, when we do make our journeys to wild places, we stand a better chance at a bit of magic—to connect across the void between species, two beings face to face, taking an interest in each other.

We need a better word than happiness
for where this ends up

" get such a thrill out of walking to get my groceries," Janet Luhrs
told me.

It seemed an unlikely choice of words. A person can surely enjoy
a walk to their local shops—but to find it thrilling? The declaration had
the ring of overstatement. Yet Luhrs, sitting in the colourfully decorated
living room of her home in Seattle, Washington, gave every impression of
being sincere. A writer and journalist, she chooses her words carefully.

I had come to Seattle to speak with people who have practised voluntary
simplicity—the deliberate choice to live with less—for decades. I wanted to
hear what the deconsumer lifestyle feels like in the long run, what kind of
humans we might become in a world that stops shopping. Luhrs's story was
archetypal. She had become a lawyer, only to leave that career behind about
two weeks later, when she realized that she didn't want her infant daughter
raised by nannies. Not long afterward, she found herself with a mortgage,
family and, in her words, "more stuff than we knew what to do with." When
she saw an advertisement for a local voluntary simplicity group, she felt the
eye of fate turn its gaze toward her. She showed up for the event, and was
surprised to find a couple hundred other people in attendance. Instantly,
Luhrs knew she would pursue a simpler life. That was nearly thirty years ago.

"It was like a love affair," she said. "It was like I craved it."

The term "voluntary simplicity" was coined in 1936 by the American social philosopher Richard Gregg. Curiously, Gregg proposed the new term not to promote simple living, but *simpler* living—a more lenient version of the pure asceticism practised by such spiritual leaders as Buddha, Lao-tzu, Moses, and the Prophet Muhammad, not to mention various legendary armies and, as Gregg put it, "occasional geniuses" such as Thoreau and Gandhi. That way of life had lost much of its meaning in an age when many people doubted the promise of a spiritual afterlife and, with the hardships of the Great Depression fresh in their minds, acknowledged that at least some consumption was valuable. "The financial and social stability of every industrialized country seems to be founded on the expectation of an ever-expanding market for mass production," Gregg wrote, recognizing the consumer dilemma eighty-five years ago. He nonetheless saw—in the "vast quantities" of advertising, "endless gadgeteering," and explosion of ten-cent shops, chain groceries, department stores and mail-order warehouses—as much need for simplicity as ever.

The term didn't reach the cultural mainstream until the 1980s, when consumer capitalism took the form that we know today, with showy displays of materialism, overwork and busyness as badges of honour, wealth as the main measure of merit, the commodification of everything, obsession with profit and growth to the exclusion of other values, and the invasion of ads and branding. The decade is remembered as a time of prosperity, but it was a highly unequal one. In 1986, with the Dow Jones soaring and "BOOM YEAR" in the headlines, Studs Terkel, who had chronicled the Dirty Thirties in his classic oral history *Hard Times*, surveyed the shuttered factories and round-the-block line-ups for job openings and said he hadn't seen such desperation since the Great Depression.

In the last years of the '80s, a trend began toward "downshifting," a form of voluntary simplicity that emphasized not only living with less, but earning less as well. The media presented the stereotypical downshifter as wealthy, white and thirty-something—what one commentator called the "yuppie conscientious objector." In fact, the phenomenon was more diverse. Some simplifiers were carrying over, or returning to, the hippie-era values of the '60s and '70s; others were young adults of Generation X, reacting against the consumer-culture circus they had grown up in. It's true that most were white, but so were eight out of ten Americans at the time. According to research by sociologist Juliet Schor, compared to the size of their populations, black and Hispanic Americans were actually more likely than their white counterparts to downshift.

Wealthier people could try simpler living without much risk. Many other downshifters began with a step into *involuntary* simplicity: they found themselves jobless or underemployed as the early 1990s slipped into a global recession. For this group, the voluntary aspect came in the choice to embrace the change. Nearly four out of ten downshifters started out pretty down to begin with, earning annual incomes of less than twenty-five thousand dollars (the equivalent of forty thousand dollars today). Lower-income downshifters were often not aware of the cultural wave they were a part of. They were merely trying, in the face of an increasingly heartless economy, to redefine for themselves what it meant to live the good life. At the peak of downshifting in the mid 1990s, one in five Americans was living with less and telling pollsters that they were happy to do so.

Their most common motivation was a desire to reduce stress and regain what today we call work-life balance—but they also stopped shopping. Most reduced their consumer spending by about 20 percent and, as Schor noted, "barely grieved" the resulting changes in their lives—even thirty years ago, it was possible for many people in richer countries to make a deep cut to their consumption and hardly notice the effects. Nearly a third of simplifiers reduced their spending further, by 25 percent, and a fifth scaled back by half or more. For these, the transformation was demanding. They had to accept being seen in timeworn clothes, to drop off the kids at school by bike or bus instead of one of the newly trending SUVs, to do without increasingly popular gadgets such as cell phones and personal computers.

It was quiet revolution. Most downshifters dressed quite a bit like everyone else and lived in ordinary neighbourhoods rather than communes or cabins in the woods. Seattle emerged as the nexus of voluntary simplicity as the growing tech industry—Microsoft's headquarters were there—made the city synonymous with the overworked, conspicuously consuming yuppie, while many other residents were still mired in a lingering recession. The result was perhaps the most deliberate experiment in stopping shopping in modern times: a whole city in which the rejection of consumerism entered the mainstream.

For nearly a decade, few aspects of daily life in Seattle were left unchanged by its shadow culture. The most influential fashion trends were "vintage" second-hand clothing and grunge, a look built around basic, durable workwear—flannel shirts, jeans, leather boots—that was worn until it wore out. Among youth, sparsely furnished apartments were *de rigueur* and displays of wealth disdained. Many cities in that era had not-for-profit, cooperatively run grocery stores; Seattle also had co-op restaurants, cafés, a mechanics' garage, a medical centre, a carpentry workshop and a midwifery service, not to mention alternative weekly newspapers that competed with the dailies and an abundance of cheap venues that showcased music rejected by corporate radio stations. For a few rare years, the consumer lifestyle was uncooled. "We were sure in the '90s that we were the up-and-coming lifestyle choice," Vicki Robin, coauthor of the downshifting classic *Your Money or Your Life*, told me. In 1995, the *New York Times* reported that eight out of ten Americans agreed with the statement "We buy and consume far more than we need." That same year, the Trends Research Institute of Rhinebeck, New York, chose voluntary simplicity as one of the top ten phenomena of the decade.

Then the global economy roared back to life, Seattle became better known for billionaires than plain living, and downshifting faded. Some people, like Janet Luhrs, carried on. They stopped shopping half of a lifetime ago. How did it change them? Are they happier than the rest of us? Do they really get a thrill out of a walk around the block? And if so, *why?*

Michael S.W. Lee, now a professor of marketing at the University of Auckland, in New Zealand, had what he described as "a sheltered upper-middle-class upbringing." Then, as he was about to embark on a PhD in marketing in 2002, he read *No Logo*, a book by Naomi Klein about the influence of corporate power and marketing. He thought the people *No Logo* described—rebels against brands and consumer culture—sounded strange and extreme. He decided to study them.

Three years later, Lee founded the International Centre for Anti-consumption Research. What Lee realized as he researched people who resist, resent or reject consumerism was that not a lot is known about them. He set out to determine whether these anti-consumers had different core values than consumers, and found that they do.

One is that anti-consumers put a much higher value than mainstream consumers do on having control over their consumption. Luhrs, who went on to write a popular deconsumer handbook called *The Simple Living Guide*, said that an important part of voluntary simplicity is understanding your-self and why you do things. "I think most people don't live mindfully; I think most people don't live deliberately," Luhrs said. "I definitely do." She has learned, for example, that she doesn't like always having to make con-sumer choices. With this tidbit of self-knowledge, not-shopping becomes not a sacrifice, but a gift.

Classical economic theory holds that consumers know what is best for themselves and act rationally in their self-interest, a perspective that remains influential today. Paradoxically, it is anti-consumers, not main-stream ones, who come closest to this ideal: they are more likely to make active, informed choices about what they do and don't want to consume, are less swayed by advertising and fads, and are less likely either to feel trapped in consumption or to use it as a means of escape. "It's not like I ever lived an austere lifestyle," Luhrs said, "but I've always had a sense of what I need."

A more obvious difference between anti-consumers and consumers is that anti-consumers place less importance on material desires. Yet the eventual results of this orientation can be surprising. Deborah Caplow, another longtime simplifier in Seattle, followed a boyfriend to the city in the late 1970s at the age of twenty-seven, with all her worldly possessions in a suitcase and a couple of boxes. Caplow was so young when she started down the path of simpler living that she doesn't remember how it felt to make the transition. When she was nine years old, her mother and father divorced. "He became well-to-do," Caplow said, "and my mother decided to make the best of having not a lot of money." She lived with her mother and sister. Once, after moving to a new town, they spent a year without furniture, sleeping on the floor in sleeping bags. Caplow's father lived in a mansion, and she came to consider him selfish and pre-occupied with status.

"I was thoroughly inculcated with this value that I didn't want to be a rich person," she said. "It's sort of a choice not to make money in your life."

Simplifiers often come to feel that they have solved Keynes's "economic problem" of meeting their absolute needs: they do so by having fewer of them. Today, Caplow lives in a neighbourhood spilling down a steep, thickly conifered hillside—here, Seattle feels more like a city of treehouses than a contemporary metropolis. The house that she shares with her husband (she formerly shared it with her daughter) is seventy square metres in size, one-third as large as the typical house built in the US today and smaller even than the average apartment. An art historian retired from the University of Washington, Caplow hasn't bought a piece of furniture that wasn't sec-ond-hand in more than twenty years. Until a recent accident took it out of commission, her car was a twenty-five-year-old Subaru that she drove less than a quarter the national average. Caplow has never owned a dishwasher (this seems to be a benchmark for simplifiers). She took the bus to work for more than two decades, gets most of her books from the library, and rarely buys new clothing other than socks, underwear and shoes. "I really love beau-tiful clothing," she said, "but I wouldn't like to be the kind of person who wears a lot of beautiful clothing."

Caplow carefully makes note of her privileges. She's white and has always felt there were few barriers to making more money if she wanted to, and if her financial situation was ever truly dire, she could have turned to her relatives for help. Yet for much of her life Caplow was, by the numbers, on the poorer side; she lived for years on an annual salary of fifteen thousand dollars or less. Despite this, she gradually came to feel "mildly prosperous." She has all the belongings she desires, has savings instead of debt, and has been able to travel, retire comfortably, and help her daughter go to college—she has a sense of financial security that people preoccupied with money often lack. When the coronavirus crisis sent the US economy into a tailspin, Caplow was struck by the realization that the crash didn't worry her. "We've managed on so much less before that we'll just do that again."

Syd Fredrickson connects this counterintuitive sense of prosperity to an even higher ideal: personal liberty. Originally from Minnesota, Fredrickson came to Seattle in 1991, as the downshift era was building to its peak. "I didn't downshift so much as I never upshifted," she told me.

Many people perceive living simply to be limiting; Fredrickson said it has always made her feel unusually free to make uncommon choices, question conformity, act spontaneously and express herself through her words and appearance. All her adult life she has watched people around her pursue careers they didn't like or stay in jobs they hated, because they would not risk ending up with a lower income. "They would say their lives were all hollow and crazy. They just thought it was too scary to do something else," she said.

Another distinction between anti-consumer and consumer is in where each one seeks happiness. As psychologist Tim Kasser predicted, most simplifiers do, in time, gravitate toward intrinsic values such as personal development and a sense of community. In the same way that consumer culture feeds back on itself in a vicious cycle, encouraging us to endlessly do or acquire new things, the pursuit of intrinsic values may push us further in that same direction, in what Kasser calls a "virtuous cycle." According to Caplow, stepping away from measuring status through material wealth eventually led her to place less importance on social status altogether. "It's just you as a human being and the other person as a human being," Caplow said. "The human interactions that I have make me really, really happy. I can adapt to different people who have different lifestyles, and I can see their points of view. I feel like I'm part of a human community. I think that does come from living simply."

Simplicity appears to beget simplicity. It's a stereotype that simplifiers seem drawn to tranquil pastimes like gardening, reading, walking and talking. Exactly why takes some explaining: Are only mellow people attracted to simple living or does living simply make you mellow? In a world without shopping, would we—even those of us who currently find such activities boring—be transformed in a way that made birdwatching or keeping a journal more appealing?

Kasser thinks we would be. "One of the things that's interesting about voluntary simplicity is there are a lot of doors into it. Some people become simplifiers because they're frustrated with work, some want more time with their families, for some it's about spirituality, for some it's ecological, for some it's a political act," he said. "But once people walk in that door, it's kind of the same house. And as they live in that house for a while, it seems to me they become more and more alike, even though they entered for different reasons."

A note about simplifiers: as a general rule, they have *time*. In the course of researching this book, I met people practising simpler living in places around the world; almost all of them felt to me like they had just stepped out of a different era—whether the past or future, I couldn't say, but certainly not the overscheduled present. They made themselves available. They let their conversations sprawl (in one memorable case, across seven hours of eating, drinking and walking in Barcelona). They were, in other words, highly unlikely to pencil you in for a fifteen-minute time slot five weeks in advance—and they are aware this marks them as strange. "I used to say to my women friends, when they were getting too busy to get together, 'Well, don't you eat breakfast? Don't you have coffee? *I'm* not too busy,'" said Caplow. "Then I realized I had to stop doing it. People think you're needy if you want to talk."

The stereotype of the free and easy simple life is to some degree an illusion: it's not that they *only* do peaceful things, but that they have room in their lives to do them. But it goes beyond exchanging an hour at work for one spent in meditation, an hour of shopping for one spent baking bread. Since intrinsically oriented activities meet psychological needs better than materialism does, simplifiers often increase the amount of time they spend on them by cutting back even their consumption of social media, TV or recorded music. It really does seem to be the case that a world without shopping would become a calmer world. The slow pace might even feel necessary, the way fast-paced life feels necessary today: if simpler living is about hearing yourself more clearly, it just might require an abundance of actual quiet. As Luhrs put it, "Once you do know yourself, you might find that all you want to do is listen to the frogs in the pond."

None of this yet explains how a walk to the grocery store becomes "thrilling." For that we need to look at what, for the moment, we will call "congruence."

Almost everyone has a psychological gap between the way they believe they *should* act in daily life and how they actually behave. The more materialistic a person is, the wider that gap is likely to be. Knowingly or unknowingly, materialists often feel conflicted over their failure to be better people—they experience a sense of incongruence between their ideal self and their real self. Simplifiers tend to have narrower gaps and greater congruence.

The idea of congruence appears throughout the history of writing about simpler living. Usually, it appears under names like "self-knowledge," "self-mastery" and "self-control"; in Abraham Maslow's famous hierarchy of needs, it shows up as "self-actualization" (and is the capstone of his pyramid). Each of these terms leaves hanging a question: What is the end result of all this knowledge, mastery and control? In materialistic societies, the goal is often said to be the realization of your fullest potential as measured in wealth, fame, accomplishment or even physical attractiveness. From a more intrinsic perspective, the answer is more nuanced: a version of yourself that, through careful exploration of heart and soul, you know is the one that you want to be. Perfect congruence between the ideal and real selves.

The idea is an old one. Another name we give to this congruence is authenticity, a term we apply to those people and things that seem inherently true to themselves. The word shares roots with the ancient Greek *authentes*, which referred to the perpetrator of an action—to be authentic is to be fully the author of one's own deeds. In the Greek view, this authenticity demanded the self-knowledge and self-mastery to know the difference between desires and responsibilities, fleeting pleasures and deep satisfaction, and to give time to each in accord with its value. Adam Smith wrote that the purpose of economic advancement was to be liberated enough from everyday worries to pursue "perfect tranquility," which he did not define as peace and quiet, but as a life free from the agitation to mind and spirit caused by avarice, ambition or vainglory—again, an inner congruence. "In the most glittering and exalted situation that our idle fancy can hold out to us, the pleasures from which we propose to derive our real happiness, are almost always the same with those which, in our actual, though humble station, we have at all times at hand, and in our power," he wrote.

One of the first scholars to research anti-consumers was the sociologist Stephen Zavestoski, who observed meetings of downshifters at the turn of the twenty-first century. Many of these simplifiers, he noted, felt "lied to and deceived" when economic success failed to deliver the happiness promised by consumer culture. Zavestoski recorded a quotation that he felt captured this widely shared feeling: "I had all the stuff that was supposed to make me successful—my car and my clothes, the house in the right neighbourhood and belonging to the right health club. All the external framework was excellent and inside I kind of had this pit eating away at me."

As a framework to understand what was missing from these people's lives, Zavestoski considered three "essential elements of the self": esteem, efficacy (having the power to achieve what we want or set out to do) and authenticity. Since many of the simplifiers he met had high-status roles in their communities and owned the kinds of homes, cars, jewellery and so on that marked them as successful individuals, he concluded that needs for self-esteem and efficacy could be met by consumer society. What was lacking was authenticity. Consumer society was drifting in a direction that steadily widened the gap between the ideal self and the real one. Zavestoski predicted that marketers and advertisers would soon deploy messages aimed at convincing consumers they could shop their way to authenticity. It was a marvellous bit of foresight: by 2016, the industry journal *AdAge* was reporting that authenticity "may be the most overused word in advertising."

Most of us understand how deeply bad it can feel to be out of true with ourselves. Few of us, however, experience very often how deeply good it feels to be congruent, to be authentic. It is this that can make it a thrill to walk to the store to buy your groceries: it is a small enactment of who you know you want to be. It is exactly the way you want to do that particular chore, and you know it, and you know why. "The quiet thrill," Kasser called it, adding, "it won't get many likes on Instagram."

There are still surprisingly few studies of longtime simplifiers and other anti-consumers. The research to date finds that they do, in fact, enjoy higher-than-average well-being, but if it is happiness, it is a complicated one. A simple life is not a talisman against the vicissitudes of fate, from illness and joblessness to the death of loved ones or abuse by others. Many simplifiers, too, struggle on the one hand with whether their lives are simple enough, and on the other with feelings of judgment against mainstream consumers who do not live as mindfully as they do. The pursuit of intrinsic values, meanwhile, does not start and end with learning to appreciate the simple things in life. Another core difference that Michael S.W. Lee found between anti-consumers and consumers is a wider "scope of concern," or regard for issues bigger than themselves and their personal needs. Anti-consumers are more likely to engage with issues such as climate change, species extinction, racial injustice and poverty—matters that can be disturbing, depressing or even frightening. Since engagement with such topics is congruent with their values, however, it makes life meaningful—but perhaps not cheerful.

Most of all, simplifiers are haunted by spending their lives as outsiders. While they have congruence with themselves, they are incongruent with consumer culture, and therefore struggle with isolation, ostracization and otherness. "I have had to fight against feelings of inadequacy because of the modesty of my way of life. For years, I was so paranoid about my clothing. For a long time I felt like my house wasn't nice enough to bring fancier people to," said Caplow. "I don't have too many relationships with people like me," she added. "I don't think there are many people like me."

Many people who try simplicity find it a hard and lonesome road, and soon give up. Those who succeed are often rebels, free spirits or iconoclasts to begin with—people who form their identity in opposition to the mainstream, rather than in favour of anything in particular. "I think anti-consumption and consumption can only exist together," said Lee. "The only question is the balance between the two." There will always be at least a little consumer in all of us, and some materialism, too. It's a reminder that no way of being human should ever be—should ever have been—allowed to take up as much space in our lives as consumerism did.

But every society needs mavericks. Take away consumer culture, and some of the people who oppose consumption today will need a new place to put their contrarian spirit. The choice is obvious: they become the rebellious overconsumers of our low-consuming future.

Now we're all shopping in cyberspace?

There's a last chance for consumerism to live on in a world that stops shopping, and that is to preserve consumer culture in the digital sphere. Do you hate to appear in public in the same outfit more than once? In a video game, you can change your appearance—in gaming parlance, your "skin"—as many times as you choose, not to mention become a warrior rabbit or a flaming zombie that dances like Michael Jackson. In a virtual world, you can own and drive a hundred cars, or wear a thousand pairs of shoes, or build a dozen castles, all while using only the tiniest fraction of the planet's resources that doing these things in real life would demand.

Would we do it? turn our backs on malls, shops, theatres, restaurants, stadiums, spas and resorts and carry on as virtual consumers? Life in pandemic quarantine seems to provide an answer, and it is an emphatic *yes*.

The big-bang expansion of online activity during the pandemic has come to be known as the "digital surge." Some of it was nearly unavoidable, such as remote work, video meet-ups with friends, or online schooling. But suddenly, people who had never done such things before were also playing poker in virtual casinos, competing in bike races in which their onscreen avatars were linked to their indoor stationary bicycles, or getting eye-to-eye with the *Mona Lisa*—usually thronged by crowds and cloistered in a glass box in the Louvre—through VR goggles. They attended concerts by supersized, animated rappers in the *Fortnite* gameworld, livestreamed DJ sets and watercolour painting lessons, and also "shopstreamed," watching videos of other people shopping in order to decide what to buy for themselves. Private Zoom-viewings at auction houses pushed some jewellery sales to record highs; a Cartier Tutti Frutti bracelet (which looks like Skittles that melted among diamonds, except that the Skittles are sapphires, rubies and emeralds) went for $1.34 million at the height of the first lockdown, nearly twice the estimated price.

We walked the streets of distant cities in Google Earth. We learned to accept ordering fruits and vegetables online, without seeing, smelling or feeling them. *Animal Crossing* sold faster than any other video game in history, then became a platform for virtual fashion, with hours-long lineups within the game to attend exclusive sales—using in-game currency—by well-known designers. When the online collectibles company CryptoKitties issued a limited run of virtual cats by the Chinese artist Momo Wang, they sold out in three minutes. Our necessity goods quickly shuffled: we bought fewer new phones and more gaming consoles and high-end televisions, more augmented-reality backdrops that gave us angels' wings and a halo when we made our video calls. We shifted so much of daily life online that, as the overall economy sank into severe recession, the employment rate in some kinds of digital work surpassed pre-pandemic levels.

Most of all, we *watched*. TV binges, autoplay rabbit holes, twenty-four-hour news channels. By the end of April 2020, after the sharpest increase in history, three-quarters of US households had subscriptions to streaming services. A survey of British and American consumers during that locked-down spring found that 80 percent were consuming more media than usual, most of it—by far—being television and video. Screen time climbed so high that the European Union asked Netflix and YouTube to lower their picture quality in order to reduce data demand and keep the internet from breaking. The average American was watching fully a quarter more television than before the pandemic, topping out at forty-one hours in front of the TV each week—and that's not counting time spent staring at the screens of their other devices.

Even before the pandemic, evidence was growing that digital consumption can stand in for the consumption of material goods. Kenneth Pike, a professor of philosophy at the Florida Institute of Technology who has written on the subject, told me he took inspiration from the bedrooms of his four children. "It strikes me just how much less cluttered they are than mine was when I was a child in the 1980s," he said. "I sometimes walk in and think it feels bare, like my children should have more *stuff*. But then I think, well, no, they shouldn't."

Pike's own childhood bedroom was filled with bins of plastic toys (he remembers action figures like He-Man and the Super Friends), decorated with posters, piled with books, graced with trophies. His children's toys and games are mostly digital, they mainly read on Kindles, and many of their trophies and awards exist only in online gameworlds. Their favourite game at the time I spoke with Pike was *Roblox*; search online, and you can easily find videos of *Roblox* players spending hundreds of real-world dollars to buy, say, a virtual monster truck, a Mustang, and a Ferrari in a single gaming session. "They are definitely digital consumers," Pike said.

Most of us now are. Almost no one still seeks out live music as their primary way of listening, for example; music streaming services are popular even in poorer parts of the globe, including rural India and all across Africa. The digital revolution left homes less cluttered by clocks, flashlights, timers, stereo equipment, calculators, fax machines, printers and scanners, not to mention collections of books, albums, encyclopedias and maps. Instead, well before the digital surge, households worldwide were filling—or rather *not filling*—with apps, ebooks, video games and photo albums that exist only in the vaporous space of the cloud.

In July 2020, Vili Lehdonvirta, a Finnish-British economic sociologist who studies how digital technology shapes economies, had an experience that hinted at a more deeply virtual future. Lehdonvirta was living in Tokyo, then a city with few coronavirus restrictions but a lingering wariness of the disease, when, one night, a favourite artist of his began streaming a gallery show in real time on Instagram.

The artist, Taro Yamamoto, makes modern art grounded in Japanese tradition—his most famous piece emulates a four-hundred-year-old folding screen depicting the classical gods of wind and thunder, but replaces them with Nintendo's Super Mario Brothers. Richly textured and made with materials such as gold leaf, which reflects light differently when seen from different angles, his artwork is hard to fully appreciate in online photos, and Yamamoto was lamenting the fact that the gallery was empty.

Lehdonvirta, who usually works from the Oxford Internet Institute, suddenly realized that he could go keep Yamamoto company; he was, after all, in the same city where the exhibition was happening. He rode the subway through the quiet megalopolis, showed up at the gallery, and spent two hours with the artist. They didn't discuss whether live audiences would return to the galleries soon, however, or how to lure them back to the physical world. Instead, Lehdonvirta told me, they talked about whether Yamamoto could take his art into the three-dimensional space of virtual reality, such as the gameworld of *Animal Crossing*, where so much more of Tokyo—and the rest of the world—was hanging out that night. The scene was quaintly surreal: two figures in living, face-to-face conversation, accepting the end of that era.

This is all potentially good news, said Lehdonvirta, who first learned to write basic code in the mid 1980s, when he was five or six years old. By the early twenty-first century, he was working in a Finnish lab to create virtual clothing and accessories that could be viewed through augmented reality devices such as camera phones; he remembers that another local company was figuring out how to do the same with virtual furniture. Today, apps that do exactly these things—allow you to test a shade of lipstick in augmented reality, or see what new shelving would look like in the corner of your living room before you buy it—are mainstream.

In virtual reality, Keynes's "economic problem" has decisively been solved. It is a world of total abundance, in which endless novelty, passing fads and planned obsolescence are rendered nearly harmless. "You can accelerate consumption. You can throw away stuff. The fashion cycle can go faster and faster without increasing material requirements or the environmental footprint," Lehdonvirta said. All you're doing when you turn one virtual garment into another is "flipping bits"—changing one kind of digital information into another.

Lehdonvirta isn't out to abandon physical reality for the matrix. Like many Finns, he typically spends part of each year in a rustic cabin ("except the mobile connectivity is always much better even than in Oxford"). He can tell an edible mushroom from a toadstool, and brings Finnish bilberries and wild game meat back to England so that he can avoid eating mass-produced food. What he pictures is a world in which much of what we do in the material economy now—telling the world who we are, exploring our identities, showing off our taste or our skill and so on—is done through virtual consumption, while real-world consumption shrinks to focus mainly on material needs.

"You can have this stable state where everyone's got connectivity, everyone's got a screen, everyone's got an input method—and that's all that's needed for virtual consumption," he said. "You're going to need to supply electricity to those devices. You're going to need to replace them when they die. But the actual growth can happen all inside of that screen."

When a small fraction of the population first began, in the 1990s, to buy virtual goods, they were widely shamed. "Money for nothing," scoffed the same people who readily paid a premium for T-shirts that differed from other T-shirts only in that they were marked with an entirely symbolic brand. "Utterly useless," said critics who were already spending much of their income in sectors of the economy driven by little else than pleasure, anxiety or status—in other words, by nothing tangible at all. A decade later, when users of virtual worlds like *Second Life* had collectively amassed digital possessions (clothing, cars, houses, toys) worth an estimated $1.8 billion, the possibility that environmentally damaging material consumption could be replaced seemed to hold real promise. "I'm saving so much money in real life, because I get the satisfaction of spending in *Second Life* and it costs almost nothing," one virtual consumer told the *Sacramento Bee* in 2006.

Second Life is now largely forgotten and, so far, most of us have not embraced virtual objects as stand-ins for the real thing. We may test-drive furniture in digital space, but in the end we buy chairs we can sit on, shelves that hold printed and bound books. Yet taking the plunge into fully virtual consumption may only be a matter of technological advance. During the pandemic, when the number of people playing video games increased across every generation, many didn't realize they had become regular buyers of virtual goods. "The revenue model of half of the games, at least, is heavily based on selling stuff within the game," said Lehdonvirta. Almost anything else a person is likely to spend that money on—food, clothes, sports, travel— would cause more environmental harm to the "corporeal world," as some gamers refer to that strange land that their physical bodies inhabit.

We can already see virtual objects in material space; augmented reality can provide us with a digital sculpture, a houseplant that never dies, or wall colours that can change shades in an instant. For now, though, we can only see such things through cumbersome pairs of goggles. If we could use lightweight glasses instead, or better yet contact lenses, we might embrace virtual possessions as eagerly as we took to recorded and disembodied voices through technologies like radio, the phonograph, and landline telephones more than a century ago.

When we do, consumer culture will be waiting for us. "That's the way capitalism works: you go where the people are and sell to them within that space. If that space looks like this"—Lehdonvirta's fingers traced the rectangular frame he appeared in during our video call—"then there's a lot that business can do to make this space more commercial. Not necessarily better, but more commercial."

So far, digital consumption has shown every sign of behaving exactly like ordinary, real-world consumption. It has endlessly increased. It devours more and more resources every year. And it consistently outpaces every effort to make it green. It is more accurate, for now, to say that digital consumption *is* real-world consumption.

The improvements in energy efficiency in digital technology are legendary. The first computer built along the same principles that we use today was called the Electronic Numerical Integrator and Computer, or ENIAC, developed by the US military in the 1940s. You certainly couldn't go shopping for one. The machine was as long as a blue whale and as heavy as a Second World

War tank. According to calculations by environmental scientist Ray Galvin, if you built a computer as smart as the typical desktop computer today, but used ENIAC technology, it would weigh five million tonnes and, if you started building it in London, pointing west, it would eventually stretch across the Atlantic Ocean and deep into Canadian wilderness. The moment you turned it on, it would devour 70 percent of the power used in the UK.

Today's computers obviously consume energy much more efficiently, and require far fewer resources to manufacture. Yet for the past two hundred years, both energy efficiency and the total consumption of energy have steadily increased, side by side. As computers and the rest of what we now call "tech" became less expensive to own and operate, they expanded into every niche of global society—a transformational rebound effect.

"Energy efficiencies in the infrastructure are important," said Kelly Widdicks, a computing researcher at Lancaster University in England, "but they are made inconsequential by the sheer growth in demand."

In 1992, the internet carried 100 gigabytes of data per day. By 2007, when the iPhone was released, it carried 2,000 gigabytes *per second*. Today, it's moving beyond 150,000 gigabytes per second. Measured across a year, that's nearly five zettabytes, an amount that is just as incomprehensible as it sounds. (In long form, it's 5,000,000,000,000,000,000,000 bytes.)

In recent years, annual data consumption has grown at a compound rate of about a quarter, and—once again in common with material consumption—the ways we consume are becoming more rather than less resource intensive. Coming in the near future is a swelling wave of data-demanding technologies, including artificial intelligence, augmented reality, virtual reality, cryptocurrencies, the smart home, self-driving cars, and the "internet of things," which will connect our internet-connected devices to each other.

We don't yet know, really, how harmful—or not—all of this is to the planet, said Widdicks. Ironically, the data on the environmental costs of data is not great. Still, there are patterns worth paying attention to. One is a feedback loop: new digital devices and services drive higher demand for data, which requires larger and faster networks, which pushes growth in internet infrastructure, such as fibre optic cables, data centres, transmission towers and personal devices. With the expanded infrastructure in place, the pattern repeats itself. The result is a constant increase in both the material and energy demands of the digital world.

The internet is still thought of as a cornucopia—a bottomless horn of plenty. "A lot of people don't really think about the internet using energy," Widdicks said. "People more think of the power consumption of charging the phone." Meanwhile, electrical demand from digital infrastructure and our devices has been growing at about 7 percent a year globally, more than twice as fast as the rate of economic growth. Conservative estimates are that about one-fifth of global electricity will be used up by information and communications technology before the current decade is over, meaning, once again, that in order to fight climate change, we need not only to produce enough renewable electricity to replace nearly all the energy we currently pump into our digital lives, but more and more and more in the future.

Widdicks humbly suggests an alternative approach: "We need to curtail the demand for internet connectivity." One way to do that, curiously enough, is to stop shopping for so many material goods: overnight, the market shrinks for upgraded phones and devices, new internet-connected lights and showers and toasters and cars, and the data consumed through online shopping itself. Another part of the solution is to have fewer but better experiences online.

While it has yet to be quantified, a lot of what we do online is "digital waste," including activities that we ourselves recognize as pointless or even detrimental to our health or self-interest. We fill the daydreaming boredom of, say, waiting for a friend at a restaurant, with the distracted boredom of the internet. Our terminology captures it: we are sucked into "black holes" of "doomscrolling," or give lifeblood to the "time vampire" of autoplay video. We did not stop at polluting the climate to watch cat videos; we now also stream videos for our cats to watch.

A few decades ago, most households shared a single TV; today, the trend is toward multiwatching, in which different people—or even individuals—watch different programs on different devices at the same time. Another recent practice is media multitasking: streaming video while online shopping, online shopping while checking social media, checking social media while online gaming. Then there is "trivial watching," or viewing things that add little or nothing to our lives—not even guilty pleasure or escapism. Widdicks and nine of her colleagues once put themselves through an exercise in digitally "living with less." For two weeks, they strived to connect to the internet only when it felt necessary to do so, turning digital consumption into something closer to a need than a want. All of them found that some of their digital consumption—streaming music at home, streaming videos while doing chores, listening to podcasts while exercising, constantly checking social media or searching miscellany on the web—could be eliminated without any inconvenience or distress, often filling the extra time with reading, cooking, chatting, creative projects, or even sleeping and bathing. "People adapt to internet disconnection," Widdicks said.

Yet she forgives us for not choosing to abstain. Once, during a period when she was writing an article about environmentally unsustainable streaming patterns, she also streamed all sixty-two episodes of the hit TV program *Breaking Bad* in her spare time. "It was just so *good*," she told me. "And obviously one of the drivers around video streaming is how it's designed—in terms of autoplay video—so you watch one and the next one is automatically loading, and you're like, oh well, may as well keep watching."

Our devices and digital services can be "undesigned" to help us use the internet less, Widdicks said. Instead of autoplay, for example, apps could have autoclose features, or be required to allow people to choose, during set-up, maximum amounts of time they want to use them. Some streaming could be shifted to broadcast TV, which is far less energy-intensive, and we could ban all marketing that promotes digital bingeing. ("How is it that *excess* is valued as neutral or even positive, in this context?" Widdicks said.) We could even choose to put limits on data demand for reasons of health or climate protection. All of these, and many other ideas for slowing digital consumption, involve the same radical redirection of society as stopping shopping: a shift away from the endless more, toward a sense of sufficiency.

Perhaps the first place we will learn sufficiency will be online. Lehdonvirta said that the sheer pace of growth and change that is possible with fully virtual consumption—the kind that takes place entirely within virtual space—could lead us to stop wanting more and more.

Already, designers of video games and other virtual realms have noticed that users don't like to be overwhelmed with too many goods or choices. Unlike real-world economists, who focus on expanding the GDP, makers of digital worlds are mainly interested in user satisfaction and enjoyment. As a result, they tend to keep the GVP—gross virtual product—stable rather than endlessly growing. Too much of a thing makes it less special, too much novelty renders every new thing meaningless, and too much of all of it stops making us happy. What happens then is that we don't want to play the game anymore.

"The bottleneck is not going to be our ability to produce virtual goods or to destroy them when they're no longer needed, but to keep coming up with virtual goods that somehow kick off a new consumer cycle," Lehdonvirta said. "There's got to be some kind of a limit to consumers' ability to adopt new fashions and trends and get excited about them—I think there must be some equilibrium. You can maybe escape the ecological limits, but I doubt that there is, even in a completely virtualized, immaterial economy, an appetite for endless growth."

On the day the world stops shopping, we really might move consumer culture into digital space, where it can grow and accelerate until we are finally ready to let it go. A warning, though: we still might be waiting a while. The idea that the consumer appetite will one day meet its natural limit, after all, is not a new one. William Stanley Jevons said the same about the material economy, more than 150 years ago.

It's like a world with fewer people
but without losing the people

Rumiko Obata likes to say that she was born in a brewery. For four generations, her family had produced sake in a long, barn-like storehouse called a *kura* on the shore of the Sea of Japan. Inside was a warren of rooms, a subterranean kingdom where musty odours hung like sea fog and Shinto shrines to the spirit of sake glittered from dark corners. As a girl, Obata would play within this labyrinth, but later dreamed of escape from so much tradition and antiquity. She wanted to march into the modern world. She wanted off Sado Island.

On a map, Sado Island looks like a lightning bolt that has turned to stone and fallen into the sea thirty storm-lashed kilometres off the west coast of Honshu. Sado feels remote, but on the clock it is just three hours by high-speed train and ferry from Tokyo. As soon as she could, Obata moved to the megacity, earned a law degree at a prestigious university, and went to work as a publicist for Hollywood films being screened in Japan.

Obata lived her Tokyo dream during the height of the bubble economy. Those were the days when young women could go to the bar without money, certain that their drinks would be paid for by Japanese salarymen; when late-night revellers would bid for taxis by holding up sheets of paper marked with exorbitant offers to the drivers; when gold flake emerged as a decoration to be eaten on desserts and drunk in cocktails. Above all, it was the time when Shibuya plaza in Tokyo became the world's vision of the future. There, giant advertising screens and spotlit billboards cast an otherworldly glow over the carnival of consumerism below. Teenage subcultures competed to debut vanguard street fashions—gigantic socks! crinolines! ultra-cute everything!—while young and old alike shopped for Versace, Dior and Louis Vuitton, creating a trend toward everyday luxury that soon spread across the globe.

By the numbers, the bubble ended on the eve of 1990, but in Tokyo, the after-party continued. Then, in January 1995, a powerful earthquake centred near the city of Kobe killed more than six thousand people. Two months later, a doomsday cult attacked the Tokyo subway system. Cult members boarded trains during the morning rush hour, then used sharp-tipped umbrellas to puncture packets of liquid sarin, a toxic nerve agent, which quickly evaporated into a deadly gas. Thirteen people died and thousands more suffered lasting injury.

While Japan is renowned for its ability to overcome adversity, the Japanese do not simply "get over it." Instead, they have tended to soul-search, to wonder at what meanings can be drawn from their traumas. When the earthquake brought Kobe's new skyscrapers crashing down, many Japanese began to question ideas of modernity and progress. The sarin gas attack left them wondering whether cultural harmony had been sacrificed at the bubble economy's altar of materialism. Writer Kenzaburo Oe, a Nobel laureate, spoke for millions when he said that the twin crises revealed that the Japanese had reached "a dead end in our soul."

A year earlier, Rumiko Obata had begun having similar thoughts. The Tokyo lifestyle she had dreamed of while growing up on Sado Island was losing its lustre for her. As 1995 unfolded under apocalyptic clouds, she had an epiphany. "I thought, if tomorrow was the last day of the world, I would want to spend it drinking sake in my small, dark brewery."

Obata has been home on Sado Island for a quarter century now. Together with her husband, who had been an editor with a major Tokyo publishing house, she has become the fifth generation in her family to oversee the production of Obata Shuzo sake. When she first returned, she said, she had been entrepreneurial, following the conventional approach of trying to expand her product's market at home and abroad. After a time, she found herself losing heart. The problem, she realized, was that she was "selling for the sake of selling."

It was only then that she noticed the island's unoccupied houses and fading villages. The shopping arcades, or *shoten-gai*, that had always lined the main streets had come instead to be nicknamed *shatta-gai*, for the shutters pulled down over so many closed storefronts.

"Sado is thirty years ahead of Tokyo," Obata told me. Caught in the folds of her pinstriped suit, she looked like a songbird; also like a songbird, she has vitality that transcends her size. Obata is an optimistic person, but the idea that remote and rural Sado is ahead of Tokyo on the future's horizon is an extraordinary claim—and a troubling one. If longtime voluntary simplifiers offer a window into who we might become as individuals after a few decades without shopping, then Sado does the same at a larger scale. And whatever your feelings about consumer culture, only the strongest misanthrope could arrive on Sado Island without feeling pangs of despair, if not outright panic.

The island's population has dwindled from a high of 120,000 to about 55,000, and it continues to fall. By demographics alone, Sado's economy has been reduced by half. Sit down with a Sado resident and a map of the island, and they will point to town after town and say "*akiya*" or "*haikyo*." Empty houses. Ruins.

One of these places, Aikawa, captures the history. In the early eighteenth century it was home to one of the world's largest gold mines, digging out so much ore that it split a mountain in two. At the time, the region Sado is a part of, Niigata, was the most populous in the country, with well over a million people, and Sado itself had more residents per square kilometre than modern Hawaii. In the twentieth century, the mine declined, but the bubble economy turned Sado into a popular getaway: it's considered an iconic example of *furusato*, the nostalgic ideal of the rural hometown. Then the bubble popped. The island soon began to experience what demographers call "double-negative population disequilibrium." People migrated to Tokyo and

other large cities in search of thrills and opportunity; those who remained
had too few babies to replace their elders as they died of old age. All across
the island you can see abandoned country homes, with their distinctive red-
brown wood and black roof tiles, staring hollow-eyed into the sunset. In
Aikawa the sense of desolation is more chilling, because it looks more like a
scene from our own times. Modern apartment blocks loom vacant over silent
streets, as if a nuclear accident had occurred. A bright blue poster on a wall
absurdly declares: POWER OF YOUTH!

Sado is often described as a mini-Japan, and sure enough, for more than
a decade, the national population, too, has been slowly declining. Japan is
what geographers call a "hyper-aged" society. Nearly a third of its people are
over sixty-five years old, and the population is declining by the hundreds
every day. Unless it opens the floodgates to immigration, the UN predicts
Japan will lose nearly twenty million people in the next thirty years. While
much of the world struggles with overpopulation, Japan worries about
depopulation. Wild boars and monkeys are rewilding forgotten villages.

Japan's economy is not shrinking, but it's treading a fine line. The first
decade after the bubble collapsed was nicknamed the Lost Decade, and the
first generation to enter the postlapsarian workforce is known as the Lost
Generation or Ice Age Generation. Three decades into the post-bubble era,
many Japanese simply talk about it all as the Lost Years.

Japan never reached the lows that Finland did, much less the misery of
post-Soviet Russia. No other wealthy nation, however, has seen its economy slow down for so long. Since the bubble ended, Japan's household
consumption rate has been a flattening curve. Government after government has attempted to get people spending again. The American economist Milton Friedman once wrote that governments could use a
"helicopter drop" of free money to stimulate their economies; Japan has
twice come close to turning that figure of speech into reality, handing out
tens of millions of shopping vouchers worth up to two hundred dollars
each. None of it has worked.

Sitting in her small, dark brewery, surrounded by vanishment, Rumiko
Obata accepted the fact that Sado Island simply was not going to return to
a growth path anytime soon. She concluded that she did not want Obata

Shuzu to succeed at the expense of other local breweries; the island had already dropped from over a hundred sake makers to only a handful. Instead, she realized that aggressive expansion, the goal of so many conventional companies, did not make sense on Sado. The island already had a cautionary tale about the potential environmental costs of boosting production of rice—the grain that is fermented to make sake—through industrial farming. The heavy use of pesticides and chemical fertilizers in the past had helped wipe out the crested ibis, or *toki*, a white, crane-like bird with such a distinctive pastel pink-orange under its wings that it is described in Japanese as *tokikala*: toki-coloured. Though the toki was formerly widespread, Sado had been the last place in Japan that the bird could be found; the species had to be reintroduced from central China. Locals still say that you can tell how many chemicals are used in a field by how often the toki visit it.

"I feel uncomfortable when people say there should be growth," Obata said. "There are two kinds of growth: one is expansion and the other is maturity. This occurs in the human body as well. As you grow up, your body is expanding. Then it becomes a matter of adding more years in a healthy way."

Curiously, Obata's new approach to business *has* resulted in growth. The company recently expanded, taking over a sunset-facing, seaside school that had been forced to close (it's an extraordinary quality of Japanese culture that they have historically built schools in scenic locations) and creating an education centre, not only for sake making, but also to bring big ideas from around the world to Sado. The sake they make there works entirely within Sado's natural limits, right down to the energy supply, which comes from solar panels; the rice is certified toki-friendly. A little less than half of Obata Shuzu sake is sold on the island, and the same amount in the rest of Japan, but the company now also exports worldwide. Obata no longer thinks of Sado's residents as castaways of history. She considers them pioneers. "I think Japan's future will come from the countryside," she said. "I'm not saying in terms of technology or money—I mean the way of thinking."

Even what is lovely or sacred—and the human hand in Japan has contributed a lot of beauty, a lot of holiness, to the landscape—is waning on Sado. I spoke to a man who had recently become the caretaker of a temple, only to find that the roof of the temple was falling apart. I asked him what would be done. Nothing would be done, he said. The roof would fall apart. There was no money to repair the temple, and no community to rally to the task. *Shikata ganai*, people say in Sado: nothing can be done about it.

Such stories can rouse hard-wired fears and sadness that the human imprint on the planet might be starting its long fade to black. Yet a lesson from Sado Island is that when a wealthy, technologically advanced country slows its consumption, the result need not be a freefall into poverty, let alone a return to the Stone Age. A previous era of human endeavour is in decay on Sado, but there is no real sense of want. The people who live there have cars and smartphones and televisions. It would be a hard place to get rich, but money still circulates—it *flows*. Many of the large, bubble-era restaurants and hotels have closed, to be replaced by neighbourhood restaurants and small inns. The permanent closure of so many shops, on the other hand, is a direct consequence of the arrival of centralized big-box stores and online ordering. There is still an economy. It is simply smaller.

There are two main groups of people on Sado Island. One is composed of longtime residents, most of them senior citizens, who remember the bubble and the gold-mine days and are generally saddened by the deterioration of the lively place they once knew. The other group is made up of more recent arrivals from younger generations who have sought out Sado Island for what it is becoming. Sado has turned generational stereotypes upside down: it's often the old who have nostalgia for progress, the young who cherish what is old.

In Japan, people who return to the countryside after living in a city are known as "U-turners"; those who grew up in a city and are trying country life for the first time are called "I-turners," for their straight-line migration from urban to rural. Shades of apocalypse have encouraged both trends. On March 11, 2011, Japan was struck by a savage earthquake and tsunami, which killed nearly twenty thousand people and triggered a nuclear disaster in the Fukushima area. Some recent arrivals to Sado left behind homes that were destroyed or irradiated, while others felt compelled by the catastrophe to question their values and lifestyles. The disaster is known as 3/11.

Motoe Oikawa moved to the island more than a decade ago as an I-turner. A former dental hygienist who tired of living in Tokyo, she has no illusions about Sado's prospects. Since she arrived, the population has declined by ten thousand.

As Oikawa stands in front of her farmhouse, "snow flowers"—huge, ragged snowflakes—are pinwheeling out of the few clouds in an otherwise blue sky, a familiar late-winter phenomenon on Sado. She wears sturdy work pants and a wool toque, but there are still hints of the Tokyo commuter about her, too: her socks are a perfect blue match for her padded jacket, and a pink scarf brightens the ensemble. Oikawa—despite starting out with minimal experience—is now a farmer, in part to put food on her own table. (Her homemade soy sauce is the earthy, savoury essence of umami.) But she also specializes in growing high-grade, "beyond organic" rice and adzuki beans, most of which she sells online and ships off the island. "I really wanted to make something good, and properly, so that overcame any intimidation," she told me. "Everyone here has some special project or technique."

The term for this in Japan is *kodawari*, a word that refers to a kind of positive obsession or deeply committed preference. We in the West might call it a person's passion—their "thing." I heard an apocryphal story in Japan about a man whose kodawari was to produce the most exquisitely engineered briefcases; he spent a year designing a latch that would shut with exactly the soft but authoritative click of a Leica camera shutter.

A consumer can have kodawari, too, and that person might also be an *aiyosha*. The word translates as "a person who uses a product lovingly." An aiyosha might seek out the highest-quality gardening hoe, sharpen the blade regularly, and take satisfaction from the way the handle subtly wears to the shape of her hands. Oikawa's customers, dedicated to eating some of the best rice in the world, are aiyosha, but so might be a person who forms a powerful attachment to their Toyota truck or Apple phone. It's not the rejection of materialism, but rather its transformation—a deeper relationship with material goods.

People still shop for the basics on Sado, too, but it's a downsized, simplified consumer culture. The winter is long and cold, and there are no streets where the cafés, shops and restaurants buzz with energy. "The Tokyo people who come here don't want the same lifestyle they had in Tokyo," Oikawa said. "They realize they had a lot of things they didn't need. There, you have more income, but you have to work. Here, you don't have as much income, but you don't spend as much money. If how much money you have is a point of status, you can't have that kind of status on Sado."

Oikawa didn't come to the island with wealth, and she doesn't expect to become wealthy. Since moving here, she has thought a lot about *yutori*, another word that has no direct translation into English, but is used in such phrases as "no yutori can be found in our daily lives." What it means, in the broadest sense, is room, in the sense of breathing room. For some, that means a financial cushion, for others, a surplus of time, a beautiful environment to live in, mental calm, a sense of possibility, some freedom to do what you want. For most people, it's a blend of some or all of the above.

In Tokyo, Oikawa says, there is a surplus of money and the things that it buys, but she now considers that a narrow expression of the concept. "I wonder if I had yutori in Tokyo," she said. "It's not a busy lifestyle here. I'm not time-strapped. There are times when it's busy, but there are times when it's slow. I have more space in my life and in my heart."

She still visits the megacity, though less and less often. "The Tokyo lifestyle feels like a trap to me now: you go there, you want things, you have to buy them. There's a lot of fun things to do, or have, or eat. But you consume it all. Here on Sado, there's nothing. You have to create it for yourself. The joy is not from consuming, it's from being a creator."

When I set out on this thought experiment, I wasn't sure what the nature of the results would be. Would there be dozens of different ways that a world that stops shopping might function, if it functions at all? Or would a consistent pattern emerge, a cluster of ways of being that overlapped and recurred among different places, people and times?

Sado Island provided an answer. Everything I heard and saw there echoed what I had heard and seen elsewhere, except that what was happening no longer had the feel of an adaptation. Instead, it felt like a system. A rudimentary system, still early in its evolution, but a system nonetheless.

At the core of the system is an economy that is smaller and slower-churning than the one we know from consumer capitalism. There is less paid work available, which has three main results. The first and most obvious is that most people earn less and buy less. The second, closely related to the first, is that there is an unusual surplus of noncommercial time, reminiscent of sabbaths and the lives of people who practise voluntary simplicity. The third is that people spend more of that time providing, in some way, for themselves. On Sado Island, with its rural character and inexpensive land, that often means growing at least part of their own food. It also—as Oikawa pointed out, and as the advocates for a more participatory and creative culture would confirm—means making more of your own fun. When one new resident, an evacuee from the Fukushima nuclear disaster zone, founded a simple, concrete-floored gathering space in a 180-year-old farmhouse, he was surprised to see locals showing up in their best clothes. Five years later, the room is sometimes a restaurant, sometimes a tea house, sometimes a theatre, bakery, comedy club or noodle-making workshop. There had been an unmet hunger for social and cultural life.

The relationship with things is different on Sado, too. People tend not to have so many of them, and they hang on to them longer. There's a lot of wabi-sabi: patched pants, faded paint, older cars. But it really is an economy of fewer, better things. The stuff people own, once again paradoxically, seems more, not less important to them—an appreciation either for how long the object will be a part of their lives or, in the case of things more fleeting, like food, its exceptional quality. Some of what people make, eat and own on the island is as good as it gets, really. It's not an economy of endless new pleasures, but of pleasures you live with for years, if not a lifetime.

To mainstream economists, growth is always a solution and never a problem: Peter Victor once surveyed a century of articles in the *American Economic Review* and found not one that focused on the costs of growth. Yet geographers are quick to recognize that an endlessly rising population can create serious problems, and regard degrowth's twin—depopulation—as a challenge, not a catastrophe. Peter Matanle, a British geographer who has been visiting Sado Island periodically since 2004, argues that a "depopulation dividend" accompanies the end of population growth. There is no struggle on Sado to find a nursery space for your children or to get into the college classes that you want. There's no housing crisis on Sado, no commuter misery; instead of rising anxiety about immigration, there's increasing openness to it. Unusually for any corner of the planet right now, the natural world on Sado Island is growing richer and more abundant every day. As Rumiko Obata put it, people may say there is depopulation, but there is growth in the number of toki.

In other ways, Sado Island is far from a vision of life after the day the world stops shopping. A declining population may mimic the effects of a drop in consumption in some ways, but it isn't the same: a deconsumer society wouldn't have the same haunted emptiness, nor the loss of capacity in the community itself. Then there is the fact that, by all accounts, Japan's national government has never accepted, planned for or taken deliberate steps to make the best of the end of growth. Instead, they have continued, against the tide of reality, to pursue a return to consumer-driven expansion, leaving places like Sado, where growth seems close to impossible, in a state of suspended animation. Finally, there is the question of whether tiny, shrinking Sado Island, with its pastoral rice fields and quiet country roads, can really hold any lessons for a place like Tokyo, the largest human settlement on Earth, still pulsing with life and light.

Perhaps it can. For now, Japan's major cities, such as Osaka and Tokyo, are still gaining population as migrants flow in from the rest of the country. Even in Tokyo, though, the slow pace of the economy casts its shadow. Shibuya plaza remains iconic: the giant screens still flicker, fashionista youth still parade the newest looks, and tourists flock to experience the "scramble," an every-way-at-once street crossing that heightens the sense of frantic urban life. Yet Shibuya hasn't changed much in forty years. The screens have an almost vintage look compared to the media architecture of today, and the buildings, made with futuristic materials that are now water-stained and weathered, look contradictory to the eye. Perhaps Shibuya still is the world's vision of the future.

In 2010, Norihiro Kato, a literary professor, published a widely read essay in which he described a new breed of Japanese youth: the nonconsumer. "In a world whose limits are increasingly apparent, Japan and its youths, old beyond their years, may well reveal what it is like to outgrow growth," Kato wrote, going so far as to call the dream of limitless growth "an earlier stage of development." In Tokyo, Kato's nonconsumers are everywhere. Faced with a seemingly permanent slowdown in the economy, many are involuntary simplifiers, wearing second-hand clothes, staying in tiny flats or with their parents, living online rather than blowing money in shops and nightclubs. Outside, their natural habitat is convenience stores like 7-Eleven, a company born in America but now based in Japan, where they eat their signature contribution to Japanese cuisine: *konbini* (convenience) food, such as one-dollar stuffed rice balls. There's no Versace or Louis Vuitton in sight; culture journalist Tyler Brûlé observed that Japan is transforming into "the world's first post-luxury economy."

These particular nonconsumers have been condemned as *hikikomori*, or shut-ins, but they are not shut in so much as shut out of the economy. What they represent is the emptiness left behind when one way of life, consumer capitalism in this case, is failing, with nothing to replace it. I heard, though, that a different vision of Tokyo's future might be seen not in its throbbing heart, but at its furthest edge.

It took more than an hour on a northbound suburban train to reach its final station, Ogawa-machi. There, Satoko Hatta was easy to find—hardly anyone else was waiting. Tucked between the wide sheepskin collars of a jacket she could have borrowed from Bob Dylan, Hatta was an unusual combination of the most genuine friendliness and a skeptical, mordant intelligence. The day was clear and cold, and she immediately made for a cozy bistro, an emphatically simple place with plywood and plaster walls. "This restaurant is like a symbol of Ogawa-machi," Hatta said.

Ogawa-machi began as a rice-paper manufacturing town that rose out of fields that flow and pool between the low hills of the Saitama district. Greater Tokyo's tideline gradually crept out to engulf the village. At its peak, some forty thousand people lived in Ogawa-machi, and the residents' main concern was that there weren't enough schools to serve all the children. Since then, it's lost 20 percent of its population. Ogawa-machi was once named one of the district's three communities most likely to disappear entirely.

Instead, people began to I-turn from downtown Tokyo to this suburb on its fringe. Most have never in their adult lives known a booming economy; in Japan, that includes people up to middle age. As Yoshihiro Nakano, a professor of development studies at Waseda University in Tokyo, said to me, "Those who are excluded from economies are condemned to create alternative economies."

Hatta's own move to Ogawa-machi happened slowly. First, she was a commuter. Then she began working in logistics for organic farms. Today, her job is to help newcomers settle and succeed. The main attraction these days is organic agriculture. In the 1970s, a pioneering farmer went organic here, and his apprentices gradually spread across the surrounding landscape. For a time, almost all of the produce was shipped into Tokyo, in much the same way that most Ogawa-machi residents rode the train downtown every day. But as Tokyo's tideline recedes, Ogawa-machi is beginning to embrace organic farming as its economic foundation. The bistro Hatta beelined to serves organic food. The supermarket is locally owned, and makes space for Ogawa-machi's growers. Just down the road, a brewery serves beer made with ingredients drawn from within a four-kilometre radius. Even the grab-and-go doughnuts at the subway station are enriched with water left over from the production of organic tofu. You can find similar businesses anywhere these days, but I had never seen them so integrated into what was once an ordinary suburb.

This is not a triumphant story of economic revival, at least not in any conventional sense. Ogawa-machi is still shrinking, Hatta said, and residents expect to get by rather than get rich. What is remarkable is that even a part of Tokyo is evolving toward the same patterns as Sado Island. More of the economy is smaller scale and local, and less is accomplished through individual participation in the cash economy. Most people, Hatta said, work in "agriculture and *x*." The *x* might be freelance design, consulting, coding, the arts, some kind of part-time job or kodawari small business. There are still commuters. Buildings, cars, clothing, the chairs in the café—everything shows signs of age, with newness a rare pleasure rather than the gloss on everyday life. It's a different way of being, but far from a bad one. When I asked Hatta how long she plans to live in Ogawa-machi, she replied, "Forever."

Do people who move there know what they're getting into? "No," said Hatta, with a wide smile. But they're tired of waiting for the old economy to change, and they're ready to try to make a new one. I asked what the most important piece of advice is that she gives them, the words that might guide anyone, anywhere, who wants to travel a similar path. She lowered her head and sank into thought.

"Instead of wanting something you don't have, look at what you do have," she said at last. "I say that often."

Koichiro Takano, who was elected the first mayor of all of Sado Island after it shrank enough to be considered a single jurisdiction, stood in the vast lobby of a seaside hotel, the giant windows looking out through wind-gnarled pines to a placid bay. The only other person in the sprawling space was the hotel receptionist, joined by a small, malfunctioning robot, which, when greeted with the words "Hi robot," peevishly replied, in digital read-out, "HIGH DEVIL." As Takano took a seat in the lounge, the brilliant white furniture seemed to swallow him whole.

Retired since 2012, Takano is a dignified, even sombre, figure, and so it feels impolite—yet surely relevant—to point out that his corduroy trousers had lost much of their ribbing, and the cuff of his sportcoat was missing a button. You could say that the former mayor's clothing looks threadbare, as Sado looks threadbare. You could as easily say that his clothes are well-worn, and Sado Island is an old soul.

As mayor, Takano had launched a public consultation about how to face Sado's crisis. What did the islanders want their economy to do? Some clamoured for growth, but most felt that was no longer the question. "It's really useless to resist," Takano said. The community decided that the main purpose of the economy was to make Sado a *sumiyasui tokoro*, or "comfortable place to live." It should have a healthy environment, good sake breweries, a growing population of toki, care and welfare for the elderly; it should maintain its traditions and restore the best of its architecture. "Our work is to ensure that the people who live here feel happy and we are building the local community—that they have a good life," Takano said.

Was it difficult to give up on growth? He didn't think there was too much to it. "Things don't change overnight—things change on something more like a ten-year span. Unless you're being really rigid, you should be able to adapt."

These days, Takano has the luxury of taking the long view. Maybe, he said, Sado Island's story is simply the story of the twentieth century: a rush into modernity, and now a return to a more timeless pattern. Four centuries ago, before Sado's gold-mining era, the island's population was about fifty thousand. It more than doubled, and now, once again, is approaching fifty thousand. "If you take away that mine period," he said, "things haven't changed that much."

He is more interested now in the roots of Japan's shrinking population. People misunderstand it, he said. They think the problem is rural depopulation, the global pattern of people leaving the country for the city. But most Japanese already live in cities, and the entire nation is losing population. Tokyo has one of the lowest birth rates, lower than Sado Island. Without migrants from the countryside, the world's largest city would be, demographically speaking, on the pathway to extinction, every generation smaller than the last. In a sense, then, it is not the country but the city—enormous, unsleeping, voracious, beguiling—that drives Japan's decline. People vanish into it. Why is it happening? Takano has thought about this question a lot.

"When a culture enters into maturity, maybe there's a tendency for human nature to try to destroy itself, to bring about its own end. Maybe we carry that inherently," he said. "Maybe there is a kind of god playing a role in reducing our number."

It is easy to wave this off as the apocalyptic vision of a man who has watched his own world fade and fall apart. But the words seem to haunt the consumer dilemma. We can't stop shopping; we must stop shopping. It isn't only that consumption is distorting the climate, felling the forests, cluttering our lives, filling our heads with a throwaway mindset, even stealing the stars from the night sky. The worst is that it leaves us with no idea of what else to do, no belief that things can be different. Whichever way we go, it leaves us doomed.

The Japanese word for consumption is *shohi*. It was created in the nineteenth century from two other words, *hi*, to spend, and *sho*, to extinguish, like a fire that burns itself to ashes. The roots of the English word are similar: to consume originally meant to utterly exhaust what existed before, to leave nothing behind, as though devoured by flame. If we are to consume more and more, it will have to be more of everything: more opportunities and more exhaustion, more experiences and more distraction, more depth but also more shallowness, more fullness but also more emptiness. We will consume time, space, life, death. We'll consume others and we'll consume ourselves. It all goes into the fire.

One hundred and fifty thousand years later . . .

The Juǀ'hoan village of Duin Pos, which is how you spell Dune Post in Afrikaans, is no longer in sight, lost somewhere in the flat scrub of the Kalahari Desert. Five women spread like a hand across the landscape, seeming to feel their way forward, lightly and quickly. It's high season for bush potatoes, wild tubers that are delicious when roasted, or sweet and refreshing—like mild sugar cane—when raw. No more than a few moments ever pass before one of the party bends to dig, vigorously, despite an air temperature that still hovers above 40 degrees Celsius in these cooler hours of late afternoon.

I had come to Duin Pos to go gathering with the hunter-gatherers—a chance to witness what the anthropologist Marshall Sahlins, fifty-five years ago, called the practice of "running below capacity." The Juǀ'hoansi tend to gather just enough to meet the needs of the moment. Even when one or another edible plant or nut is at its peak of abundance, they will not lay away stores against the future beyond a day or two. Sahlins wondered at the "inner meaning" of this way of life, and what it might say to outsiders whose wants appear to be infinite, and who are forever stretched thin from reaching toward the limits of their productivity. I wondered the same thing, and also where that inner meaning might lead us a hundred, a thousand, many thousands of years after the world stops shopping.

When I arrived in Duin Pos, three hours' drive from Namibia's paved highway network into the Ju|'hoan territory of Nyae Nyae, the idea of running below capacity, here, seemed to me to be risky indeed. From the low summit of the village's namesake dune, the spreading Kalahari, blurred by afternoon heat, looked almost like the sea: blue and with gentle swells. It is, of course, the opposite, a parched and searing landscape. It's a difficult place to survive at the best of times, and even harder near the end of a rainy season that hadn't brought any rain in months.

There was no store-bought food in the village, and probably no money, either. They had their government rations of cornmeal, but everything else they ate came from the bush. It had been two days since the women last went gathering, and they planned to go as soon as the sun began to lower its gaze. "Even if I have food from the shop and government, I still *want* to eat bush food," a woman named ||Uce (sounds a bit like "Lucy") told me. She was dressed in a knit hat, pastel pink shirt and bright pink skirt, all second-hand, all as neat and clean as if this fact alone could erase the hardships of desert life.

When it was time, the women were ready in a matter of moments. They only needed to pick up their digging sticks, which these days are typically metal rods with one end beaten flat, then tie on wraps either as shoulder bags or to backpack their babies. They found their first foodstuff three minutes after setting out, when ||Uce spotted a delicate whorl of bush-potato vine poking up through a low shrub.

Gathering is skilled work. Before we left the village, ||Uce had pointed to a plant sprouting just beyond the circle of people gathered around a fire that had burned down to embers. It was a gemsbok cucumber vine, she said, which produces spiky-looking fruit filled with refreshing pulp, but has a poisonous root. (Children also use the vines as skipping ropes.) The Kalahari cucumber vine looks nearly the same, but has a tasty root. ||Uce can tell one from the other at fifteen paces.

Still, it is the blood, death and danger of hunting that have always dominated the wider public's imaginings of hunter-gatherer life. Even the anthology of papers from the 1966 conference that revolutionized Western scientists' view of hunter-gatherers was titled *Man the Hunter*, though a key finding of that conference was that gatherer-hunters might be the more accurate term. (Richard B. Lee found that 60 to 80 percent of the Ju|'hoan diet at the time was made up of wild plants, mainly harvested by women.) ||Uce shrugs it off. A gatherer is just as likely as a hunter to run into a lion, leopard or elephant in the bush, she told me. She showed the hollow on her forearm where, while digging out a tuber, she had once been bitten by "the snake that can bite from both sides." Known in English as Bibron's stiletto snake, the Ju|'hoan name comes from the fact that the snake can rotate its fangs so that they stick out either side of its mouth. Fortunately, the venom usually is not fatal—it only causes severe pain and swelling on its way to carving out a pocket of dead tissue in your flesh.

For an hour and a half, the women search the desert. Between finds, they discuss their discoveries or make jokes or point out the fresh footprints of an elephant, which are huge and yet so softly set down that it seems the enormous animals could easily sneak up behind you. A thrill ripples through the group when ||Uce, digging beneath a tangled bush, flushes out another snake-that-can-bite-from-both-sides. Overhead, a crowd of clouds walks the sidewalks of the sky, each with an air of independence. They carry rain, but they are carrying it elsewhere.

And then, suddenly, the gathering trip is over. The women arc back toward the village, somehow knowing its exact position in a desert that to my eyes looks featureless. They have collected a few dozen bush potatoes, a handful of other tubers, and a stack of juicy poison-onion greens (only the root is poisonous). It is enough to feed the village for a day or two.

I am surprised by my own reaction to the women's decision to go home with so little food. To me, it seems to stray well beyond simple living and into a danger zone. Why not stay out until sundown, get enough food for a month, fill a storehouse while the bush potatoes are plentiful? In such an unforgiving land, how could it possibly make sense *not* to maximize productivity when a surplus of resources is available?

Over the decades, people who study hunter-gatherer life have explained away these kinds of questions in various ways. Some concluded that the Kalahari Desert was an unexpected paradise of abundance, in which food was always available to the knowledgeable hunter or gatherer and there was no need to think of the future. In fact, while the Kalahari is often surprisingly fertile, its riches are also unpredictable, and periods of hardship or suffering are not uncommon, especially during droughts. As a result, the Ju|'hoansi historically moved around within their territories to take advantage of scattered and seasonal food resources. This became another explanation for running below capacity, because why would they carry burdensome loads of possessions or food when they have to travel by foot? Yet there is little doubt the Ju|'hoansi could have carried more than they did, or cached supplies and belongings in places they always returned to.

Many hunter-gatherer cultures are now known to employ measures to avoid overharvesting; leaving bush potatoes behind in high season, for example, might give more of the plants a chance to reproduce. Perhaps running below capacity is an act of economy in the older sense: the prudent use of resources in order to sustain them into the future. Then there is the fact that long hours of work undermine the Ju|'hoan notion of the good life. Like voluntary simplifiers, but more so, they solved Keynes's "economic problem" by having few enough needs that they can meet them relatively easily, even in the heart of the Kalahari Desert. The reward for living with less is meant to be a plenitude of leisure time.

Anthropologist James Suzman points out that people in the West have long imagined that they, too, would someday satisfy their material desires and embrace a life of leisure. The problem has not been a failure to reach that satisfaction, but to grasp it. In 2008, political scientist Robert E. Goodin and his colleagues found that, by working only enough to live just above the poverty line and keeping household chores to a basic standard of social acceptability, people in the rich world could enjoy abundant free time. Most choose instead to work toward second homes, renovations, more clothes, furniture in the latest style, the newest gadgets, adventure travel—and dream of the day, forever postponed, when technology finally liberates them from daily toil.

Each theory about why the Ju|'hoansi live simply probably contains its grain of truth, but none makes clear to me why the women foraged only enough food for one or two days, when, with a little more effort, they could have brought back enough for a week. What's more, they did so during a drought—the kind of precarious circumstances that, as we saw in the pandemic, inspire many of us to hoard food, supplies and even entertainments.

It all seems even more inexplicable in light of another unmistakable difference between the Ju|'hoansi and global consumer society: the Ju|'hoansi take sharing very, very seriously.

Back in the village, the women pile the gathered food together and take seats on the blankets around the fire. A few small logs are burning now, a nod to the lengthening shadows; the desert heat dissipates quickly with the approach of sunset, and by midnight it will be almost cool. A sense of well-being suffuses the scene. There is a tendency in the West to think of any African who lives in a hut as the picture of desperation. Here, the people look emphatically healthy; their skin glows. An old man, nearly blind with cataracts, taps a walking stick down a fence line to join the group, but even he looks strong, and makes wisecracks to his neighbours as he settles in. Everyone will eat together, and everything will be shared.

Would a world without shopping become one in which wealth is distributed more evenly? Throughout history, many people have thought so; it's the assumption built into that old catchphrase "Live simply, so that others might simply live." In capitalist countries, it rarely if ever works out that way. Live simply, and it's much more likely that the wealth you've forsaken will end up in the hands of someone who was better off to begin with.

The Ju|'hoansi, on their long journey through time, rejected this outcome. Again, it's hard to say exactly why. Perhaps they learned along the way what modern social scientists have also shown—that inequality aggravates rates of consumption—and saw that too much consumption in a place with finite resources would end in disaster. Whatever the reason, they, like many other hunter-gatherer cultures, became radically egalitarian, not only in the distribution of wealth but in rights and freedoms for individuals.

The word "sharing," as applied to the Ju|'hoansi, is not as warm and fuzzy a concept as you might assume. Even the term "redistribution of wealth" doesn't quite describe what they do. In most countries, wealth is distributed either through taxation and wage laws enforced by the state, or through charity handed out at private donors' discretion. Among the Ju|hoansi, sharing involves both rights and responsibilities. If someone has something you don't, it is your right to ask for a share, often quite bluntly—anthropologists call it "demand sharing." If you acquire something, you have a responsibility to make yourself available to share it. The Ju|'hoansi are guided by the general principle that what you have, regardless of how you came to have it, should be shared with those who have less if they adhere to that same belief. In the words of Megan Laws, an anthropologist at the London School of Economics and Political Science who has studied sharing as it is carried out today in Nyae Nyae, people are expected to make themselves "vulnerable to others."

Sharing among the Ju|'hoansi is notoriously difficult for outsiders to comprehend, but it is certainly conspicuous. Hand a Ju'|hoan a cigarette—smoking is deeply rooted in Ju|'hoansi culture, and tobacco is only the most recent expression of the habit—and chances are good it will be smoked by five or more people, while still "belonging" to the person you gave it to. Similarly, hunters "own" the meat they bring back from the bush, but failing to share it would be unthinkable. When I asked one hunter how many people a springhare (an animal that resembles a kangaroo the size of a tomcat) would feed, he was perplexed. It would feed as many people as it was supposed to, he replied, even if each one received only a small share. To do otherwise would invite mockery and gossip.

The introduction of the cash economy and the weaker social bonds of town life have led to greater inequality in Nyae Nyae and shaken sharing traditions. One relatively well-to-do Ju|'hoan explained to me how he navigates the new times. Since he lives in the town of Tsumkwe, he said, he doesn't have a village to share with day by day. Instead, he shares with a network of dozens of people. How much he shares with each depends on the strength of their mutual relationship, his own wealth at the time, and the need of the person involved; he might give groceries or money to one and offer no more than a cigarette to another. In return, he often gets things he can't easily procure for himself, such as hunted meat, fresh milk or bush vegetables. It is as imperfect as any system made up of individual personalities, he said. Some people are overly generous and others "walk in a zigzag"—away from you when they have, and toward you when they have not. But he felt no need to give *everything* away. It was enough to make himself available to others and to take their circumstances into account. He had been able to buy a phone, a television with satellite connection, and a car, without public condemnation.

In many villages in Nyae Nyae, there is still next to no difference in the material wealth of each resident. The Ju|'hoansi describe themselves as "people who help each other," and say that the best among them are those who "just give to people." As for outsiders, several Ju|'hoansi told me they've met enough of us to know that most of us are not good at sharing.

It's often said that the difference between the simple life and poverty is that one is a choice and the other is not. The distinction isn't always so straightforward. In the case of the Ju|'hoansi, it is difficult—probably impossible—to parse where traditional simplicity continues by preference and where it persists as a result of dispossession. They have long faced racism, segregation and unequal treatment in Namibia, making it far easier for them to end up underconsuming than overconsuming. It's equally clear, however, that long-standing ways of being remain vital among the Ju|'hoansi. Many still accumulate less money and fewer possessions than they could with more effort, and limit their wants mainly to a fair share of what the landscape makes available. Seeing this, outsiders often dismiss the Ju|'hoansi as holdovers, forever struggling to apply their ancient lifeways to a world in which they no longer make sense. If they weren't stuck in the past, they would surely stop running below capacity and give in to the cash economy, nine-to-five jobs, store-bought goods. They would gather all the bush potatoes they can, and keep them for their own security and betterment.

It is as though the Ju|'hoansi *refuse* to step off the razor's edge. Which, as it turns out, may be something close to the truth.

Sharing and running below capacity have one effect in common: they sustain a delicate balance between security and precarity. Taking only what is needed maintains a state of "just enough." Sharing, as described in Laws's research, does much the same, preventing anyone from accumulating a surplus of the available wealth, or the power and status over others that can confer. In secure times, people are reminded of their precarity; in precarious times, they feel more secure. Everyone is constantly made to recognize that—to borrow a phrase from the Urarina people of the Peruvian Amazon—they "stand leaned together."

Somewhere in the mists of the past 150,000 years, the Ju|'hoansi apparently determined that perhaps the single most important condition for survival in the long run is never to forget that we need one another.

Consumer culture was supposed to be irresistible. Back in 1984, Gary Larson published a cartoon that reflected what was then an emerging belief about the fate of hunter-gatherer cultures. His drawing showed a caricatured bone-through-the-nose tribe rushing to hide their lamps, phones, TVs and video recorders. One of them shouts out a warning to the others— "Anthropologists! Anthropologists!"—as safari-suited researchers paddle up to their huts.

That same year, Rick Wilk, an American anthropologist, presented a paper titled, "Why Do the Indians Wear Adidas?," which is now something of a cult classic in the field. In the 1960s, after researchers had told the rest of the world that the hunter-gatherer lifestyle was actually much better than anyone else had imagined, people like the Ju|'hoansi had thrust upon them many people's romantic need to believe—without making any serious changes to their own pursuit of material wealth—that there still were cultures untouched by the corrupting forces of consumerism. For a time, introductory textbooks in the field gave the impression that, as one critic put it, hunter-gatherers had "near-perfect lives." The hunter-gatherers, meanwhile, were going shopping.

"It's hard to describe just how divorced the anthropology we were trained in was from what we saw when we actually got out into the world," Wilk told me. In 1979, he arrived to do graduate fieldwork among the Q'eqchi' culture in Belize. "Day one, I'm living in the village and I'm watching mules laden with cases of Coca-Cola heading off to more distant villages."

Wilk's paper, co-written with Eric J. Arnould, gathered similar observations from around the globe: Indigenous people in Peru who carried rectangular rocks painted to look like transistor radios; Banna people in a remote corner of Ethiopia paying for the chance to look through a View-Master at a 3-D Disney slideshow entitled "Pluto Tries to Become a Circus Dog"; White Mountain Apache puberty ceremonies in Arizona involving "the massive redistribution of soda pop." To many in the West, these reports were disappointing signs that Eden had truly and finally fallen. For others, they confirmed that consumer culture itself was progress, and the only thing that decided whether people fully became consumers was how much access they had to goods and services, and how much money they had to pay for them.

What the research actually showed is that, as the world's kaleidoscope of cultures engaged with the global consumer economy, consumerism was proving to be far from inevitable. Some cultures consumed a great deal, others very little; some consumed collectively, others privately; some put materialism at the heart of their societies, and others on the periphery. What did seem to be the case, however, is that consumer culture as most of us know it is an increasingly powerful force. "It thrives in situations of instability and contradiction, on social disruption and individual mobility," Wilk said. It's hard to miss the fact that these conditions define the current world order. Consumer culture creates the circumstances that create consumer culture.

The Ju|'hoansi are not stuck in the past. Instead, it seems they look at the world around them today—a world of instability and disruption—and see, as they always have, a precarious place to live. It is a place where, maybe more than ever, it remains important to make ourselves vulnerable to each other. As so quickly became clear during the pandemic, when a random disease was allowed to hurt some far more than others through no fault of their own, if we give up on each other when the going is good, it can be hard not to do the same when the going gets tough. For all of their struggles, there is a sense among the Ju|'hoansi that they have the fundamentals right.

With the horizon dipping into the golden yolk of the sun, a big pot of food is on the fire in Duin Pos. Already, the children are eating roasted beetles as an appetizer. The whole village, now, is together on the blankets, aloft in conversation and laughter. Loneliness here seems impossible. Almost every person is in physical contact with at least one other. Legs across legs, hands on shoulders, children across laps, backs leaned against backs. The mood is so festive, in fact, that I begin to wonder. Is this a special gathering, unusual for some reason?

The young woman whom I ask looks confused by my question. She pauses to take in the scene. "No," she replies at last. "This is the normal way."

Maybe she's right. Maybe it is. Perhaps, 150,000 years after the day the world stops shopping, the rest of us will have come to the same conclusion: above all, we need to need one another. A simpler life leads to a still simpler one and a simpler one after that, until we gradually relearn how to live in such a way that, even if we discover how to make our resources infinite, we might find we don't want to consume every last thing. What will our current age of consumption look like then? A misstep. A puzzling failure to return to normal. A moment of disconnection before we rejoined the long timeline of human history, and in so doing gave ourselves a future.

There's a better way to stop shopping

An unexpected result of writing a book about consumption is that I found myself shopping *more.*

I bought an almost comically ethical pair of jeans, for example, made in a revived jeans factory in Wales, using durable denim from what may be the most environmentally minded denim mill in the world, and dyed grey with the natural waste products of some kind of palm tree. I invested in a fifty-dollar broom with an estimated lifespan of twenty years, built by hand in Vancouver on antique machinery powered only by two leanly muscled sisters, Mary and Sarah Schwieger—a deconsumer business if ever I have seen one. ("Our economy is based on constant growth, which we are not," Mary told me.) I purchased second-hand clothes, and a safety razor that will get me through the rest of my life without ever having to buy another disposable one.

My shopping binge was the result of clarity. The act of consuming, I realized, had become so complicated and weighted with issues that I often avoided it entirely; now, having done a lot of research on the subject, I knew what I wanted my consumption to look like. I wanted the things I owned to serve their purpose well, to last for as long as I wanted them to, to be made in ways that were in keeping with my values, and to provide an enduring sense of satisfaction. I also did a lot of not-shopping. I had a trench coat retailored to bring it up to date. I resoled shoes, fixed my own toaster, sewed up ripped seams in my clothing, replaced lost buttons, had my phone repaired instead of buying a new one. As the Depression-era saying goes, I used it up, wore it out, made it do, or did without. Of all the things I wanted to buy but didn't, I remember only one (a new sleeping bag), which I take to be a sign of how fleeting these desires usually are. Looking around my home, there is nothing I've purchased recently that I regret or that goes unused. I rest easy with my choices.

My focus as a consumer is now fewer, better *everything*: goods, travels, activities, YouTube videos, hours on social media. In the time I've gained from making these choices, I've done more of the simple things—reading, walking, talking with people—that I already knew I find satisfying. I do feel these changes are making my life better, and I do feel materialism weakening its grip. But I haven't stopped working long hours too often, can't get comfortable with the idea of living on less income in such precarious times, haven't really learned to sit quietly with my thoughts—at least not yet.

There are good reasons why you, too, might want to stop shopping. Perhaps consumerism is hurting you financially, cluttering your life with things you don't need or love, using up time and attention that you could put to better use, or contributing to planet-wide ecological crises that you care deeply about. Maybe you see in simplicity a chance to have more unscheduled time, freedom, calm or connection. Your consumption may feel hollow—a parade of distractions that never seems to lead anywhere. By all means, slow down. Stop. Like many others, you may discover that living with less is one secret to a happier life.

But can you bear with me through one more contradiction? When you or I stop shopping, it doesn't bring us any closer to a lower-consuming society. History tells us, in no uncertain terms, that the forces stacked in favour of consumerism—from social inertia, to pressure to conform, to governments that rise or fall on a percentage point of economic growth, to the vast machineries of advertising and multi-trillion-dollar markets with investors to serve—have always been a stronger influence than popular movements urging us to live simply.

The Puritans, the religious sect that fled in disgust from the corrupted morals and materialism of Europe, began anew in America, living plainly and with piety. Within a generation they were immersed in land speculation, the pursuit of fortunes and conspicuous consumption.

The early American patriots, who would become the founding fathers of the United States, practised simplicity as a model of the higher American ideals they believed would surely follow the overthrow of the British. After their successful revolution, they despaired as their new country descended into vanity, selfishness and extravagant consumption.

Henry David Thoreau, in the mid-nineteenth century, propounded "simplicity, simplicity, simplicity"—including as a way to free us from giving so much of our lives to bosses and drudgery. Even in his own time, his ideas were widely admired but rarely followed. Thoreau himself once admitted that his words spoke more loudly than his actions. "Those things I say," he said, "others I do."

And so it has continued, with back-to-the-land movements, reconnect-with-nature movements, fads for decluttering, manias of worry about the nerve-fraying pace of modern life, all rising time and again only to be swept away by a rush of consumption unlike anything seen before. The hippies became the boomers. Generation X rejected the conspicuous consumption of the 1980s only to take up what psychologist Geoffrey Miller called "conspicuous precision," or the public display of artisanship, quality, provenance and ethical virtue—drawing more sophisticated lines around positional consumption than ever before. Millennials famously bought fewer things and more experiences, and often *increased* their ecological footprints. When the pandemic shuttered the consumer economy, and we told ourselves nothing would ever be the same again, history was quietly laughing.

Surveying what he called this "metronome behaviour," tick-tocking between eras in which simplicity became trendy or was utterly ignored, historian David Shi concluded that simple living was "destined to be a minority ethic." In every era it would appeal to some people, and sometimes to many people, but never to most of them. Less would never be more. When it comes to reducing consumption, you can be the change you want to see in the world, but it will not change the world.

This is a problem, of course, because shopping is destroying the planet we live on.

Fortunately, our repeated failures to simplify do not render our situation quite as hopeless as it seems. There is another way to read these setbacks, and it is this: since a deconsuming world will not be achieved by individuals making the choice to live with less, something else must be tried. A world that stops shopping is not something we will *do*, but something we have to *make*.

I gave a magic wand to Amanda Rinderle of Tuckerman & Co., maker of probably the world's most sustainable dress shirts. If she could use it, I asked, to change one thing in order to help create an economy of better but less, what would that one thing be? Rinderle thought for a while (overnight, in fact) and then got back to me, apologizing that her answer was not magical, but rather quite technical: she would make prices tell the whole truth. "It would have to be one hell of a wand," she said.

Right now, prices reflect demand for goods and services and the costs of producing them: materials, energy, manufacturing, marketing, shipping. Mostly excluded are the *consequences* of production and consumption, from pollution to soil erosion to carbon emissions to habitat loss and onward to the human health effects of all of these, the incredible destruction wrought by wildfires, floods and storms in the age of climate chaos, the burden of two billion tonnes of garbage each year, and the incalculable moral injury of driving million-year-old species into extinction.

For now, these costs are mainly shouldered not by producers, investors or consumers, but by society at large—economists call them "externalities," since they are accounted for outside the chains of supply and demand. And just like the wealth an economy creates, its externalities are never fairly shared: recall the people of Bangladesh, bearing the brunt of flooding, cyclones, toxic air and water. The most savage of consumerism's ironies is that those who consume the least often suffer far more of consumption's harms than those who consume the most.

Climate change is the ultimate externality: a cost of consumption that was left off the books until it threatened the future of civilization. British economist Nicholas Stern dubbed it "the greatest and widest-ranging market failure ever seen." Now, governments around the globe are beginning to assign climate pollution a price, often by charging a tax on carbon emissions, in order to make industries and shoppers pay something closer to the true cost of the fossil fuels burned up for their benefit. A similar approach to other natural resources, Rinderle said, would make Tuckerman & Co.'s shirts more cost-competitive. Maybe then organic cotton, grown in ways that regenerate rather than deplete the soil, would cost the same or less than cotton raised with polluting fertilizers and pesticides. A long-lasting shirt would suddenly be more penny-wise than a dozen disposable shirts, each with its heavy social and ecological footprint.

The same is true of any product. Forests store water, provide homes to thousands of species, stabilize the climate, and offer pleasure and consolation to the people who live in or visit them. If the right to cut down trees came at a higher price, wooden shelves would be built to last rather than thrown away and the wooden frames of demolished houses would never end up in a landfill. If the value of the rare earth minerals found in our digital devices included the cost of the land and waterways ruined to mine them, then your phone would be made to be repaired or updated, not discarded and replaced every two years.

If you want fewer, better things, you can certainly buy them. More and more businesses make high-quality goods. Your purchase, however, does little to change the fact that the system is stacked against those businesses and against you as their customer. As with organic food and green consumerism, we probably can shop our way to a niche market of premium-priced, long-lasting products that few people are willing or able to buy; we can't shop our way to a world that stops shopping.

Nearly every aspect of deconsumption turns out to demand changes beyond what can be achieved through an individual's choice to consume less. I can take breaks from earning and spending, for instance, but it takes a whole community, if not a nation, to bring back noncommercial time. I can become a deconsumer, but it will make me an outsider from society, or even an outcast, making it unlikely I'll stick with the change. When I reduce my personal consumption, it does not pressure governments to require that products be made repairable, address the income inequality and insecurity that fuels overconsumption, or think beyond GDP growth. It won't create the infrastructure for citizenship, participation or any other social role to replace that of the consumer. Intrigued by the research of Wouter van Marken Lichtenbelt and Elizabeth Shove, I have, as an experiment, chosen to live within a wider range of natural temperatures in my home. As the science predicts, I've come to enjoy the shifting patterns of heat and cold through a day or the seasons—but I've accomplished exactly nothing to change the social and technological trends that steadily increase the energy demands of temperature control.

Fortunately, ideas already exist for how to achieve every aspect of deconsumer society that appears in this book. Lifespan labelling can encourage product durability; new tax regimes and regulations can favour repair over disposability; job-sharing programs and shorter work days or work weeks can keep people employed in a slower, smaller economy. Redistribution of wealth can reverse inequality, or prevent it from worsening in a lower-consuming world. A guaranteed basic income makes it possible for people who are willing to live simply to spend less time on the job or withdraw from the workforce entirely. In a culture of consumer capitalism, such a choice is often condemned as laziness or lack of ambition; in a deconsumer society, it might be admired for its sufficiency—success in achieving enoughness.

I set out on my thought experiment as an observer. I wanted to see for myself where a world that stops shopping would lead, rather than be guided by others' theories. In the end, both approaches arrive at the same place. Movements for degrowth and a well-being economy—one measured not by GDP but by its ability to improve the quality of life of citizens—have been steadily refining a set of ideas and ways of life that could free us from the need for relentless, and relentlessly damaging, economic expansion. The alternative to consumer capitalism is not a constellation of possibilities, but increasingly a convergence.

It is still reasonable to reduce your consumption for personal reasons alone. But there are many more roles that individuals can play. A world that stops shopping needs new products and services, new theories of how an economy can function, new ways of making meaning in our lives, new models for doing business, new habits, new policies, new protest movements, new infrastructure. As Kris De Decker said, "We have to rethink *everything*."

Nearly everyone on Earth is familiar with this scale of change. We live in an age of innovation, from the introduction of goods like the car, computer and smartphone, to services like space tourism and overnight global shipping, to system shifts like worldwide internet connectivity. Even before the pandemic, we were swept up by changes in every sphere of existence, many of them thrilling. A transition to a lower-consuming society would be just as wide and deep a transformation.

We live, too, in an age of disruption, which capitalism continues to lay claim to as a right. The transfer of manufacturing from richer countries to poorer ones left behind whole regions of rust-belt abandonment; online shopping led to such widespread closures of brick-and-mortar businesses that it has been dubbed the "retail apocalypse." There's no indication that we're approaching the other changes on our near horizon with any more caution than these earlier ones: artificial intelligence and virtual reality are just two emerging technologies that promise to cause major social upheaval. (Goodbye truckers, hello self-driving vehicles.) This is not to say that it's the right way to go about things, only that it's the usual way. Any slowdown in consumption risks economic repercussions as grave as any we've faced in the course of human history, and should be undertaken with care for those who are vulnerable. At the same time, solving the consumer dilemma is the most urgent challenge of our times, the problem that begets all our other biggest problems. We've been asked to endure sweeping changes many times for lesser reasons.

What about those technological solutions that have so far been held out as our best and only hope to save the planet? What about renewable energy? What about recycling, water conservation, organic farming, bicycle paths, electric cars, walkable cities and all the rest of it? Their potential to reduce the consumption of resources is as important as ever, or more so. The critical difference is that, if they are no longer as deeply undermined and counteracted by consumer culture, they may finally achieve their end.

Technology can reduce the degree to which we need to cut back consumption; reducing consumption narrows the gap technology needs to span. Each buys time for the other, and for us.

This book began with a question: Can we solve the consumer dilemma? The answer is yes, we can. In slowing an economy bound to endless expansion, we only rejoin the longer trend of more gradual growth seen throughout most of history; with ingenuity, we can adapt. The more personal question—whether we want to go down this path—is harder to answer. The evidence suggests that life in a lower-consuming society really can be better, with less stress, less work or more meaningful work, and more time for the people and things that matter most. The objects that surround us can be well made or beautiful or both, and stay with us long enough to become vessels for our memories and stories. Perhaps best of all, we can savour the experience of watching our exhausted planet surge back to life: more clear water, more blue skies, more forests, more nightingales, more whales. Many people will see, in the day the world stops shopping, a world they want to live in. Others will see a dystopia.

Suppose we start with a more humble goal: to reduce consumption by 5 percent across the rich world. That would take us back to the lifestyle of a couple years ago, a shift we might hardly feel. Yet everything would begin to change, from our desires to the role of economics to the future of the planetary climate. It might be the end of the world as we know it. It will not be the end of the world.

ACKNOWLEDGEMENTS

'd first like to thank everyone that I interviewed as I worked on this book, for sharing their insight and experience, and for playing along with some imaginative nonfiction. Whether you are named in these pages or not, please trust that your contribution was invaluable, and that I greatly appreciate your openness to participate in the human conversation.

This book was written in the tradition of nonfiction thought experiments and fictional reimaginings of reality. Two books from that canon were particularly important to me: *The World without Us*, by Alan Weisman, and *News from Nowhere*, by William Morris.

Several people went above and beyond to smooth my access to potential sources or the logistics of my travels. They are: at Levi Strauss & Co., Amber McCasland and Phil Zabriskie; in Ecuador, Juan Andrés Portilla; in Finland, Vera Schoultz, Anu Partanen, Anna Alanko and Saska Saarikoski; in the UK, Jenny Poulter, Jamie Burdett, and the Adland voices who gathered one memorable night in London but are not otherwise named in this book (Jonathan Wise, Lucy Clayton, James Parr); for Seattle, the writer Emma Marris provided helpful contacts; for Japan, the insightful research of geographer Peter Matanle led me to Sado Island; and I was shown further generosity by Tetsuo Ikeda, Yoshihiro Nakano, Andrew Sutter and Yasuyuki Sato; for Namibia, I received essential guidance from James Suzman and Megan Laws. I'd also like to thank the always prompt staffs of the US Bureau of Labor Statistics, Bureau of Economic Analysis,

University of British Columbia Library and Vancouver Public Library. Libraries have always been models for a lower-consuming society.

I worked directly with several people as colleagues along the way. The marvellous Joanne Will helped me with the groundwork. Maho Harada was my interpreter, translator and fixer in Japan; most of all, I appreciate her friendship. In Namibia, Oma Leon Tsamkxao and Steve |Kunta were my guiding lights. Tuomo Neuvonen and |Ailae Fridrick |Kunta contributed translations. I'd also like to acknowledge Tilman Lewis, Aline Bouwman and Deirdre Molina for their deft assistance with the final edits.

Friends, too, went out of their way to help me in ways that I never seem to find any way to properly repay. Thanks very much to Jennifer Jacquet, Lara Honrado, Joanna Wong, Yoshi Sugiyama, Vanessa Timmer, Paul Shoebridge, Michael Simons, Ronald Wright and Ruben Anderson. I'd also like to express my deep appreciation to the readers on my mailing list for their enduring support and useful suggestions (you can join the list by emailing me through the contact page at jbmackinnon.com).

In the writing world, Jim Rutman provided critical early feedback, after which he and his colleagues quite literally made this project possible. Matt Weiland is just plain one of the best people you will meet in the business. For her timely support, I thank Emma Janaskie. My editors made this book much better and helped me guide it closer to my original vision than any other book I've written to date; thank you, Anne Collins, Sara Birmingham and Stuart Williams. Some of the developmental work for this book appeared in the *New Yorker* and *The Atlantic*; I am especially grateful to Jeremy Keehn and Michelle Nijhuis for their outstanding editorial guidance. I remain indebted to all members of the Vancouver FCC.

My lifelong appreciation to Alisa, for everything, just everything.

Finally, my apologies and thanks to whomever I've forgotten. As for those whom I've named here, they are responsible only for the best of the book; the worst of it, including any errors, is mine to bear alone.

I am grateful to have received funding support at critical stages of this project from Access Copyright Foundation, a nonprofit copyright licensing organization representing writers and other creators.

SOURCE NOTES

What follows, listed by chapter, are principal sources that informed or influenced my writing or thinking. If you have further questions about the origin of any specific fact, please contact me directly at jbmackinnon.com.

Two books bear special mention for their contribution to multiple chapters, and they are Frank Trentmann's history of consumption, *Empire of Things* (Allen Lane, 2017); and Thomas Piketty's *Capital in the Twenty-first Century* (Belknap, 2014). My statistics on personal consumption in the United States usually derive from United States Bureau of Economic Analysis (BEA) and US Bureau of Labor Statistics (BLS) data; similar data at the global scale are generally from United Nations sources (e.g., the UN Department of Economic and Social Affairs) or the World Bank. I have frequently benefited from reports in the *New York Times* and *The Guardian* newspapers.

PROLOGUE: We must stop shopping but we can't stop shopping

Besides the books, reports and studies listed below, various facts included in this chapter are drawn from Global Footprint Network, UN Food and Agriculture Organization, International Energy Agency, Carbon Brief, White House Archives, National Bureau of Statistics of China, and World Economic Forum.

Elhacham, Emily, Liad Ben-Uri, Jonathan Grozovski, Yinon M. Bar-On, and Ron Milo. "Global human-made mass exceeds all living biomass." *Nature* 588 (2020): 422-444.

Ellen MacArthur Foundation. *A New Textiles Economy: Redesigning Fashion's Future.* Ellen MacArthur Foundation, 2017.

Kaza, Silpa, Lisa Yao, Perinaz Bhada-Tata, and Frank Van Woerden. *What a Waste 2.0: A Global Snapshot of Solid Waste Management to 2050.* World Bank, 2018.

Laws, Megan. "All Things Being Equal: Uncertainty, Ambivalence and Trust in a Namibian Conservancy." PhD diss., The London School of Economics and Political Science, 2019.

Lee, Richard Borshay, and Irven DeVore. *Man the Hunter.* Transaction, 1968.

MacKinnon, J.B. "Can We Stop Global Warming and Still Grow?" *New Yorker*, March 27, 2017.

Mueller, Paul D. "Adam Smith's Views on Consumption and Happiness." *Adam Smith Review* 8 (2014): 277–89.

Oberle, Bruno, Stefan Bringezu, Steve Hatfield-Dodds, Stefanie Hellweg, Heinz Schandl, et al. *Global Resources Outlook 2019: Natural Resources for the Future We Want.* UN Environment Program International Resource Panel, 2019.

Remy, Nathalie, Eveline Speelman, and Steven Swartz. *Style That's Sustainable: A New Fast-Fashion Formula.* McKinsey & Company, 2016.

Rose, A., and S. B. Blomberg. "Total Economic Impacts of a Terrorist Attack: Insights from 9/11." *Peace Economics, Peace Science, and Public Policy* 16, no. 1 (2010): 2.

Shi, David E. *The Simple Life.* New York: Oxford University Press, 1985.

Suzman, James. *Affluence without Abundance.* New York: Bloomsbury, 2017.

Zalasiewicz, Jan, Mark Williams, Colin N. Waters, Anthony D. Barnosky, John Palmesino, et al. "Scale and Diversity of the Physical Technosphere: A Geological Perspective." *Anthropocene Review* 4, no. 1 (2017): 9–22.

CHAPTER 1: What we give up and what we hang on to

Additional sources include Levi Strauss & Co., US BEA and the National Bureau of Economic Research.

Dittmar, Helga, Rod Bond, Megan Hurst, and Tim Kasser. "The Relationship between Materialism and Personal Well-being: A Meta-analysis." *Journal of Personality and Social Psychology* 107, no. 5 (2014): 879-924.

Jacobs, Meg. "America's Never-Ending Oil Consumption." *The Atlantic*, May 15, 2016.

Jacobs, Meg. *Panic at the Pump: The Energy Crisis and the Transformation of American Politics in the 1970s.* New York: Hill and Wang, 2016.

Lee, Michael S.W., and Christie Seo Youn Ahn. "Anti-consumption, Materialism, and Consumer Well-being." *Journal of Consumer Affairs* 50, no. 1 (2016): 18–47.

Miller, Daniel. *The Comfort of Things.* Cambridge: Polity, 2008.

Miller, Daniel. *Consumption and Its Consequences.* Cambridge: Polity, 2012.

Museum of Modern Art. *Fashion Is Kale* (symposium), New York. Filmed October 19, 2017.

Putt del Pino, S., E. Metzger, D. Drew, and K. Moss. "The Elephant in the Boardroom: Why Unchecked Consumption Is Not an Option in Tomorrow's Markets." Washington, DC: World Resources Institute, 2017.

Trentmann, Frank. *Empire of Things.* London: Allen Lane, 2017.

Wilk, Richard R. "Consumer Cultures Past, Present, and Future." In *Sustainable Consumption: Multi-disciplinary Perspectives,* edited by Alistair Ulph and Dale Southerton, 315–36. Oxford: Oxford University Press, 2014.

CHAPTER 2: We don't shop equally, so we won't stop equally

Additional sources include the Government of Ecuador, Economic Policy Institute, UN Development Program, US Census Bureau, World Bank, Worldwatch, World Happiness Report and Happy Planet Index.

Jacobs, Meg. *Pocketbook Politics: Economic Citizenship in Twentieth-Century America.* Princeton: Princeton University Press, 2005.

Steinbeck, John. *Log from the Sea of Cortez.* New York: Viking, 1941.

Trentmann. *Empire of Things.*

York University Ecological Footprint Initiative and Global Footprint Network. National Footprint and Biocapacity Accounts, 2021 edition.

CHAPTER 3: It's not that time turns weird, it's a different kind of time
This chapter also benefited from the records of the US Supreme Court.

Cohen, Lizabeth. "From Town Center to Shopping Center: The Reconfiguration of Community Marketplaces in Postwar America." *American Historical Review* 101, no. 4 (1996): 1050–81.

Laband, David N., and Deborah Hendry. *Blue Laws: The History, Economics, and Politics of Sunday-Closing Laws.* Lexington, MA: Lexington Books, 1987.

MacKinnon, J.B. "America's Last Ban on Sunday Shopping." *New Yorker,* February 7, 2015.

Mass-Observation and R. Searle. *Meet Yourself on Sunday.* London: Naldrett, 1949.

Shi. *The Simple Life.*

Shulevitz, Judith. *The Sabbath World: Glimpses of a Different Order of Time.* Random House Incorporated, 2011.

Trentmann. *Empire of Things.*

CHAPTER 4: Suddenly we're winning the fight against climate change
Special thanks to Damon Matthews, Concordia University research chair in climate science and sustainability, and Trissevgeni "Jenny" Stavrakou of the Royal Belgian Institute for Space Aeronomy. Additional sources include the *New York Times,* International Energy Agency, NASA Scientific Visualization Studio, Global Carbon Project, Carbon Brief and the air-pollution technology company IQAir.

IEA. *World Energy Outlook.* Paris: IEA (multiple years).

Jackson, Robert B., Josep G. Canadell, Corinne Le Quéré, Robbie M. Andrew, Jan Ivar Korsbakken, et al. "Reaching Peak Emissions." *Nature Climate Change* 6, no. 1 (2016): 7–10.

Knight, Kyle W., and Juliet B. Schor. "Economic Growth and Climate Change: A Cross-National Analysis of Territorial and Consumption-Based Carbon Emissions in High-Income Countries." *Sustainability* 6, no. 6 (2014): 3722–31.

Masson-Delmotte, V., P. Zhai, H.-O. Pörtner, D. Roberts, J. Skea, et al., eds. *Global Warming of 1.5°C: An IPCC Special Report on the Impacts of Global Warming of 1.5°C above Pre-industrial Levels and Related Global Greenhouse Gas Emission Pathways, in the Context of Strengthening the Global Response to the Threat of Climate Change, Sustainable Development, and Efforts to Eradicate Poverty*. IPCC, 2019.

Meadows, D.H., D.L. Meadows, J. Randers, and W.W. Behrens III. *The Limits to Growth: A Report for the Club of Rome's Project on the Predicament of Mankind*. New York: Universe Books, 1972.

Mian, Atif, and Amir Sufi. *House of Debt*. Chicago: University of Chicago Press, 2014.

Ward, James D., Paul C. Sutton, Adrian D. Werner, Robert Costanza, Steve H. Mohr, and Craig T. Simmons. "Is Decoupling G.D.P. Growth from Environmental Impact Possible?" *PloS One* 11, no. 10 (2016): e0164733.

Wiedmann, Thomas O., Heinz Schandl, Manfred Lenzen, Daniel Moran, Sangwon Suh, et al. "The Material Footprint of Nations." *Proceedings of the National Academy of Sciences* 112, no. 20 (2015): 6271–76.

York, Richard. "De-carbonization in Former Soviet Republics, 1992–2000: The Ecological Consequences of De-modernization." *Social Problems* 55, no. 3 (2008): 370–90.

CHAPTER 5: We need to get used to the night again

Other sources include NASA, International Dark-Sky Association and the Kennedy Space Center, and the *New York Times* from February 21 and 24, 1962. Analyst Thomas Liles of Rygard Energy and entomologist John Wallace also provided valuable information.

Bundervoet, T., et al. "Bright Lights, Big Cities, Measuring National and Subnational Economic Growth in Africa from Outer Space, with an Application to Kenya and Rwanda." Policy Research Working Paper WPS7461, World Bank Group, 2015.

Davies, Thomas W., and Tim Smyth. "Why Artificial Light at Night Should Be a Focus for Global Change Research in the Twenty-first Century." *Global Change Biology* 24, no. 3 (2018): 872–82.

Elvidge, Christopher D., Feng-Chi Hsu, Kimberly E. Baugh, and Tilottama Ghosh. "National Trends in Satellite-Observed Lighting." *Global Urban Monitoring and Assessment through Earth Observation* 23 (2014): 97–118.

Falchi, Fabio, Pierantonio Cinzano, Dan Duriscoe, Christopher C. M. Kyba, Christopher D. Elvidge, et al. "The New World Atlas of Artificial Night Sky Brightness." *Science Advances* 2, no. 6 (2016): e1600377.

Glenn, John H., Jr. "Description of the MA-6 Astronomical, Meteorological, and Terrestrial Observations." *Results of the First U.S. Manned Orbital Space Flight February 20, 1962*. NASA: 1962.

Green, Judith, Chloe Perkins, Rebecca Steinbach, and Phil Edwards. "Reduced Street Lighting at Night and Health: A Rapid Appraisal of Public Views in England And Wales." *Health & Place* 34 (2015): 171–80.

Henderson, J. Vernon, Adam Storeygard, and David N. Weil. "Measuring Economic Growth from Outer Space." *American Economic Review* 102, no. 2 (2012): 994–1028.

Hough, Walter. "The Development of Illumination." *American Anthropologist* 3, no.2 (1901): 342–52.

Kyba, Christopher C.M., and Franz Hölker. "Do Artificially Illuminated Skies Affect Biodiversity in Nocturnal Landscapes?" *Landscape Ecology* 28 (2013): 1637–40.

Kyba, Christopher C.M., Theres Kuester, Alejandro Sánchez De Miguel, Kimberly Baugh, Andreas Jechow, et al. "Artificially Lit Surface of Earth at Night Increasing in Radiance and Extent." *Science Advances* 3, no. 11 (2017): e1701528.

Shaw, Robert. "Night as Fragmenting Frontier: Understanding the Night That Remains in an Era of 24/7." *Geography Compass* 9, no. 11 (2015): 637–47.

Steinbach, Rebecca, Chloe Perkins, Lisa Tompson, Shane Johnson, Ben Armstrong, et al. "The Effect of Reduced Street Lighting on Road Casualties and Crime in England and Wales: Controlled Interrupted Time Series Analysis." *Journal of Epidemiology and Community Health* 69, no. 11 (2015): 1118–24.

Trentmann. *Empire of Things*.

CHAPTER 6: The end of growth is not the end of economics

A further resource was the JFK Library. Below is a short reading list of quality books that raise important questions about growth.

Blyth, Mark. *Great Transformations: Economic Ideas and Institutional Change in the Twentieth Century.* Cambridge: Cambridge University Press, 2002.

Kallis, Giorgos, Susan Paulson, Giacomo D'Alisa, and Federico Demaria. *The Case for Degrowth.* Oxford: Polity, 2020.

Jackson, Tim. *Prosperity without Growth: Foundations for the Economy of Tomorrow,* 2nd ed. Routledge, 2017.

Hickel, Jason. *Less Is More: How Degrowth Will Save the World.* London: Penguin Random House, 2020.

Pilling, David. *The Growth Delusion.* Tim Duggan Books: New York, 2018.

Raworth, Kate. *Doughnut Economics: Seven Ways to Think Like a Twenty-first-Century Economist.* White River Junction, VT: Chelsea Green Publishing, 2017.

Victor, Peter. *Managing without Growth: Slower by Design, Not Disaster,* 2nd ed. Cheltenham, UK: Edward Elgar, 2019.

CHAPTER 7: The consumption disaster begins, the disaster of everyday life is over

I relied greatly for this chapter on the expertise and research of University of Helsinki scholars including Päivi Timonen at the Centre for Consumer Society Research; Anna Alanko at the Centre for Research on Addiction, Control, and Governance; historian Juha Siltala; media studies researcher Anu Kantola; and Matti Kortteinen at the Helsinki Institute of Urban and Regional Studies. I'm also indebted to journalist Saska Saarikovski and the Finnish home economics organization Martat. A further source is the World Health Organization.

Barro, Robert J., and José F. Ursúa. *Macroeconomic Crises since 1870.* No. w13940. National Bureau of Economic Research, 2008.

Barro, Robert J., and José F. Ursúa. "Rare Macroeconomic Disasters." *Annual Review of Economics* 4, no. 1 (2012): 83–109.

Fligstein, Neil, Orestes P. Hastings, and Adam Goldstein. "Keeping Up with the Joneses: How Households Fared in the Era of High Income Inequality and the Housing Price Bubble, 1999–2007." *Socius* 3 (2017).

Hennigan, Karen M., Linda Heath, J. D. Wharton, Marlyn L. Del Rosario, Thomas D. Cook, Bobby J. Calder. "Impact of the Introduction of Television on Crime in the United States: Empirical Findings and Theoretical Implications." *Journal of Personality and Social Psychology* 42, no. 3 (1982): 461-477.

Jonung, Lars, and Thomas Hagberg. *How Costly Was the Crisis of the 1990s?: A Comparative Analysis of the Deepest Crises in Finland and Sweden over the Last 130 Years.* No. 224. Directorate General Economic and Financial Affairs, European Commission, 2005.

Riihelä, Marja, Risto Sullström, and Matti Tuomala. *What Lies behind the Unprecedented Increase in Income Inequality in Finland during the 1990s.* Working Paper 2, Tampere Economic Working Papers Net Series. University of Tampere, 2001.

Salokangas, Raimo. "Why Recessions Lower the Impacts on Mental Health." *Duodecim* 111, no. 16 (1995): 1576.

Schor, Juliet. "Do Americans Keep Up with the Joneses?: The Impact of Consumption Aspirations on Savings Behaviour." (Courtesy of the author.) May 1997.

Schor, Juliet B. *The Overspent American.* New York: Basic Books: 1998.

Solnit, Rebecca. *A Paradise Built in Hell.* New York: Viking Penguin: 2009.

Veblen, Thorstein B. *The Theory of the Leisure Class.* Oxford: Oxford University Press, 2009 [first published 1899].

CHAPTER 8: Can advertising turn into the opposite of itself?

Additional sources include Glimpse Collective (weglimpse.co), Levi's historian Tracey Panek, Patagonia, Inc. and Jon Alexander of the New Citizenship Project (newcitizenship.org.uk).

Kotler, Philip, and Sidney J. Levy. "Demarketing, Yes, Demarketing." *Harvard Business Review* 49, no. 6 (1971): 75–77.

MacKinnon, J.B. "Patagonia's Anti-Growth Strategy." *New Yorker,* May 21, 2015.

Okazaki, Shintaro, and Barbara Mueller. "The Impact of the Lost Decade on Advertising in Japan: A Grounded Theory Approach." *International Journal of Advertising* 30, no. 2 (2011): 205–32.

Picard, Robert G. "Effects of Recessions on Advertising Expenditures: An Exploratory Study of Economic Downturns in Nine Developed Nations." *Journal of Media Economics* 14, no. 1 (2001): 1–14.

Ridgeway, Rick. "The Elephant in the Room." Patagonia.com. Fall 2013.

Sekhon, Tejvir S., and Catherine A. Armstrong Soule. "Conspicuous Anti-consumption: When Green Demarketing Brands Restore Symbolic Benefits to Anti-consumers." *Psychology & Marketing* 37, no. 2 (2020): 278–90.

Trentmann. *Empire of Things.*

CHAPTER 9: We adapt to not-shopping more quickly than you think

Special thanks to Sam Geall of *China Dialogue* (chinadialogue.net/en). Additional information from the World Bank and *China Dialogue*.

Brown, Kirk Warren, Tim Kasser, Richard M. Ryan, and James Konow. "Materialism, Spending, and Affect: An Event-Sampling Study of Marketplace Behavior and Its Affective Costs." *Journal of Happiness Studies* 17, no. 6 (2016): 2277–92.

Dittmar et al. "The Relationship between Materialism and Personal Well-being."

Geall, Sam, and Adrian Ely. "Narratives and Pathways towards an Ecological Civilization in Contemporary China." *China Quarterly*, 236 (2018): 1175–96.

Kasser, Tim. "Materialistic Values and Goals." *Annual Review of Psychology* 67 (2016): 489–514.

Kasser, Tim, Katherine L. Rosenblum, Arnold J. Sameroff, Edward L. Deci, Christopher P. Niemiec, et al. "Changes in Materialism, Changes in Psychological Well-being: Evidence from Three Longitudinal Studies and an Intervention Experiment." *Motivation and Emotion* 38, no. 1 (2014): 1–22.

Keynes, John Maynard. "Economic Possibilities for Our Grandchildren." 1930.

Lekes, Natasha, Nora H. Hope, Lucie Gouveia, Richard Koestner, and Frederick L. Philippe. "Influencing Value Priorities and Increasing Well-being: The Effects of Reflecting on Intrinsic Values." *Journal of Positive Psychology* 7, no. 3 (2012): 249–61.

Offer, Avner. *The Challenge of Affluence.* Oxford: Oxford University Press, 2006.

Nasr, Nada. "The Beauty and the Beast of Consumption: A Review of the Consequences of Consumption." *Journal of Consumer Marketing* 36, no. 7 (2019): 911–25

Wang, Haining, Zhiming Cheng, and Russell Smyth. "Wealth, Happiness and Happiness Inequality in China." In *Wealth(s) and Subjective Well-being,* edited by Gaël Brule and Christian Suter, 445–61. Springer, 2019.

CHAPTER 10: We may need to see the ruins to know it's time to build something new

Burawoy, Michael, and Kathryn Hendley. "Between Perestroika and Privatisation: Divided Strategies and Political Crisis in a Soviet Enterprise." *Soviet Studies* 44, no. 3 (1992): 371–402.

Burawoy, Michael, Pavel Krotov, and Tatyana Lytkina. "Involution and Destitution in Capitalist Russia." *Ethnography* 1, no. 1 (2000): 43–65.

Eichengreen, Barry. *Hall of Mirrors: The Great Depression, the Great Recession, and the Uses—and Misuses—of History.* Oxford: Oxford University Press, 2015.

Gessen, Masha. "The Dying Russians." *New York Review of Books,* September 2, 2014.

Greasley, David, Jakob B. Madsen, and Les Oxley. "Income Uncertainty and Consumer Spending during the Great Depression." *Explorations in Economic History* 38, no. 2 (2001): 225–51.

Kindleberger, Charles P., and Robert Z. Aliber. *Manias, Panics, and Crashes,* 6th ed. Palgrave MacMillan, 2011.

Oberle et al. *Global Resources Outlook 2019.*

Southworth, Caleb. "The Dacha Debate: Household Agriculture and Labor Markets in Post-Socialist Russia." *Rural Sociology* 71, no. 3 (2006): 451–78.

Romer, Christina D. "The Nation in Depression." *Journal of Economic Perspectives* 7, no. 2 (1993): 19–39.

Terkel, Studs. *Hard Times: An Oral History of the Great Depression*. Pantheon: New York, 1986 [first published 1970].

York. "De-carbonization in Former Soviet Republics."

CHAPTER 11: A stronger, not a weaker, attachment to our things
I received helpful guidance from members of the Sustainable Consumption Research and Action Initiative (scorai.org).

Cooper, Tim, ed. *Longer Lasting Products: Alternatives to the Throwaway Society*. CRC Press, 2016.

Cooper, Tim, Naomi Braithwaite, Mariale Moreno, Giuseppe Salvia. *Product Lifetimes and the Environment: Draft Conference Proceedings*. Nottingham: Nottingham Trent University, 2015.

Dupuis, Russell D., and Michael R. Krames. "History, Development, and Applications of High-Brightness Visible Light-Emitting Diodes." *Journal of Lightwave Technology* 26, no. 9 (2008): 1154–71.

Karana, Elvin, Owain Pedgley, and Valentina Rognoli, eds. *Materials Experience*. Butterworth-Heineman, 2014.

Krajewski, Markus. "The Great Lightbulb Conspiracy." *Spectrum, IEEE* 51, no. 10 (2014): 56–61.

Jackson, John Brickerhoff. *The Necessity for Ruins*. Amherst, MA: University of Massachusetts Press, 1980.

MacKinnon, J.B. "The LED Quandary: Why There's No Such Thing as 'Built to Last.'" *New Yorker*, July 14, 2016.

MacKinnon, J.B. "Trying to Solve the LED Quandary." *New Yorker*, Oct. 5, 2016.

Mostafavi, Moshen, and David Leatherbarrow. *On Weathering*. Cambridge, MA: MIT Press: 1993.

Trentmann. *Empire of Things*.

Weiser, Harald, and Tröger, Nina. "The Use-Time and Obsolescence of Durable Goods in the Age of Acceleration." BEUC/ European Consumer Organization, 2015.

CHAPTER 12: Fast fashion cannot rule but it may not have to die

An additional source is the Worker Rights Consortium (workersrights.org).

Ashmore, Sonia. "Handcraft as Luxury in Bangladesh: Weaving Jamdani in the Twenty-first Century." *International Journal of Fashion Studies* 5, no. 2 (2018): 389–97.

Berg, A., M. Heyn, E. Hunter, F. Rölkens, P. Simon, and H. Yankelevich. *Measuring the Fashion World*. McKinsey & Company, 2018.

de Wit, Marc, Jelmer Hoogzaad, Shyaam Ramkumar, Harald Friedl, and Annerieke Douma. *The Circularity Gap Report*. Circle Economy, 2018.

Ellen MacArthur Foundation, *A New Textiles Economy*.

Leitheiser, Erin, Syeda Nusaiba Hossain, Shuvro Sen, Gulfam Tasnim, Jeremy Moon, et al. "Early Impacts of Coronavirus on Bangladesh Apparel Supply Chains." RISC Briefing, Danida—Ministry of Foreign Affairs of Denmark, 2020.

Majima, Shinobu. "Fashion and the Mass Consumer Society in Britain, c. 1950–2001." PhD diss., University of Oxford, 2006.

Putt del Pino et al. "The Elephant in the Boardroom."

Remy, Speelman, and Swartz. *Style That's Sustainable*.

ThredUp. *Resale Report*. ThredUp, 2019.

Trentmann. *Empire of Things*.

US Bureau of Labor Statistics. *100 Years of US Consumer Spending: Data for the Nation, New York City, and Boston.* US Department of Labour, 2006.

CHAPTER 13: Business plays the long, long, long, long game

Other sources include Toraya Group archives, The Henokiens (henokiens .com), INSEAD Wendel International Centre for Family Enterprise, Fairphone and *Low-tech Magazine* (lowtechmagazine.com and solar.lowtechmagazine.com).

Anthony, Scott D., S. Patrick Viguerie, Evan I. Schwartz, and John Van Landeghem. *2018 Corporate Longevity Forecast: Creative Destruction Is Accelerating*. Innosight, 2018.

Daepp, Madeleine I. G., Marcus J. Hamilton, Geoffrey B. West, and Luís M. A. Bettencourt. "The Mortality of Companies." *Journal of The Royal Society Interface* 12, no. 106 (2015).

Pilling, David. *Bending Adversity: Japan and the Art of Survival.* New York: Penguin, 2014.

Mulgan, Geoff. *Good and Bad Innovation: What Kind of Theory and Practice Do We Need to Distinguish Them?* London: Nesta, 2016.

Wang, Yangbo, and Haoyong Zhou. *Are Family Firms Better Performers during the Financial Crisis?* SSRN Working Papers Series, 2012.

CHAPTER 14: If we're no longer consumers, what are we instead?

Additional sources include Participatory City Foundation (participatorycity .org), Every One Every Day (weareeveryone.org), New Citizenship Project (newcitizenship.org.uk), Greater London Authority and Redefining Progress (rprogress.org).

Britton, Tessy. *Hand Made.* 2010.

Open Works. *Designed to Scale.* n.d.

Participatory City Foundation. *Made to Measure: Year One Report.* Participatory City Foundation, n.d.

Participatory City Foundation. *Y2: Tools to Act.* Participatory City Foundation, n.d.

CHAPTER 15: We are still consuming way too much (part one: inconspicuous consumption)

Additional sources include the DEMAND Centre (demand.ac.uk) and *Low-tech Magazine.*

Ackermann, Marsha. *Cool Comfort: America's Romance with Air-conditioning.* Washington and London: Smithsonian Institution Press, 2002.

C40 Cities, Arup, and University of Leeds. *The Future of Urban Consumption in a 1.5 C World.* 2019.

Cabanac, Michel. "Physiological Role of Pleasure." *Science* 173, no. 4002 (1971): 1103–7.

Cooper, Gail. *Air Conditioning America.* London: The Johns Hopkins University Press, 1998.

de Wit et al. *The Circularity Gap Report* (2018).

de Wit, Marc, Jacco Verstraeten-Jochemsen, Jelmer Hoogzaad, and Ben Kubbinga. *The Circularity Gap Report 2019.* Circle Economy, 2019.

Heschong, Lisa. *Thermal Delight in Architecture.* Cambridge, MA: MIT Press, 1979.

Hui, Allison, Theodore Schatzki, and Elizabeth Shove, eds. *The Nexus of Practices: Connections, Constellations, Practitioners.* Taylor & Francis, 2016.

Oberle et al. *Global Resources Outlook 2019.*

Shove, Elizabeth. *Comfort, Cleanliness and Convenience: The Social Organization of Normality.* Oxford: Berg, 2003.

Trentmann. *Empire of Things.*

van Marken Lichtenbelt, Wouter, Mark Hanssen, Hannah Pallubinsky, Boris Kingma, and Lisje Schellen. "Healthy Excursions Outside the Thermal Comfort Zone." *Building Research & Information* 45, no. 7 (2017): 819–27.

van Vliet, Bas, Heather Chappells, and Elizabeth Shove. *Infrastructures of Consumption.* Earthscan, 2005.

CHAPTER 16: We are still consuming way too much (part two: money)

Bataille, Georges. *The Accursed Share, Vol. 1: Consumption.* Zone Books: New York, 1988 [first published 1949].

Dütschke, Elisabeth, Manuel Frondel, Joachim Schleich, and Colin Vance. "Moral Licensing—Another Source of Rebound?" *Frontiers in Energy Research* 6, no. 38 (2018).

Hood, Clifton. *In Pursuit of Privilege.* New York: Columbia University Press, 2017.

Fouquet, Roger, and Peter J.G. Pearson. "Seven Centuries of Energy Services: The Price and Use of Light in the United Kingdom (1300–2000)." *The Energy Journal* 27, no. 1 (2006).

Fouquet, Roger. "Historical Energy Transitions: Speed, Prices, and System Transformation." *Energy Research & Social Science* 22 (2016): 7–12.

Inoue, Nozomu, and Shigeru Matsumoto. "An Examination of Losses in Energy Savings after the Japanese Top Runner Program." *Energy Policy* 124 (2019): 312–19.

Jevons, William Stanley. *The Coal Question.* 1865.

Kallis, Giorgos. *Limits.* Stanford, CA: Stanford University Press, 2019.

Kropfeld, Maren Ingrid, Marcelo Vinhal Nepomuceno, and Danilo C. Dantas. "The Ecological Impact of Anticonsumption Lifestyles and Environmental Concern." *Journal of Public Policy & Marketing* 37, no. 2 (2018): 245–59.

Makov, Tamar, and David Font Vivanco. "Does the Circular Economy Grow the Pie?: The Case of Rebound Effects from Smartphone Reuse." *Frontiers in Energy Research* 6 (2018).

Mueller. "Adam Smith's Views on Consumption and Happiness.".

Murray, Cameron K. "What If Consumers Decided to All 'Go Green'?: Environmental Rebound Effects from Consumption Decisions." *Energy Policy* 54 (2013): 240–56.

Smith, Adam. *The Wealth of Nations.* 1776.

Stepp, John Richard, Eric C. Jones, Mitchell Pavao-Zuckerman, David Casagrande, and Rebecca K. Zarger. "Remarkable Properties of Human Ecosystems." *Conservation Ecology* 7, no. 3 (2003).

Trentmann. *Empire of Things.*

Welch, Evelyn. *Shopping in the Renaissance.* New Haven and London: Yale University Press, 2005.

CHAPTER 17: We finally, actually, save the whales

Other sources include the International Union for Conservation of Nature (IUCN), Convention on International Trade in Endangered Species of Wild Flora and Fauna (CITES), International Fund for Animal Welfare, Samoa Conservation Society and the National University of Samoa Centre for Samoan Studies.

Drury, Rebecca. "Hungry for Success: Urban Consumer Demand for Wild Animal Products in Vietnam." *Conservation and Society* 9, no. 3 (2011): 247–57.

310   J.B. MacKINNON

Duffy, Rosaleen. *Nature Crime*. New Haven and London: Yale University Press, 2010.

Filous, Alexander, Alan M. Friedlander, Haruko Koike, Marc Lammers, Adam Wong, et al. "Displacement Effects of Heavy Human Use on Coral Reef Predators within the Molokini Marine Life Conservation District." *Marine Pollution Bulletin* 121, no. 1–2 (2017): 274–81.

Kraus, Scott D., and Rosalind M. Rolland (eds.). *The Urban Whale*. Cambridge, MA: Harvard University Press, 2007.

MacKinnon, J.B. "It's Tough Being a Right Whale These Days." *The Atlantic*, July 30, 2018.

MacKinnon, J.B. "The Rich Meals That Keep Wild Animals on the Menu." *The Atlantic*, March 19, 2020.

Parry, Luke, Jos Barlow, and Heloisa Pereira. "Wildlife Harvest and Consumption in Amazonia's Urbanized Wilderness." *Conservation Letters* 7, no. 6 (2014): 565–74.

Pirotta, Vanessa, Alana Grech, Ian D. Jonsen, William F. Laurance, and Robert G. Harcourt. "Consequences of Global Shipping Traffic for Marine Giants." *Frontiers in Ecology and the Environment* 17, no. 1 (2019): 39–47.

Serra, Gianluca, Greg Sherley, S. Afele Faillagi, S. Talie Foliga, Moeumu Uili, et al. "Traditional Ecological Knowledge of the Critically Endangered Tooth-Billed Pigeon *Didunculus strigirostris*, Endemic to Samoa." *Bird Conservation International* 28, no. 4 (2018): 620–42.

Stirnemann, R.L., I.A. Stirnemann, D. Abbot, D. Biggs, and R. Heinsohn. "Interactive Impacts of By-catch Take and Elite Consumption of Illegal Wildlife." *Biodiversity and Conservation* 27, no. 4 (2018): 931–46.

Truong, V. Dao, Nam V.H. Dang, and C. Michael Hall. "The Marketplace Management of Illegal Elixirs: Illicit Consumption of Rhino Horn." *Consumption Markets & Culture* 19, no. 4 (2016): 353–69.

Quintus, Seth, and Jeffrey T. Clark. "Ritualizing Hierarchy: Power Strategies and Pigeon Catching in Ancient Samoa." *Journal of Anthropological Research* 75, no. 1 (2019): 48–68.

York, Richard. "Why Petroleum Did Not Save the Whales." *Socius* 3 (2017).

CHAPTER 18: We need a better word than happiness for where this ends up

Additional sources include the US BLS and the International Centre for Anti-consumption Research (icar.auckland.ac.nz).

Belk, Russell W. "Worldly Possessions: Issues and Criticisms." *ACR North American Advances* 10 (1983): 514–19.

Brown, Kirk Warren, and Tim Kasser. "Are Psychological and Ecological Well-Being Compatible?: The Role of Values, Mindfulness, and Lifestyle." *Social Indicators Research* 74, no. 2 (2005): 349–68.

Gregg, Richard B. "The Value of Voluntary Simplicity." *Pendle Hill Essays* 3 (1936).

Lee and Ahn. "Anti-consumption, Materialism, and Consumer Well-being."

Miller, Geoffrey. *Spent.* New York: Viking, 2009.

Oral, Cansu, and Joy-Yana Thurner. "The Impact of Anti-consumption on Consumer Well-being." *International Journal of Consumer Studies* 43, no. 3 (2019): 277–88.

Psychology & Marketing 37, no. 2 (2020). Special Issue on Anti-consumption.

Schor, Juliet B. "Voluntary Downshifting in the 1990s." In *Power, Employment, and Accumulation: Social Structures in Economic Theory and Practice,* edited by Jim Stanford, Lance Taylor, Ellen Houston, and Brant Houston, 66–79. M.E. Sharpe, 2001.

Seegebarth, Barbara, Mathias Peyer, Ingo Balderjahn, and Klaus-Peter Wiedmann. "The Sustainability Roots of Anticonsumption Lifestyles and Initial Insights Regarding Their Effects on Consumers' Well-being." *Journal of Consumer Affairs* 50, no. 1 (2016): 68–99.

Zavestoski, Stephen. "The Social–psychological Bases of Anti-consumption Attitudes." *Psychology & Marketing* 19, no. 2 (2002): 149–65.

A short reading list on voluntary simplicity in the 1990s:

Andres, Cecile. *The Circle of Simplicity.* New York: HarperCollins, 1997.

Dominquez, Joe, and Vicki Robin. *Your Money or Your Life.* New York: Viking, 1992.

Elgin, Duane. *Voluntary Simplicity.* Quill, 1998.

Luhrs, Janet. *The Simple Living Guide.* New York: Harmony, 1997.

Schor, Juliet B. *The Overspent American.* New York: Basic Books, 1998.

CHAPTER 19: Now we're all shopping in cyberspace?

Special thanks to Danny Goel, CEO of PrecisionOS, and Dan Burgar, president of the Vancouver VR/AR Association. The sources of many of my details on the "digital surge" are the *New York Times* and *The Guardian* newspapers.

Belk, Russell W., and Rosa Llamas. *The Routledge Companion to Digital Consumption.* New York: Routledge, 2013.

Devine, Kyle. *Decomposed: The Political Ecology of Music.* Cambridge, MA: MIT Press, 2019.

Galvin, Ray. "The ICT/Electronics Question: Structural Change and the Rebound Effect." *Ecological Economics* 120 (2015): 23–31.

Lehdonvirta, Vili. *Virtual Consumption.* Series A-11. Turku, Finland: Turku School of Economics, 2009.

Lehdonvirta, Vili, and Edward Castronova. *Virtual Economies: Design and Analysis.* Cambridge, MA: MIT Press, 2014.

Pike, Kenneth R., and C. Tyler DesRoches. "Virtual Consumption, Sustainability and Human Well-Being." *Environmental Values* 29, no. 3 (2020): 361–78.

Preist, Chris, Daniel Schien, and Paul Shabajee. "Evaluating Sustainable Interaction Design of Digital Services: The Case of YouTube." In *Proceedings of the 2019 CHI Conference on Human Factors in Computing Systems*, 1–12. 2019.

Widdicks, Kelly. "Understanding and Mitigating the Impact of Internet Demand in Everyday Life." PhD diss., Lancaster University, 2020.

Widdicks, Kelly, and Daniel Pargman. "Breaking the Cornucopian Paradigm: Towards Moderate Internet Use in Everyday Life." In *Proceedings of the Fifth Workshop on Computing within Limits*, 1–8. 2019.

World Economic Forum, Global Web Index, and Visual Capitalist. "This Is How COVID-19 Has Changed Media Habits in Each Generation." 2020.

CHAPTER 20: It's like a world with fewer people but without losing the people

Degrowth scholars Andrew Sutter and Yoshihiro Nakano also provided important guidance and research.

Kishida, Ittaka. "Preparing for a Zero-growth Economy." *Forum Report 008: Reexamining Japan in Global Context Forum*. Tokyo, Japan, May 26, 2015.

Matanle, Peter. "Towards an Asia-Pacific 'Depopulation Dividend' in the Twenty-first Century: Regional Growth and Shrinkage in Japan and New Zealand." *Asia-Pacific Journal: Japan Focus* 15, no. 6 (2017).

Matanle, Peter, and Yasuyuki Sato. "Coming Soon to a City Near You!: Learning to Live 'Beyond Growth' in Japan's Shrinking Regions." *Social Science Japan Journal* 13, no. 2 (2010): 187–210.

Pilling. *Bending Adversity.*

Salsberg, Brian, Clay Chandler, and Heang Chhor, eds. *Reimagining Japan: The Quest for a Future That Works*. San Francisco: McKinsey & Co., 2011.

CHAPTER 21: One hundred and fifty thousand years later . . .

The Washington, DC-based Institute for Policy Studies hosts an excellent reading list on inequality at Inequality.org.

Dittmar et al. "The Relationship between Materialism and Personal Well-being."

Goodin, Robert E., James Mahmud Rice, Antti Parpo, and Lina Eriksson. *Discretionary Time: A New Measure of Freedom*. Cambridge: Cambridge University Press, 2008.

Kaplan, David. "The Darker Side of the 'Original Affluent Society.'" *Journal of Anthropological Research* 56, no. 3 (2000): 301–24.

Laws. "All Things Being Equal."

Oishi, Shigehiro, Kostadin Kushlev, and Ulrich Schimmack. "Progressive Taxation, Income Inequality, and Happiness." *American Psychologist* 73, no. 2 (2018): 157.

Partanen, Anu. *The Nordic Theory of Everything*. New York: HarperCollins, 2016.

Payne, Keith. *The Broken Ladder: How Inequality Affects the Way We Think, Live, and Die*. New York: Penguin Random House, 2017.

Suzman. *Affluence without Abundance.*

Wilk, Richard R., and Eric J. Arnould. "Why Do the Indians Wear Adidas?: Or, Culture Contact and the Relations of Consumption." *Journal of Business Anthropology* 5, no. 1 (2016): 6–36.

Wilkinson, Richard, and Kate Packett. *The Inner Level: How More Equal Societies Reduce Stress, Restore Sanity and Improve Everyone's Well-being*. New York: Penguin, 2019.

EPILOGUE: There's a better way to stop shopping

Cohen, Maurie J. *The Future of Consumer Society*. Oxford: Oxford University Press, 2017.

Cohen, Maurie J., Halina Szejnwald Brown, and Philip J. Vergragt. *Social Change and the Coming of Post-consumer Society*. Milton Park, UK: Routledge, 2017.

Kallis et al. *The Case for Degrowth.*

Pilling. *The Growth Delusion.*

Raworth. *Doughnut Economics.*

Roscoe, Philip. *I Spend Therefore I Am*. Toronto: Random House Canada, 2014.

Shi. *The Simple Life.*

INDEX